Charles Pelham Villiers

The Free Trade Speeches of the Right Hon. Charles Pelham Villiers, M.P.

Charles Pelham Villiers

The Free Trade Speeches of the Right Hon. Charles Pelham Villiers, M.P.

ISBN/EAN: 9783744724067

Printed in Europe, USA, Canada, Australia, Japan

Cover: Foto ©ninafisch / pixelio.de

THE

FREE TRADE SPEECHES

OF THE

RIGHT HON. CHARLES PELHAM VILLIERS, M.P.

WITH A POLITICAL MEMOIR

EDITED BY

A MEMBER OF THE COBDEN CLUB

Under circumstances of infinite difficulty, the cause of total and immediate Repeal was first and solely upheld by the terse eloquence and vivid perception of Charles Villiers—DISRAELI'S *Life of Lord George Bentinck*

IN TWO VOLUMES—VOL. II.

LONDON
KEGAN PAUL, TRENCH, & CO., 1 PATERNOSTER SQUARE
1883

CONTENTS

OF

THE SECOND VOLUME.

Errata.

Page 220, line 12, *for* '250' *read* '254.'

" " " 13, *for* '1842' *read* '1844.'

FREE TRADE SPEECHES.

XV.

HOUSE OF COMMONS, May 9, 1843.

Not a shadow of the apathy that once had proved a more serious obstruction to the progress of the repeal of the Corn Laws in the House of Commons than the most active opposition itself was perceptible when May 9, 1843, for which day Mr. Villiers had given notice of his Annual Motion, arrived. The debate on the Motion, 'That this House resolve itself into a Committee for the purpose of considering the duties affecting the importation of foreign corn, with a view to their immediate abolition,' was anticipated with keen interest. It lasted five nights. Mr. Gladstone fell back on the worn-out drain of bullion, and agricultural labourers' fallacies, and again urged that the Ministry 'would be guilty of a great injustice to a large portion of the community, and exhibit themselves to the world as having acted with great imbecility, and unworthy to conduct the Government of a great and mighty empire, if they were to adopt the Motion.' Sir R. Peel commended the Sliding Scale that he had himself introduced, and in his turn took up the thin fallacies of the Malt Tax and peculiar burdens on land as a justification of Protection. At the conclusion of his speech the clamour and confusion in the House caused by the Monopolists became so great that Mr. Cobden, who was expected to reply, decided to wait till the next night; and ultimately an Adjournment was carried. Lord J. Russell adhered to his 8*s.* fixed duty, but was deserted by Lord Howick, who declared in favour of immediate Repeal. The division showed a considerable falling off in the Monopolist majority: the numbers being 381 against the Motion, to 125 for it.

I RISE to propose the Motion of which I have given notice. It is the same that I have proposed before to this House; and but for this circumstance I believe that I should have shrunk from the task now I have always felt myself incompetent for it, and I never felt more conscious than I do at the present moment that there are persons in the House far more fitted to undertake it than I am.

I know that the subject is distasteful to the House; I fear, indeed, that it is offensive to the majority from the question of their own interest which it involves. And it is not on that account rendered attractive to me: I had rather propitiate than offend this assembly if I could; but under existing circumstances this is, unfortunately, to be done by diverting rather than by attracting public attention to the Corn Laws. My reason for moving in the matter, however, is the same now that it always has been: a deep conviction in my own mind that in the whole range of public questions that can engage the attention of the House there is not one of equal importance with that which it is the object of my Motion to decide. With this conviction I have at different times brought the Corn Laws under the consideration of the House when others have been indisposed to do so, and during an interval when the public were complaining less of their effects; and now, when millions are expressing their interest in them, I regret that one abler than myself to represent their feelings is not the mover of the question. In fact, I could hardly have undertaken the task had I not been aware that there are those around me who have the talent and knowledge requisite to supply my many deficiencies.

It is said that the subject is exhausted, that nothing new can be said upon it. This is true: it was so in the year 1815 after the first Corn Law had been enacted; for there was nothing said then that ought not to have weighed as much as what is said now. But the Corn Laws exist, and as long as they do there will be something to say about them; but the importance of what is said will depend upon the numbers and intelligence of those out of this House who are attending to the matter. And in this respect, rare as any novelty in connection with the Corn Laws may be, there is something new; for without exaggeration it can be asserted that since the Laws were passed they have never been so much discussed, so much examined, so much inquired about, so thoroughly mastered by the great body of the middle classes, as at present.

I may add, moreover, that there is now no other question that maintains itself so firmly on their attention; that apparently produces such unanimity in discussion; and on which they now speak with such confidence. And the result is an unqualified impression on their minds that the Corn Laws have no national object whatever in view; that they are without any public grounds of defence; that they are the occasion (as their purpose indicates they must be) of great privation to the most numerous class; that they are a great check to the progress of the people and of serious injury to their morals; that they disturb the business of the country; that they limit the commerce of the country and impair the sources of revenue; in a word, that they have been the prominent cause of the embarrassment, depression, misery, and loss that this country has experienced for the last four years. As such they are regarded as unwise, unjust, repugnant to humanity, and at variance with every precept of the Christian faith; and in this view the educated portion of the mechanical classes and such of them as have access to the ordinary sources of information cordially join, with this conviction superadded, that the more difficult the acquirement of the necessaries of life is made to them the more dependent they must become upon the capitalist and employer of labour.

Nor is this statement controverted by the fact that at some public meetings where the subject has been discussed, men assuming the garb of working-men have entered and by violence and noise stopped the proceedings. The number of those who have thus degraded themselves to become the tools of tyranny has seldom exceeded twenty or thirty, and they have never obtained a majority. Whenever any honest men have been parties against a public meeting of this kind it has never been the object of the meeting with which they have quarrelled, but always with the means to secure that object, which they feared would be insufficient: the Laws in question have been unanimously condemned by them.

And here in pointing to the state of opinion upon this question, I must not omit to name a very important change that has occurred among a portion of the middle classes. I allude to those for whose interest the Corn Laws are declared to be maintained: namely, the farmers. It is a fact beyond dispute, and it is a new and striking feature in this great social movement, that this class now fearlessly examine the question; they may have shrunk from it before; but the change has already been manifested in public places and will soon be rendered more clear in their open avowal of the utter delusion under which they have laboured in supposing that the profit of laws that gave artificial value to land could belong to any-one but the owner of the land.

If it be asked what has occasioned this change in opinion, I should certainly refer it to the efforts of that intelligent, energetic, and persevering body, who, though they may find little favour in this House, will ere long not only be duly appreciated in the country, but from the aid they give to the cause of freedom generally, will also be entitled to the gratitude of mankind. I allude to the Anti-Corn-Law League. Usefully and effectively the League has drawn the attention of the people to the subject of the Corn Laws at a time when they are suffering and seeking the cause of their suffering; and it has brought conviction home to their minds. In this it has doubtless been aided by the course that was pursued by the House last year; for there is, I believe, hardly a ground upon which the Corn Laws had up to that time been rested that was not then abandoned by those who are responsible for their maintenance.

The majority of the middle classes in this country, absorbed in the pursuit of their own affairs, are much in the habit of deferring to authority; hitherto they have been reluctant to believe that men in high station would state what was untrue, or that they would really sacrifice the great interests of the country to serve the sinister interests of a class, and so they were lulled into submission to the Corn Laws by the things they were told about them. They heard that these were Protective Laws ; that they had retained labour in employment and secured industry its reward ; that they enabled the farmer to obtain profit in his business and indemnified the land-owner for great national burdens which he had taken on himself ; that they preserved us from dependence upon foreigners and gave to agriculture its best encouragement. They were told also that the repeal of these Laws would convulse the country to its furthest point and disturb all the engagements into which the proprietors had entered ; and that, looking at the vast interests of the country and the complication of its affairs, it could not be worth while to imperil so much in the vain hope of drawing a higher prize in the lottery of legislation. These were the things that were said, and the influence of which I have at times regretted to observe, though from their hollowness I did certainly not expect they could endure ; and if the House remembers when this question was last before it, it will see that my expectation has not been disappointed.

Last year I had no longer to ask that it should resolve itself into Committee. When the abolition of the Corn Laws was then demanded the House was already in Committee deliberating upon them ; not certainly to proclaim their efficiency, not to point to their success, but, in the full acknowledgment of their mischievousness, avowing that they ought to have been altered long since; that we had become habitually dependent upon foreigners for supply; that the people were rapidly increasing, and through the Corn Laws deteriorating in their condition; that the limit of taxation on the necessaries of life had been reached; and that the Revenue depended upon the condition of the people. And this year we have heard that 'peculiar burdens' were never much relied upon.

There is one fallacy however still adhered to: that the farmer and his labourer are interested in this legislation, and that with the view to their interest it is wise for Parliament to endeavour to regulate the price of produce. 'Do not blight his hopes, do not chill his expectations,' said the Right Hon. Baronet at the head of the Government, 'while he is endeavouring to supply you adequately at a price between 54*s.* and 58*s.* a quarter. To protect him against the foreigner till the price reaches 61*s.* is the object of my Bill.' 'This will prevent the displacement of capital and labour, this will keep land in cultivation and the labourer in employment,' said the Member for Nottinghamshire; 'while should wheat ever fall to 47*s.*, acres without end would return to waste and people without number would lose their occupation.' And so strongly was this felt by proprietors to be the intention of the Laws, that the Duke of Richmond told his tenants in the summer that he was not the man to hold them to agreements made in the expectation of a price assured to them by law, and to refuse to release them if the law should fail in its promise; and that he would accept surrenders of leases from every tenant if the prices they expected were not obtained in the following year. This was honourably said, and I do not see how the example could now be rejected by any landlord who was a party to the Corn Laws; for certainly the Imperial averages, and not the Corn Law League, have already blighted the hopes which the Laws were intended to raise.

Such things, however, having been said, is it wonderful that the people should now ask why Laws, no longer defended upon any public ground and resting solely upon favour to a particular interest which they have utterly failed to secure, should be maintained an hour longer? The fact is, the Corn Laws are condemned by public opinion; justice, humanity, and policy have all borne testimony against them; and now a kind of retributive experience is reaching their promoters; in truth, these Laws only wait the final sentence of the House to be buried for ever with those other Acts that have had private interest at the expense of public good for their end; and it is the object of this Motion now to ask you to pass this sentence.

I do not come here to haggle about the best mode of effecting a compromise with a bad principle: satisfied of its badness, I oppose it entirely. I cannot propose terms when I know that none should be accepted. If there is a right to claim the repeal of the Corn Laws it is or ought to be based on truth and justice. I contend that it is; and such are the grounds on which we have hitherto relied: to make any concession at variance with these principles would be wholly out of the question.

Besides, the hour is passed for tampering with the food, the health, the life, and the rights of millions of our fellow-creatures. The time is come when the great mass of the community consider themselves aggrieved and injured by these Laws, and only insulted by the defence that is offered for them ; and they call for their abolition as they would for that of any other nuisance or evil with which they might be afflicted. No argument resting on the particular interests that have grown up under them could be advanced for their continuance that would not equally apply to the perpetuation of any abomination ; or that might not equally be claimed for any injustice or the continuance of any of the greatest curses that could befall humanity.

In truth the Corn Laws have no purpose, no advantage for their supporters, unless they tend to produce one of those evils that man has always been most anxious to avert, and from which the Deity has always been invoked to protect him : I mean famine. The very object of the Laws is the approximation of misfortune, and in the opinion of their promoters they fail of their object if this is not accomplished.

The inadequate supply of food is an evil that in a primitive state of society must always excite the greatest alarm ; but it is equally a matter of the gravest concern to a people in the most advanced state of civilization. Now, to the effect of the Corn Laws as they operate upon a community like ours I would here call the attention of the House, as I do not believe that the consequences of any approach to scarcity in this country have been duly appreciated. Not only is a constantly increasing supply of food essential to a population constantly increasing like our own; but it is the condition of that minute division of labour which results in our great wealth and the various industries that tend to the adornment and comfort of life, and which is therefore necessary to the continued progress of a people. For it is only after the assurance of an adequate supply of food is felt that this distribution of the national labour occurs; and if after the distribution has taken place anything should occur to diminish or prevent a sufficient supply, then all those engaged in the production of other things than food are at once disturbed in their business, and the demand for the results of their industry ceases or diminishes: the prior demand for food having exhausted or reduced the means available for their consumption. And hence those engaged in producing the conveniences and luxuries of life are driven to seek for themselves a more direct mode of obtaining food, which they usually do by a return to the occupation of land; or, in such countries as our own, by a resort to mendicity, to public relief, to emigration, to crime. All this may be said to be obvious, but if so why has it been forgotten? It really lies at the bottom of the question that we are considering; and had it been heeded, the Legislature would never have attempted through scarcity to raise the price of produce lest they should deprive those engaged in manufacture, or occupied otherwise than in the production of food, of the means of living.

Equally obvious is it that the more abundant and accessible food is, the greater will be the demand for all other results of industry. If any man would satisfy himself of the truth of this rule let him only inquire what would be the effect, in a country like this, of the great mass of the population's having easy access to food; let him learn whether it would not instantly occasion greater demand for the comforts and decencies of life; and whether the effect with which this would be attended would not of necessity be an increased demand for the labour of those who could be employed in the production of such objects—thus occasioning a better market for manufactures at home, and consequently rendering the manufacturers' business a better market for labour.

And if this would be the case, what can be more worthy of the attention of those responsible for the state of the country than to discover in what way the supply of food can be most abundantly increased, in order to cause an adequate demand for the additional labour of the country? For on this, it is manifest, hangs the physical condition of the people, and on the physical condition depend their morals, their education, their general well-being and contentment. And in this country above every other it is important to increase the demand for manufactures now that it has been ascertained and established beyond question that all future additions to the population must look for employment in manufactures or other employments t han agriculture

Let men with these principles in their mind examine the facts that are afforded to them by this country: the facilities for ascertaining anything that affects our economical condition are great, and the opportunity was never better than at present, when we are at the termination of a period during which there have been years of scarcity and abundance of equal duration. I would ask any man who rises from such an inquiry, whether he will not admit that while a mass of evil and misery has followed in close connection with the period of dear or scarce food, comparative prosperity has not seemed to result from the years of cheapness; whether as food became dear the occupations unconnected with its production did not become worse; and whether thousands of those so employed have not been driven to seek food in some other way?

It is well known that between 1834 and 1838 there was a comparative abundance of food and that the great body of the people had access to food of good quality in greater amount than before. And it is not disputed that during that period all occupations connected with manufacturing industry were never more prosperous; that commerce was active; that the Revenue was flourishing; that Poor Rates were reduced; that crime diminished; that all the businesses connected with the distribution of wealth were in a prosperous state; that the habits of the people, which had been deteriorating during the years 1829 and 1830, began to improve; and that the general aspect of the community was good. But in 1838 the harvest failed and wheat, which in the beginning of that year had been 51*s.*, rose in September to 73*s.* From that moment till the harvest of 1842 the effects of a high cost of food upon a highly-civilised, commercial, manufacturing community, annually augmenting in number like our own, may be observed.

From the autumn of 1838 to that of 1842 we had high prices, which means scarcity of food; and it cannot be questioned that during that period the whole business of the country was, as it still is, deranged and depressed. Nor is this concurrence of high-priced food and bad trade a mere coincidence and not the necessary connection of cause and effect: it would be easy to show that it is impossible that it should be otherwise.

In the first place, if we take the average cost of wheat in the beginning of 1838 and the average amount consumed, we shall get the rate at which the community was paying for this food before the prices rose. Assuming that sixteen millions of quarters are consumed, and that the price was 56*s.*, the yearly expenditure would be about forty-five millions. If the price rose to 73*s.*, the cost would then be fifteen millions more; and if we take the average of the four years, we shall find that during that period sixty millions more were required for food than were required for the four preceding years. Indeed, my Hon. Friend the Member for Paisley stated last year that other things, such as tea, coffee, and sugar, having risen in price at the same time, an additional expenditure on necessaries equal altogether to 100 millions had been caused.

What then should we expect to be the effect of abstracting so large an amount of the public means from the expenditure on manufactures? Could it do other than greatly injure the home market, and thus diminish the demand for goods compared with that of cheap years? What is the account that intelligent men connected with the staple manufactures of the country and dependent alike upon Home and Foreign Trade, would give on this point? Why, that the effect of the price of food rising was felt immediately on the home market for manufactures, and that, as at first it was inconvenient and almost impossible to stop the manufacturing processes, they continued to produce without reference to the demand; so that the stocks were thereby increased beyond the demand at home, and they were obliged to consign their goods on their own account to foreigners abroad. This soon caused the markets abroad to be overstocked—a circumstance that was much aggravated by our inability to effect exchange with foreign countries growing food, and prices fell to a ruinous point here; and in 1842, the foreign markets being glutted, while the home market remained unimproved, a period of unexampled depression followed in this country. There was one continued course of sacrifice, bankruptcy and ruin steadily increasing throughout that most unfortunate year; and, as we know only too well, such were the wretchedness, destitution, despair, induced by diminished profit and diminished reward of labour that an outbreak of a serious character occurred, which was rendered all the more alarming by the circumstance that it found many of the middle class, on whom the peace and well-being of the State greatly depends, in a condition to care little for its result.

Considering all the details of what has occurred during this progress of misery and ruin for three years past, while every evil that physically and socially can befall humanity has been suffered by millions of our people, I believe that nothing that war or pestilence could bring would have been worse, or that anything ever exceeded what was endured in England at that time. It is difficult to measure the misery of such a period in this country; the mental agony of persons sinking in their station and the moral ruin entailed upon whole families of innocent persons by the demoralizing influence of poverty, hurrying, as it were, multitudes of unconscious men and women into habits of vice and crime. It is vain to talk of educating the people or of raising their moral state while laws attended periodically with these consequences are suffered to exist. There are moments when people's morals and habits are moulded for their remaining life —when the moral being of millions is determined; and not all the education, not all the vigilance of all the clergy could redeem many of those who have been so reduced and degraded, and subjected to such trials and privations as we have witnessed.

Hon. Members should judge of the Corn Laws in connection with these practical results; for there is a way of viewing them apart from their purpose and their necessary effect; gentlemen talk of them as of some abstraction that may form a chapter in political economy, or excite the interest of the student, not as having any practical bearing. But they must learn that it is precisely by their distressing consequences that the Corn Laws are known and felt by the industrious classes, who on this account, not unreasonably, consider the supporters of them as the authors of their misery.

It is the observation of those who are brought in contact medically with the working classes that there is nothing that determines their health and well-being to such an extent as the facility with which they obtain food. Indeed, as public men are reproved for the strength of their language in condemning the Corn Laws when they have termed them murderous Laws, it is well that it should be known that this is the view that is taken by medical men when treating them more calmly. I will quote here from a medical man who has had much experience in the treatment of the poor. He says:—

> The Poor Law preserves from death, but it does not, it cannot preserve them from gnawing anxiety and destructive toil, from exposure to the weather, whilst seeking far from home for work—from suffering cold, from insufficient clothes, the best having been sold or pawned for bread—from crowding several families into one small dwelling to save expense of rent—from choking up every avenue for air to obtain warmth without expense of fuel. Nothing can preserve the infant from unwholesome milk, when its mother is harassed by care, and stinting herself of food that her little ones may eat. Nothing can save men from disease and death with insufficient and unwholesome food—with garbage to stay the cravings of hunger, and seeking in the excitement of gin a brief respite from despair. Such are means by which the Corn Laws kill.

Again, I have here an extract from a work on 'Vital Statistics.' [Sir J. Graham: 'Who is the author?'] Dr. Hawkins. I will read a few passages from it that will show the estimation in which these Laws are held by even men of moderate opinions :—

> The price of corn has a most remarkable influence on the movements of population and of disease. We have not a sufficient number of data to enable us to estimate the exact amount of its influence, but we shall assuredly not be mistaken in classing it among the most energetic causes which press upon the operations of life. This influence extends not only upon deaths but upon births; it affects also the number of marriages, of diseases, and even crimes. Variations in the price of food, then, form one of the most serious changes that can occur on the surface of a State; they may insensibly lead to the most unexpected, the most formidable result; and we may affirm with confidence that one of the most important duties of a Government is to temper, and to diminish, as far as possible, all the circumstances which promote these fluctuations in the price of the most necessary article which man can produce.

Thus it is acknowledged that the price of food not only has a great influence on the comfort and condition of the people, but that its variations and fluctuations are amongst the greatest and most important changes that can occur in any State, and may insensibly lead to the most unexpected and formidable results. These are the opinions of persons held in considerable estimation as medical writers who have published several valuable statistical works; and the soundness of their statements is fully confirmed by the increase of crime and the amount of poverty and disease that have taken place lately amongst the poorer classes of this country.

One of these writers shows that during the four

dearer years 14,657 more patients applied for medical relief in the manufacturing districts than during the same period of cheap food; and that 1,177 more had died, or 196 per year, showing that the proportionate increase of mortality was much greater than the increase of admissions. In ten divisions of England only, the deaths from starvation within the year were 116, and in Ireland, Scotland, and Wales there were three times as many. The annual deaths from starvation were two in every 100,000, or 560 of the whole population.

The increase of crime is also frightful to contemplate. I find that in 1835 the number of commitments was 20,731.

In 1836 they had increased to	20,984
,, 1841 ,, ,, ,, ...	27,760
,, 1842 ,, ,, ,, ...	31,760

During the last four years the Poor Rates in Marylebone, one of the most populous parishes of this rich metropolis, have increased to an alarming extent.

	£
In 1840 the amount was	27,000
,, 1841 ,, ,, ...	31,000
,, 1842 ,, ,, ...	36,000
,, 1843 ,, ,, ...	40,000

Thus showing in one parish alone an increase of 13,000*l.* in the expenditure for the relief and support of the poor. I also find that the number of casual poor relieved by the City of London, which in 1836 amounted to only 925, had increased in 1842 to 29,933.

Nor is this state of things confined to one place; it is general throughout the country. At the alms-houses at Durham, for instance, the number of persons relieved has increased 40 per cent. during the same period. Surely these are matters that should at least be weighed and considered by men who, subjected to no privations themselves, sit here and deliberately legislate against food and purposely make it scarce! And this they can accomplish only at the risk of producing the consequences to which I have referred, thereby impairing the morals, the health, happiness, and general well-being of the people, and thus adding fearfully to all the elements of discontent and disorder in the State.

Moreover, it should be noted that it is not solely during the periods of bad seasons that general distress and its attendant evils occur; but that under our present circumstances it is more or less the constant condition of the country. In fact, even when the harvests are good we are without a sufficient supply of food—at least of food of the better kind, such as we all desire to consume ourselves; and the great mass of the people have not at any time food of good and strengthening quality within their reach. It has been said in former discussions—and it may be repeated this evening—that in ordinary years there is an adequate supply of food; this I deny: the supply is never adequate; there is more at one time than at another, but there never is enough.

I have here a calculation that has been made at a great cost of trouble with the view of obtaining an accurate account of the distribution of the largest quantity of wheat that has been allotted to general consumption. The largest quantity is about sixteen million quarters, which shows that ten millions of the population, the number named by some advocates of the Corn Laws, never consume wheaten flour at all. The estimated distribution is as follows :—

Population				Quarters yearly
500,000	people at	7	oz. per day	166,666
1,500,000	,,	10½	,,	750,000
3,000,000	,,	14	,,	2,000,000
3,000,000	,,	17½	,,	2,500,000
4,000,000	,,	21	,,	4,000,000
5,000,000	,,	24½	,,	5,833,333
17,000,000				15,249,999

Besides these, I find that there are four millions who live on oatmeal, and six millions who 'rejoice' on potatoes. These ten millions of people are without the first great necessary of life. Is it not a scandal and a disgrace to this country which boasts of its wealth and greatness, which boasts of its charity and its Christianity, to suffer these things to be while we know that across the Atlantic a pestilence was nearly occasioned by food rotting on the quay for want of a market? I allude to what actually occurred at New Orleans.

Really, if it were not lamentable, it would be almost ludicrous to hear people who are parties to the Corn Laws observe upon and regret some of its most obvious consequences. For instance, it is not unusual to hear in this House a sort of lamentation that of late years the labouring classes have been getting poorer while other particular classes and individuals have become richer; and that while those who live luxuriously seem to prosper, those who are wanting comforts are becoming more necessitous.

This was observed upon by the Right Hon. Baronet at the head of the Government when he introduced the Income Tax; and he seemed to state it as a reason why he should exempt the poorer classes from the tax. The same observation was again pressed upon the House by the Vice-President of the Board of Trade, who regretted the great accumulation of capital and the simultaneous spread of poverty. Another Member of the Government, the Secretary of the Admiralty, made the subject the leading topic of an address to his neighbours and constituents last winter. I will just read his words. He said:—

> The truth is, we none of us feel sufficiently the responsibility of wealth, and the duties which the possession of property entails on us; we forget we are trustees for our poorer brethren, and this whether the property possessed be great or small. Look at the state of society in England, and we must be struck by the necessity of making efforts equal to the emergency of the case. It must be evident to all who have paid attention to the working of our system, that whether owing to our laws and institutions, or to some other cause, great changes have taken place at the ends of the social scale, wealth being at one end greatly on the increase, and poverty as rapidly increasing at the other, the rich becoming still richer, and the poor becoming every day more numerous and more poor.

Now assuming that those who express their regret at this circumstance are sincere, I would just put a case to them to aid them in solving the difficulty as to the cause of the evil. I will imagine a very much smaller community than our own, say one of a few thousand; and I will suppose that only fifty persons have the supply of the necessary food of the people. What do these gentlemen think would be the condition of the people, as well as of those possessing the Monopoly of food, if their numbers gradually increased, while the supply of food did not increase in proportion? Do they doubt that while those who had the supply of food grew gradually rich, those who were compelled to depend upon them for food and were increasing in number, would gradually become poor; that the proprietary represented by the fifty would gradually acquire a greater control over the mass of the people—over their labour, their services, their resources; and that according as these were given in greater proportion for food, the people dependent on the Monopolists would have less to expend on other things; the whole resulting in what the speaker referred to calls 'the rich becoming richer, and the poor poorer'? This is my solution of the increasing disproportion between rich and poor, which all observe and say they regret; but which if Monopoly in the supply of food continues will be manifested more each year.

The population cannot multiply as ours does and not be deteriorated if the supply of food does not increase in a corresponding degree. And that this is the state of the people now, that their condition is already greatly impaired and daily becoming more and more so through want of food, and the demand for employment of the same kind far exceeding the supply, is admitted both by those who resist the repeal of the Corn Laws and those who have other projects than Repeal for the improvement of the people. They say that the people are impoverished; that a greater supply of food is required for them; and they seek to improve their condition either by foreign colonization or home colonization. But what is the assumption on which both these schemes are proposed but that the difficulties of obtaining the means of life are increasing and that it is politic either to send the people where there is more food or to encourage those now engaged in manufacturing pursuits to produce food for themselves in this country? Each scheme assumes that the people must withdraw from the employments which they are engaged in or desire to obtain, in order to raise food themselves in this country or in the colonies. The friends of foreign colonization think to alleviate the condition of the ill-paid weavers by sending them to be shepherds at the Antipodes; and the friends of home colonization invite the destitute operatives, or those who are only half employed, to leave the forge and the loom for the plough, and to till the waste lands of this country in the hope of raising by that means food for themselves and their families. I do not impugn the motives of these persons: I believe that they all are animated by a desire to relieve the destitution that they hear of or that they witness. But I cannot help observing to them that since they acknowledge the condition of our people to be that of wanting food and wanting the means of procuring it, they should be heard on this occasion calling loudly for the repeal of Laws that exist only to prevent food entering this country, and to hinder those who have it to sell from purchasing our manufactures in exchange; for it is solely to realize the object proposed by their colonization schemes that we seek to repeal the Corn Laws. They say that we want new markets; that we want to employ our redundant people; and for this their plan is to colonize them. Our plan, on the other hand, is to suffer them to work at home for food which those who take their work would give them in exchange, but which these Laws deprive them of. For if the food that is kept out of this country by the Corn Laws were to come in, it could only be received in exchange for articles that would be produced by our people with a view to such trade. As long as there are ten millions in this country who exhaust their means in the purchase of food, and are therefore inadequately supplied with manufactures, there are the means of a new market within the limits of our own land, which we could call into existence and which would manifest themselves immediately if the law would allow industry and commerce to be free; an abundant supply of food would then appear, and the present redundant labour would be absorbed by an increased demand for manufactures and by an extension of all the businesses incident to them: so that these ten millions would be like a new State with whom we should have a new trade. In short, the Home Market would be improved as much as it is at present injured by the Corn Laws. Home Trade is more convenient in some respects for those engaged in it than Foreign Trade, and it is precisely the Home Trade that the Corn Laws are peculiarly calculated to injure.

It is no preference for Foreign Trade over Home Trade that induces me to call for the repeal of the Corn Laws. I never said that it was. I object to the Corn Laws on the ground that they stop exchange between man and man respectively producers, and, by artificially raising the cost of food, limit the command of the community over the comforts of life. It is idle for those who maintain these Laws to question the benefits of allowing trade to be free, for their whole argument and all their fears are based on the expectation of them. It is precisely to prevent the merchant from having his share in the supply of the community with food that the Corn Laws are maintained: the merchant who is ready to embark his capital for this purpose, who is prepared, in fact, to take out the results of our native industry, of which we hear so much, in exchange for it, but who is deterred from doing so by this most mischievous meddling with his business. The supporters of the Laws are therefore precluded from the use of both arguments: first, that too much food would come in; and secondly, that no food would be imported. Their fears are founded upon the anticipation of too much food; and it is to prevent excess that they are legislating. Otherwise there is no purpose in the Corn Laws; for their interference to protect the capitalist is ludicrous, either on the supposition that the merchant requires to be protected by the landlords from his own enterprise, or on the assumption that with our commercial facilities—with the whole world from the valley of the Nile to the valley of the Mississippi before us, the merchant would not be able to dispose of our manufactures for food and to keep our markets supplied with the first necessaries of life. If the present system were not grossly impolitic as regards the community, it would still be abominably unjust to those who having capital that they could employ in providing food for the people, are not at liberty to do so equally with the agriculturist. A man has just as much right to the free use of his money or his ships, which he may inherit or acquire and may choose to employ for the purpose of feeding the people, as the landlord has to his acres for the same purpose; and the community are only aggrieved, and never can be benefited, by any restraint in this respect. On this ground, therefore, even if there were no other, the Corn Laws ought to be repealed as a gross infringement of the right of our traders in their business, to supply the community with the things they require. Monopoly can never offer a substitute for the unvarying operation of competition.

Where, then, is the excuse for this flagrant violation of the ordinary rules of policy? Is it that what is termed agriculture requires favour for its success in this country? I am happy to think that in the whole list of pretexts and fallacies resorted to in the defence of these Laws, there is not one more weak and indefensible than this; and that there is now almost unanimity, as far as one can collect the opinions of independent and intelligent agriculturists, that the cultivation of the soil depends upon the skill, science, and arrangements of those who bring their capital to this business, and not upon favouritism, Monopoly, or what is termed Protection. I believe that the men who have given most attention to this subject do not stop with the opinion that such interference is not needed. They go further and assert that it is positively mischievous; and that so long as the cultivator is diverted from attending to his own resources by relying on the promise of Parliament, agriculture will never thrive in this country. The case as I apprehend it is this: the law holds out an expectation that by excluding foreign competition a high price will be obtained for a particular grain; this induces the farmer to give special attention to the particular grain, and to reckon upon the expected high price for it in the engagement that he makes for the use of the land; the effect of constant disappointment in getting this price has ended in making him generally unwilling to seek a lease, and at the same time political reasons frequently render the landlord unwilling to give one.

The agriculture of this country is certainly very defective and needs many things to be done to improve it; but for this purpose patience, expense, and enterprise are required; and the best improvements of later years need considerable outlay and time to prove their efficacy. Now the present system is exactly qualified to make men timid in laying out money, for while they rely upon the promise of Parliament to maintain remunerative prices, they cease to depend upon their own exertions for the improvement of their lands. I confidently assert that they have been made timid, and that their confidence has been shaken; that the science of agriculture, as well as the interest of the cultivator, needs no other reliance than that on skill and enterprise; and that both are prejudiced by the results of Protection. Indeed upon every inquiry into the distress of the agriculturists, it has been shown that those who had put little faith in the Corn Laws, and trusted chiefly to their own skill and resource, had not suffered; while those who having relied on the promise of the Corn Laws, were bound by heavy pecuniary engagements to the owner of whom they hired the land, were precisely those who were most distressed. This was testified by the farmers of Scotland who gave their evidence in 1836; and they showed that they had thriven from the moment that they had cast off all reliance on the Laws, and made arrangements with their landlords adapted to those circumstances. It is chiefly from reflecting upon all the testimony collected at the Inquiry of 1836, that some of the most scientific men have been led to the conclusion that low prices steadily maintained would afford the best stimulus to improvements, and be alike advantageous to the occupier of the land and the community; and that this is most likely to be accomplished by freedom of trade. I find this stated by some men, and broadly hinted by others, who perhaps fear the unpopularity of broaching the doctrine among the proprietors. In fact until lately, when I examined the matter more closely than I had before, I was not aware how strong the presumption is in favour of the success of the principle of Free Trade as applied to agriculture above any other branch of industry. The cultivator in this country has an advantage over his foreign competitor in all that is essential to his business, and his disadvantages seem to begin with and to spring from the Laws that profess to protect him. He has larger capital, better labour, more manure, better implements, nearer markets than the foreigner; but he has an artificially high price to pay for his land, he has heavy Poor Rates rendered so by food being scarce, and all that portion of the produce required for consumption on the farm is consumed at a greater sacrifice than would occur if it were cheap, while at the same time the Laws impair the condition of his customer. I agree with the most intelligent men conversant with this subject, that if the farmer had fair play and, like men in other businesses, were allowed free competition, he would succeed in rivalry with the foreigner of any kingdom in the world. Nor am I here speaking without book: in support of what I have said of the change of opinion among the farmers, and to prove that I am not misrepresenting their opinions in what I state, nor calling for the entire removal of Protection in disregard and neglect of their interest, I will refer to a very intelligent work that has recently been published by a man who is a farmer himself—one with whom I am personally acquainted, whose family and connections have been entirely bound up in interest with the agricultural class, and who would have everything to lose in character and property if he were wrong in what he said. Mr. Welford is the author of the work in question; and treating in the first place the subject of rent, he says :—

I firmly believe that if the trade in corn was to be thrown open to-morrow there would be no real necessity for any important reduction of rents, except upon heavy wheat land; and there, it would only be required in order to allow the tenant time to adapt himself to a state of low prices likely to be permanent and steady, rather than from any difficulty in cultivating such lands, under a proper system, at the present rents, let the price of corn be ever so low.

Then as regards the moment for effecting the change, he says :—

Now, then, is the time to repeal the Corn Law. Home competition has reduced the price of grain to a moderate rate, and if we are blessed with a good harvest wheat may, and probably will, fall lower than it was in 1835. The most sensitive agricultural alarmist will therefore be unable to conjure up any phantom of greater abundance than that produced by the home growth. The repeal of the Corn Law would now create no panic, and Free Trade, by a gentle and gradual measure, would direct the exertions of farmers towards that intelligent system of husbandry wherein their permanent prosperity is alone to be found. All the beneficial effects which free trade in corn is fitted to produce on commerce and manufactures would at once begin to operate, and a clearer prospect of national prosperity, a prospect more free from adventitious circumstances whether of good or evil, will be opened, than has ever been hitherto attained.

On the other hand, if, either through public indifference or from the half measures of party politicians, the Corn Laws be allowed to linger on the Statute Book—practically inoperative, as we have seen, to prevent agricultural distress in abundant years, until the cycle of the season shall bring round two or three deficient crops, it is certain that a total and instant repeal will be quickly forced upon the Government of that day. But this will not be effected until all the evils of scarcity have again been endured by the community, new engagements at high rents entered into by farmers, wheat culture again unduly extended, monetary derangements and ruinous corn speculations once more rife, and, finally, an agricultural panic which the experience of several years may be required to allay. It is plain there never was a time, especially as regards the interests of the agriculturists, more favourable for the decisive step than the present. What do we fear? Is it cheap corn? If so, we have it notwithstanding the Corn Laws. But the mischief is, that though for this year we may have abundance, a bad harvest must half starve us before we can get relief.

That the British agriculturist is by no means so ill prepared to adopt the only stable means of success, as some of his self-styled friends would have believed, a brief survey of the present state of English husbandry will make manifest. Perhaps there is no source from which I could take a statement of the actual condition of English agriculturists (for in Scotland farmers have become pretty well alive to the exigencies of the times) so little open to suspicion or cavil as the article by Mr. Philip Pusey, M.P., one of the Members for the agricultural county of Berks, 'On the Progress of Agricultural Knowledge during the last four years,' which appears in the last number of the 'English Agricultural Society's Journal,' published in January of the present year. The purpose of the article is to inquire what has been the progress of agriculture since the establishment of the society; and it completely confirms the views I have taken of the comparatively backward condition of the heavy soils. Mr. Pusey justly remarks that the foundation of all improvement upon wet lands is drainage; and in the foregoing pages I have shown that the owners and occupiers of wet and heavy soils are those who are most frequent and loud in their demands for Protection.

And he proceeds to show how recently this improvement had even been recommended:—

It is only seven years since we heard in England, chiefly through the present Speaker of the House of Commons, that a manufacturer in Scotland, now well known as Mr. Smith, of Deanston, had found the means of making all land, however wet and poor it might be, warm, sound, and fertile; and that this change was brought about by two processes, thorough draining and subsoil ploughing.

Mr. Welford further quotes Mr. Pusey to confirm his own views of the improbability that these modes of improvement will be adopted under the present system of Land Tenure. After enumerating the many disadvantages of wet clay land the citation concludes :—

If I were a working farmer, nothing would induce me to enter on a cold, wet farm, unless there were a fair prospect of its being drained, either with my own money under a long lease, or with the aid of the landlord. But what farmer—continues Mr. Welford—who intends to remain solvent and independent five years hence, would now venture to take a long lease of 'a cold, wet farm,' knowing, as he does, that he would be obliged to engage to pay a rent calculated on prices he may not obtain five years out of twenty? And while such lands can be let without draining, the landlords—the majority of whom cannot afford the outlay—will never, to any great extent, furnish the means. Here and there individual landholders may promote such improvements at their own expense; but looking at land in the aggregate, its permanent improvement will only take place in the hands of occupiers. To enable the occupiers of the clay lands of England to become improvers, the first requisite plainly is steadiness of price, which can only result from a free trade in corn.

And in support of this opinion he points to the time when the protected agriculturists began generally to talk of improvement :—

Now, though individual cultivators had been for some time in the practice of enlightened systems of husbandry, and were thereby enabled to bear up against the ruinous fluctuations caused by the Corn Laws; yet it was not until that complete disclosure of the real origin of agricultural distress, and of the hollowness of all expectations of profit founded on protective laws, which were made in 1836, that any general movement was communicated to agriculture. Then a desire for improvement, to counteract the effects of low prices, arose amongst the landed gentry; one of the consequences of which was the formation of the English Society, whose proceedings have diffused the knowledge of useful practices already in operation.

And now before I close this valuable work, I cannot help reading the conclusions that the author considers to be legitimately drawn from all the evidence and experience that the past and present state of agriculture under the Corn Laws affords. And I read them in the hope of their going forth to the public, and giving agriculturists an opportunity to gainsay or refute Mr. Welford's views if they can be refuted; for the truth alone is what I desire in this matter. Mr. Welford, amongst others, comes to the following conclusions:—

That the rise of rents which has occurred in modern times has been consequent upon the growth of manufacturing industry in this country.

That the most complete Monopoly of the home market will not secure permanently high prices to the British agriculturist.

That the Monopoly prices promised by the Corn Laws, both of 1815 and 1828, were never practically enjoyed for any considerable period by the occupiers of land in Great Britain, whilst all their fixed money engagements have been calculated with reference to the promised, not to the real prices of grain; and besides, that the community will not bear in times of scarcity an effective maintenance of the Corn Monopoly for a period sufficiently long to compensate the farmer for the unnatural depression prices undergo in years of abundance.

That though the farmer, who by accident had taken his farm during a low range of prices, if his rent had been fixed with reference to the then existing prices, might be apparently benefited by even a short period of high prices; yet that, in fact, he is no gainer, for the competition of farmers for farms enables landlords and land agents, in practice, to disregard the very low priced years, and to calculate money rents with reference to the prices of seasons of comparative scarcity, and to the Act-of-Parliament price of corn.

That the Corn Laws have prevented timely adjustments of rent, and have thereby permanently injured the landlord and tenant, more particularly on those soils which were formerly almost exclusively regarded as 'wheat lands;' that they have induced farmers to rely for profit upon a great breadth of wheat, to the neglect of stock farming and improved systems of husbandry; and that they have created a habit in the minds of those connected with land, of looking to the Legislature for some undefined or unattainable remedy for occasional distress, rather than to their own energy and enterprise.

That the uncontrolled power which the landed interests have had to legislate for the Protection of agriculture has not enabled them to prevent the periodical recurrence of real and severe distress amongst the tenantry.

That it is not for the interest of the farmer that prices of corn should be high, for whether they are high or low, *the existing competition for farms* would prevent him from realizing more than the ordinary rate of profit, after payment of rent and other outgoings, calculated according to the actually existing prices; but it is most important to him that prices should be steady, without fluctuation beyond what must follow from variations in the seasons; and that such steady prices would be best secured by a constant and regular importation of grain.

That all recent improvements in agriculture have taken place in spite of the Corn Laws, and by pursuing plans directly the reverse of those which the Corn Laws have tended to encourage.

That the immediate repeal of the Corn Laws is not only desirable, as the means of placing agriculture upon a sure foundation, by at once enforcing those improved systems of husbandry, and adjustments of engagements, which alone can make agriculture permanently prosperous; but that the present time, from the comparatively low prices and the healthy appearance of the growing crops, is peculiarly favourable for the adoption of free trade in corn.

And, finally, that the high value of land in this country has always been coincident with, and is directly attributable to, the great wealth created by our commercial and manufacturing industry, and the comparatively wide diffusion of that wealth amongst the mass of the community; but not to any artificial restrictions, which have been shackles and obstructions on, not aids to, our productive power.

These are conclusions deliberately arrived at by a farmer. And people must not suppose that he is a person unknown to the body of farmers: after publishing this work he presided at the great meeting lately held in the county of Hertford—where he is well known as a farmer—at which the farmers had assembled from different parts of the country to hear the subject of the Corn Laws discussed, and to which many had come with no friendly feeling to the speakers on Free Trade; and he was unanimously elected to fill the chair.

It is, then, the condition of improvement, and the condition of the safe pursuit of this business by the farmer, that prices should be low and that trade should be free. What, then, is the objection to the change? It will occasion panic among the farmers, say some. I say it is the circumstance that no panic is likely to occur that renders the present moment so specially fitting for the change. The farmers could not, to begin with, apprehend any great fall in the price; nay, at first they might expect the contrary from the stimulus it would give to trade.

Moreover, I remember that last autumn there was a laudable endeavour on the part of some persons to prepare the way, as I hoped, for some further change, and excellent advice was tendered to the farmers in a series of speeches in different counties that, from the manner in which they were received, showed this class to be as open to conviction as any other.

My Hon. Friend the Member for Winchester addressed them in a speech that, according to the report, met with nothing but success. And, apparently, he succeeded in convincing them that the worst day that could befall the farmers, as well as the country at large, would be when the manufacturing interest should in any way decline; and that agriculture must look to the extension of our commerce as the most friendly circumstance that could befall it.

Again, the Member for Somersetshire was extremely well received when he, about the same time, announced to his constituents assembled to hear him, that the time was now come when the British farmer must abandon his reliance on Protection and stand upon his own prudence and skill.

And lastly came a gentleman who, I think, had represented or did then represent a division in the county of Sussex—Mr. Goring, who said that the farmer had nothing to fear; that he had great advantages in the circumstances of this country; and that Protection was useless to him.

I observed that all these speeches were well received; and I never could understand why a sudden stop was put to the continued utterance of such excellent counsel, or why the policy of preparing the farmers' mind was at once abandoned. I was induced at the time, I remember, to consider whether there was not some connection between it and the news from China; because from the moment that some revival of trade was expected on account of it the salutary lecturings were stopped, which looked a little as if Monopoly was to be clung to so long as it was possible ; but that if trade did not improve and the pressure from without were only sufficient, it might in the opinion of its supporters be abandoned without danger. Aye, and as many of them almost admit, with positive advantage to themselves ; for the Corn Laws are a measure that has for its purpose not only to prevent importation, but, as Mr. Welford shows, to prevent improvement and to check production. There is the same imaginary interest in doing both. What is essential to the success of a Corn Law is to limit the quantity, for that is the only way by which price can be maintained ; and that may be defeated as much by rendering the soil more productive as by importation.

Indeed, of late it has been avowed that the defect of the Laws is that they are not sufficiently restrictive, that some clause is required to limit the quantity of corn grown. This was openly stated the other day in the 'Morning Post,' which is the special organ of the proprietors who support the Corn Laws ; it has been repeated in effect by the 'Standard,' which is the organ of the Government. And I observed in a speech made by the Member for Dorsetshire when he addressed his constituents, that he almost ridiculed the idea of the farmers adopting the later and the best improvements in agriculture recommended to them, asking in derision where they were to obtain the money to effect them, and whether if the landlords advanced the money they were likely ever to be repaid.

And yet the object and effect of such improvements is to supply the deficiency of food that the Corn Laws have caused from the first, and always will cause. Nothing can secure price but limiting quantity, and nothing in some years can effect that unless improvements are checked, or special powers employed in certain quarters for the purpose of destroying the produce or controlling its amount. Mr. Whitmore sarcastically told the agriculturists at some meeting that there ought to be a Burning Clause in their Acts, to be enforced whenever, by the bounty of heaven, the harvests are too abundant; and I think he alluded to its having been gravely contemplated at an agricultural meeting in 1822. And these are really the views taken by the party represented by the Member for Wallingford, with whom a large majority of the other House, I believe, warmly sympathizes.

But if the farmers would not be frightened, and if improvements would not be prevented by Repeal, is there a pretence for the assertion that the land would go out of cultivation, which is constantly urged as a reason against it? It is reiterated year after year, and I ask the House candidly if there has ever been the slightest pains taken to show any ground for it—whether there is really the least pretence to expect such a result? Look at the foolish predictions that have been made from time to time and brought forward as a reason for these or some other Corn Laws, and how regularly they have been all falsified by experience. Last Session only, as

I said before, the Member for Nottinghamshire declared that if the price of wheat should fall to 47*s.* vast tracts of land must go out of cultivation. And yet is there an acre expected to go out of cultivation, though prices were never lower than at this moment, or does anybody expect any to go out? What was the case in 1822 and 1836? Was any labour displaced, as it is called, in consequence of land being deserted or returned to waste? Why, it was in one of those years that a Mr. Ellis or Ellman, who is a favourite witness whenever it is thought necessary to call an agriculturist in favour of more Protection, said that it was very extraordinary that during those years which were designated as periods of unparalleled distress the demand for land was as great as ever, both by those who wanted to occupy land and those who desired to have more; and that none had gone out of cultivation. We all know that at no period have Enclosure Bills been stopped, and that between the years of 1832 and 1836 nearly 100 were passed.

But if this solicitude for the labourer lest he might be displaced is sincere, how ready a mode does this land that hitherto has been productive and that is expected to lie waste, offer to provide for the destitute labourer! Let us only have an account of the land that is to be thrown out of cultivation, and we shall know how to provide for the labourer. At present the calculation is that there are three labourers for 100 acres. Is it likely that these 100 acres divided among the three labourers would not maintain them somewhat better than they are maintained at present? Here surely is an answer to those who pretend that their only fear in repealing the Corn Laws is on account of displacing labour. I doubt, if all the labourers that are to be so displaced were to be maintained magnificently at the public expense, whether it would be so costly to the community as 1*s*. a quarter added to the price of the grain consumed in this country.

But it is nothing more or less than a cruel mockery of the labourers to talk of their interest in Laws that diminish the quantity of food to be distributed amongst their class; and from the results of which they have been the invariable sufferers, and always more intensely in proportion as the Laws have succeeded in their object.

It has been with difficulty that these labourers have been restrained at various times from breaking the peace in consequence of their discontent at the results of the Corn Laws. The average price of wheat from 1794 to 1814 was 84*s*. a quarter, and during that time there were several occasions of rioting in the country districts simply owing to the high price of food.

Again, whether we make inquiry in these districts ourselves, or look to the evidence that has been collected by Committees, how could the labourer be worse off than he is at present after the Laws have existed for twenty-eight years? What occurred only the other day in one of the wealthy counties in the centre of the kingdom? A Report was lately made by the surgeons appointed to examine the convicts in the hulks when they arrive there from the prisons, and they expressed their opinion that the condition of the prisoners showed the insufficiency of their previous diet; they had every appearance of having been kept on bad and insufficient food. In consequence of this, the Right Hon. Baronet the Secretary of State issued an order to all the gaols directing an improvement in their dietaries. But when the magistrates came to consider it they exclaimed against it, and, speaking from their local acquaintance with the condition of the peasantry, declared that the criminals would in future be far better off as regarded food than the labouring poor. Thus showing that those who were in a condition only just above that which precludes sickness and disease arising from bad living, were in a condition superior to that prevailing amongst our agricultural population for the maintenance of which gentlemen, as friends of the poor, plead the continuance of the Corn Laws. I have here a specimen of what is the condition of those poor labourers in one of the midland counties where they are said to be less indigent than elsewhere; it is from a paper published in Worcestershire:—

The advocates of the Corn Laws say that their repeal would reduce the labourers' wages; others that their wages are already at the starvation point, and cannot be reduced. We give a case in point:—A labourer named Smith was recently brought before the Worcester bench, charged with an offence against the Highway Act, and when the magistrates were considering the case, it came out that he was engaged as cowman, from *Michaelmas last year* till *Ladyday this, at* 16*s*. 6*d*., besides his board and lodging, and had to pay for his washing himself. It further appeared that for the two years previous to Michaelmas he had worked *for 7s. per week*, and found everything, saving in harvest time, when he had dinner and drink. Under these circumstances, the bench mitigated the penalty to 1s. and costs, or one day's imprisonment. Smith's case is not solitary, but one of a rapidly increasing class.

Now, under these circumstances, with evidence of the wretched condition of the agricultural labourer in this country within every man's reach, I do really hope that gentlemen will be more careful than they commonly are in what they allege in defence of the Corn Laws, for it really almost amounts to insult to those who are suffering the severest privation, to tell them that laws injurious to everybody else are kept to benefit them. I do not suppose that the supporters of these Laws will much heed what I say on this point; but I assure them that there is now an intelligence abroad on the subject that will utterly preclude the success of any of those fallacies that have been used before, and that everything that is said will be carefully scrutinized and judged by men well informed on the matter. Let them remember what has been the consequence of urging that there are peculiar burdens on the land as a pretext for the Corn Laws. Inquiry into its truth was demanded. Two Motions were made in this House for it. But they were not carried. No, the House shrank from them. And why? Because after the matter had been thoroughly sifted it was found that so far from there being exclusive charges, there were shameful exemptions.

With regard to the Tithes which were urged as a plea for raising rent by law; some were induced to accept that plea through the confusion that was artfully created in their minds between a right reserved in the land as old as its appropriation, and a public burden specially borne by the present owners of the soil. Tithe is only an ancient right to a portion of the profits of the land applicable for the purposes of religion: a right that, I trust, the State will never part with, and for which the landlord has no more claim to indemnity than he has a claim to be recompensed for not possessing another man's property. That there were inconveniences and some check to improvement in the old way of collecting the Tithe or exercising this right is well known; but we are talking at a time when the commutation for a fixed pecuniary payment of the Tithe so collected has been nearly completed, and the inconvenience or mischief no longer exists. And to talk of a Corn Law as an indemnity for Tithe, when in Scotland no Tithe is paid, when in England more than one quarter of the country is Tithe free, and a large portion of the Tithes belong to the landlords themselves, is, in my judgment, an extravagant absurdity.

As for the Land Tax, it is doubtless a deduction from rent, but one to which the State is entitled; and surely, considering the manner in which the landlords in Parliament have dealt with it since it was imposed, it never can be for their interest to have it discussed or inquired into: no man can learn that history without almost feeling that as a class the land-owners have proved themselves utterly unworthy of public trust. Nothing ever was more shameless than the manner in which the State has been deprived of its due amount of the Land Tax by a gross violation of the bargain the land-owners made with the Crown when it was imposed. It was strictly in lieu of the feudal services by which alone their lands were held, and for which 4*s.* in the pound on the rental were required—clearly an inadequate commutation for the inconvenience to which such services would have exposed them; but which, did it yield what it ought, would now cover the whole amount of the Excise, and thereby dispense with it. If the Land Tax now paid its proper quota, it would yield thirteen millions a year instead of little more than one million; and by causing the assessment to be fixed upon the valuation of the land made 150 years since, the public have been defrauded of the difference. But the plea of a special burden borne by the landlords of England is unquestionably the most barefaced pretext for the Corn Laws that was ever put forward: it is matter of history that there is no country in Europe where the feudal system has prevailed, in which the land-owners and the aristocracy have made such favourable terms with the Crown as in England. In every other, whether Austria, Italy, Prussia, Belgium, France, they have submitted in lieu of services to a considerable direct tax on their land, bearing a large proportion to the whole taxation of the country.

But in calling for the great act of policy and

humanity that will free the supply of food to the community now obstructed by law, I will not descend to discuss the miserable pretence for Monopoly in a parcel of local liabilities which attach to property. I demand on the part of the community some reply to the question which is here proposed: Upon what principle of justice or wisdom is the trade in the people's food not allowed to be free, when on all hands its taxation as accessory to the Revenue is repudiated, and when it is avowed by the Minister that from the deteriorated condition of the people the limits of taxation on the necessaries of life have been already passed? I do hope that on this occasion the Right Hon. Baronet will not content himself with fencing with small details, and taking advantage of the slight errors or inaccuracies of unguarded opponents; but that he will give us his general views of the present economical condition of this country and apply himself to the main feature of the question that I have submitted to him: namely, that the people are not adequately supplied with food, that their numbers are increasing, and that the Corn Laws exist purposely to make food scarce. Let him tell us in answer whether he considers that the people are adequately supplied with food in this country, and if not how he can justify the maintenance of Laws having such a purpose as the Corn Laws, which the men who maintain them, and who know the object of those who passed them, admit to have been enacted for their interest.

The people well know that Lord Fitzwilliam has

openly declared that these Laws were made for the interest of the landed aristocracy: 'The painful confession must be made that our own benefit is the true object for which this obnoxious code is established,' were his very words. Nor can we forget that the late Prime Minister, Lord Melbourne, in the other House, reminded their Lordships in a friendly way that the pinch of the question was that they were legislating for their own pockets. Then, Lord John Russell, in the face of the citizens of London, declared that the Laws were made not for the community but for a particular class, and that he opposed them because he wanted to liberate our commerce, and to unchain the industry of the country. And lastly, we have had Lord Mountcashel's view of their necessity: he, in his simplicity, uttered the truth plainer than other men, for he said that he wanted the Corn Laws to enable great men to pay their mortgages.

With such authority as to the object of the Corn Laws, and with a long experience of their effects, what can be said to satisfy the people that they ought not to call for their repeal? Briefly, the case stands thus: these Laws avowedly passed with a partial object, still continue; the people are hourly increasing in number; they are wanting more food; there is no lack of food in the world; there is no lack of means in this country to procure it; and if the Corn Laws did not prevent food coming into the country, they would be utterly useless to those who maintain them. And let it be remembered also that the general opinion out of doors is that the continuance of such Laws is nothing less than an outrage on humanity, and a scandal to Christendom. On these grounds, then, I ask the House to resolve itself into a Committee of the whole House to take the Corn Laws into its consideration, with a view to their immediate repeal.

XVI.

COLCHESTER, July 8, 1843.

Very great importance was, at the time, attached to the Colchester meeting held on July 8, 1843, in support of the repeal of the Corn Laws. Colchester was a stronghold of Conservatism; and so successful was the canvass of the leading land-owners and the clergy, and the Agricultural Associations of Essex, which went on throughout the county for days before the meeting, that a large majority in favour of Protection was confidently reckoned on by the Protectionists. Special constables were sworn in, as violence to the advocates of Repeal was anticipated. And, apparently, not without reason. Thousands of people assembled from all parts of the county; and at one time the proceedings seemed about to terminate in a scene of uproar. The farmers, at first, positively refused to listen to Mr. Cobden. But before the end of his speech he won their attention if not their complete acquiescence; and Mr. Villiers, who followed Sir John Tyrrell, and who was received with great cheering, closed his speech amidst tumultuous applause. The victory of the Free Traders was unquestionable: the farmers' interest was carried, and Sir John Tyrrell had disappeared utterly discomfited.

I WILL make the Chairman quite easy about the time that I shall occupy in speaking. I was just about to quit the hustings, having pretty nearly satisfied my purpose in attending the meeting; and only on the suggestion of Mr. Cobden am I induced to address you now. He considers that it would be respectful for me to do so, because I am the person who from the beginning has brought forward in the House of Commons the Motion that the Laws which you are discussing should be totally repealed.

The truth is, I did not come here to make any address: I came simply to get at the truth as to the genuine feeling in the agricultural districts ; for I was told that this is a sort of fountain-head of opposition to the repeal of the Corn Laws. But perhaps the thing that really determined me to come was an accidental meeting with Sir John Tyrrell yesterday. The first thing he asked me was whether I intended to show at Colchester. You all know that Sir John generally looks in pretty good humour with the world, not altogether forgetting himself; but there was something so very confident in his tone yesterday, something so like 'come if you dare,' that I was almost afraid that if I did not come it would look like shrinking from the challenge.

Moreover, I quite thought, from Sir John's manner, that if I came I should hear something new. I thought that there was to be a new set of arguments brought out in Colchester in favour of the Corn Laws, by which, if I had any candour in my composition, I should allow myself to be converted. I need not tell you, therefore, with what interest and anxiety I have followed the proceedings. I heard Mr. Cobden state his case ; but then I knew Sir John was present, and I trembled for my friend. I have now heard Sir John's reply, and, thanks to Sir John, who for some reason proposed to you to decide before you heard his speech, I have pretty well ascertained your feeling on the subject. Why, was not the amendment put, and was it not negatived by a decided majority ? ['Yes.'] Well, then, now that you have heard Sir John's speech, are you inclined to vote differently ? ['No, no.']

By-the-by, his speech was not quite to the point of his amendment, though you may think differently; for, if I mistake not, his amendment asked you to support the Corn Laws on the ground of what he called the heavy charges on land; but after the speech began, and when everything had been said on the subject, there was very little proof of those heavy charges. And the argument for the Corn Laws was found in some black bread which he pulled from his pocket [A cry: 'It was gingerbread.'] and threw among you, hoping to make you believe that all bread would be of the same colour if the Corn Laws were repealed.

Now, which objection does he intend to stick to, the peculiar burdens or the black bread—for they have not much to do with one another? Or did Sir John hope to carry you by storm in the character he gave to Mr. Cobden's speech—for that seemed to be one reason for the amendment which he did not carry? He did not think it worth a reply. He said that it was the weakest and most impotent speech that he had ever heard. You did not seem to think so. And I, who have often heard Mr. Cobden speak, thought I had never heard him speak better. Indeed, if his speech was an impotent speech, I hardly know what an impotent speech means. But if it means avoiding the real point in question in a long ramble about everything else in the world; if it means being personal to those you cannot answer, and beating about the bush for topics to take up time, I think I have heard a more impotent speech than Mr.

Cobden's not long ago, if I am not mistaken. [A voice: 'That's for you, Sir John.']

Well, you have heard Sir John's reply to Mr. Cobden; I doubt whether he came here to show that which I came here to learn: namely, what the Corn Laws have done for the farmer and the farmer's labourer. Do you think he has settled that question? ['No, no.'] Does anybody remember precisely what he said upon the subject? Does anybody remember a single proof that the Corn Laws have benefited you, or ever could do so? ['No.']

The answer to this question is very important, let me tell you. What you wish or feel on the matter is, in fact, of much greater importance than you think. Perhaps you do not know it, but you are very mighty people in the House of Commons. You do not know, probably, from what you experience down here, how much great people care for you up there. Why, you are everything when the Corn Laws are mentioned; nobody else is talked of.

Some people change their opinions so fast, that perhaps you do not know that the Corn Laws, of which you have heard so much, are not so well thought of in high places as they used to be. In 1841, as you are aware, the Corn Laws were the cause of England's glory. We had become great with them, and we might become greater if we kept them. At all events, it would be madness to risk them in the vain hope of drawing a grander prize in the lottery of legislation. A little time afterwards, however, these famous Laws lost favour with our rulers; and since the beginning of 1842 they have been treated at best as a sort of necessary evil. If we could but begin again they never should be inflicted on the country. They diminish the Revenue and interrupt commerce; and for the future we must —as the Duke of Wellington said—look habitually for the importation of food from abroad. These and many other things that were denied before, are admitted now.

But perhaps, as you used to be told that they were for the general good, you do not know why the Corn Laws are still maintained. We sometimes tell them in the House that the special object of the Corn Laws is to keep up rents. But they always say in reply that this is a vulgar view of the question; that if rent were the object of the Corn Laws, there would be no difficulty in getting rid of them; that country gentlemen would give them up at once. What is the object, then? They say that the farmers and farm labourers are so well pleased with these Laws for the good they have done them, that they won't hear of their being abolished. That they are really the people for whom the Corn Laws are wanted. The farmers depend upon them for profit, and the labourer gets good work and good wages by means of them. [' No.'] Nevertheless, from the beginning to the end of a discussion on the Corn Laws in the House of Commons, we hear of nothing but of your interests. Is it not, therefore, consistent with our sincerity in this cause that we should come among you, and face to face talk over the matter, and so learn your real feelings on the subject—because, be it remembered, all are agreed now on the mischief that the Corn Laws do to all other classes, and, as I have already said, you alone are made the pretext and excuse for their continuance? Is it not then reasonable and laudable in Mr. Cobden to come here to discuss the question with you, when there are so many things afloat to make one believe that you are not properly represented?—when people declare that the Corn Laws have done you so much good?—when, as he says, you and your landlords are all jumbled up together in a sort of family party, called the landed interest, and are said to be so prosperous on account of them?

I have never believed that they did you good. But before bringing them under the notice of the House of Commons I have almost invariably made a point of consulting some proprietor or some occupier of land, in order to be quite sure that I was not doing anything unwise or unsafe in proposing the consideration of them; for, God knows, I bear no ill will to the landed interest—by birth I am connected with it—and I have no kind of connection whatever with manufactures.

I remember that, in 1839, I inquired of one well versed in agricultural matters, what he considered to be the value of the Corn Laws to farmers, and whether they did not really secure them a good price for their wheat. He said that there was no need to go so far for information; that we had a very good agriculturist in the House of Commons—the Speaker of the House of Commons, in fact, who in 1836 was Chairman of the Committee then appointed to inquire into agricultural distress, and who had published the conclusions that he drew from the evidence given on that Committee. My friend advised me to go and look at what the farmers had said for themselves on that occasion, as well as the Speaker's conclusions.

Well, first of all I looked to see what the Speaker had said, and one of the first things that I came upon was this: the people found to be in the greatest distress were the occupiers of wheat land—the very men who had depended on the Corn Laws to secure them prosperity! This statement was not made to prejudice the Corn Laws. It was simply a fact elicited upon the general inquiry into the state of agriculturists throughout the country. And subjoined to it was the Speaker's opinion, that the farmer, like every other man, had to depend upon his skill and prudence, and nothing else, for success in his business.

I looked also into the evidence; and I will read you the names and opinions of a few who were called on the occasion, and you will then be able to determine whether I was wrong in contending that there was at least a question as to the good the Corn Laws had done you. As Mr. Cobden has already alluded to two of the witnesses from this county, I will refer to those only who were from other places.

The first land agent examined was Mr. Thomas Neve, a resident in Kent:—

Comparing the state of the farmers in that district of the

country at the present time with their state in 1833, do you consider it better or worse?—I think where they are dependent principally on corn they are in a worse condition.

Then Mr. John Houghton, land agent on property in Lincoln, Bucks, Middlesex, Surrey, Sussex, Northampton, and Suffolk, gave his evidence:—

Do you find that the capital of the farmer has been diminishing?—Certainly.

Have the farmers been paying their rent out of their produce or out of their capital?—If you take the heavy clay lands, certainly out of their capital. When I have been paying workmen in provincial towns, they have said, 'You have all the money of the place for rents, and the tenants cannot pay us.'

Next we have Mr. W. Cox, of Scotsgrove, Buckinghamshire:—

Are the farmers doing well or ill?—A great part have failed; and more than half the rest, if they were to reckon, would be insolvent.

Then Mr. John Rolfe, Beaconsfield, Bucks, was examined:—

Do you mean to say that one-half of the tenantry in your district are insolvent?—Yes, I do..

Mr. William Thurnall, Daxford, Cambridge, follows:—

What, in your opinion, is the condition generally of the tenantry in your neighbourhood?—I think verging on insolvency, the most desperate state that men can be in; not only in Cambridge, but, generally speaking, in a great part of Norfolk, Suffolk, and Essex.

Mr. Thomas Bowyer was asked:—

What is the condition generally of the tenantry in Huntingdonshire?—They are at a very low ebb indeed. I think nearly half of them have next to nothing.

Then we come to Mr. Evan Daird :—

Is there much distress among the farmers in Glamorganshire ?—Yes, very much ; the capital of the tenantry has been disappearing in the last ten, twelve, or fifteen years.

Are there many insolvent now ?—Many have become insolvent, and I could enumerate several others whose losses have been very great. I should say nearly 45,000*l*. has been sunk by four-and-twenty farmers within ten miles of me.

Mr. Charles Howard, East Riding, Yorkshire, was also examined :—

Are the present wages of labourers paid out of the profits of the farmer or out of his capital ?—Out of his capital.

And Mr. J. G. Cooper, Blythburg, Suffolk :—

What is the state of the farmer ?—The condition of the farmer I consider to be bordering on ruin.

There was much more to the same effect. Would the witnesses tell a very different tale now, think you?

With respect to the labourers I do not believe that they are benefited by these Laws, because I find that in some counties their wages are under eight shillings a week, and hardly anywhere are they above eleven shillings ; one-eighth of the population in the agricultural districts is receiving parish relief, and there are numbers every year who wish to leave their parishes because they cannot find employment and do not want to go into the workhouse.

When I turn to Ireland, the agricultural portion of the Empire which is said to be protected by the Corn Laws, I find that three millions of the people are not able to earn more than fivepence-halfpenny a day—and this pitiful sum for only six months in the year—whilst two millions are utterly destitute.

These are all authenticated facts. Where then, I ask, is the evidence that the agricultural labourer benefits by the Corn Laws which are said to protect him? Why, there are millions who never see any wheaten food whatever. [A voice from the Tories: 'That is false.'] Well, if it is, the falsehood is not mine; it is that of the party to which that gentleman belongs. A Tory of note, dining at a Tory dinner in the county of Buckingham, stated the other day, and I believe quite truly, that there are ten millions, and no less, in that condition. But perhaps I am wrong. They do see it. They see the corn when they sow it; they see it when they reap it, when they thrash it, when they stack it; and then they see it no more.

It is upon these grounds, then, that I and my friend Mr. Cobden come into the agricultural districts to be satisfied. We want you to tell us what are the blessings, or the advantages, which you connect with the Corn Laws. We show you what reason we have to doubt what your friends say for you in London; and we ask you for a set-off in your own condition to the enormous evil which the Laws inflict on the other productive classes. And do not underrate this evil, for if the Laws did you ever so much good, you could not justify their continuance.

Hear how the Corn Laws have been described by a Peer in the House of Lords—one who is no particular friend of the League—in stating the effects of preventing the industrious classes from exchanging their labour when they could find custom for it. Hear the consequences of it, as he described them to be found in the densely peopled manufacturing districts of this country. He says :—

> In Leicester, Shropshire, Staffordshire, Warwickshire, Lancashire, and Yorkshire, wages are reduced, houses left untenanted, rents have fallen one-half or less, able-bodied and healthy men —at least men who were once in health—men well skilled in their respective branches of trade, men able and but too anxious for work, are thrown out of work by thousands. Wages are reduced in some instances to 6*d*. a week, rather less than one penny for each and every day. The Poor Rate has increased in some places four-fold, and in other places double that amount, and the defalcation of rateable property has gone on from 20 to 30, 40, and sometimes 50 per cent. There have been found such occurrences as seven, eight, and ten persons in one cottage, I cannot say for one day, but for whole days, without a morsel of food. They have remained on their beds of straw for two successive days, under the impression that in a recumbent posture the pangs of hunger were less felt. Members of religious congregations have been frequently taken from places of worship, fainting from illness and weakness, brought on from want of proper sustenance.

[Cries of 'Name, name.'] Lord Brougham made this statement to the House of Lords, and he offered to prove what he said, but no one contradicted him.

And these are the people that Sir John sneers at. ['No,' from Sir John.] You talked of their violence last year. [Sir John : 'Yes ; and I say it again.'] And would not you speak out also if you were in equal distress?

I have here—and I will read it—a short extract from a Report which was made by a Commissioner of Sir Robert Peel's, sent down into those districts to inquire into the state and character of the people, and you shall judge from it whether the people do not deserve respect, and a better fate. He said :—

They were, in intelligence, already much in advance of the other orders of working people, and still growing with the general growth of education. On the occurrence of general distress they are neither a pauperized mass, nor readily admitting pauperism among them, but struggling against adversity, beating far and wide for employment, and, in many cases, leaving their country for foreign climates, rather than depend upon any other resources for subsistence than those of their own industry and skill. Those who have not been able or willing to leave a place where their labour is of little or no value, have been found enduring distress with patience, and abstaining, sometimes to the injury of health, from applying for relief; whilst others, driven reluctantly to that extremity, we have seen receiving a degree of relief sufficient only to support life, with thankfulness and gratitude, often without murmur or complaint.

[Mr. Cobden : 'That is a description of the operatives of Stockport, and it is perfectly true.' A voice : 'And yet you get your money out of these people.' Mr. Cobden : 'I do no such thing.' My business is twenty-five miles from Stockport, and I have nothing more to do with that borough in the way of trade than you have.'] If these men work for low wages, and enable others to make large fortunes—as somebody remarked they do—whose fault is it? Is it theirs, or that of the people employing them? Is it not because there is not sufficient demand for their labour, and is not that demand checked by the very Laws that we are considering? Are there not people ready to barter with them, who can give food in exchange for their manufactures? And does not this Act of Parliament say that they shall not exchange?

And with such consequences as I have stated, is not that a scandal and a shame?

Now, mark what the case is as it stands before you and awaits your decision. Hear the claim and the story of your industrious fellow-subjects engaged in manufactures, before you again lend your names and voices in favour of such Laws.

The population in this country is rapidly increasing; every additional man must find employment in manufactures or other business—for in agriculture there is room for no more. In order to be able to find employment in manufactures there must be a demand for what is made, and to support the people there must be an adequate supply of food. What say the manufacturers? They say: 'Give us food and take our manufactures, and we would sooner exchange with you than with foreigners. But if you cannot consume our manufactures, and cannot supply us sufficiently with food, let us go where we can find customers for our manufactures who will give us the food we want in exchange.' That is the request of the manufacturers. Is it unreasonable? ['No, no.'] And what is the answer to it? Has Sir John Tyrrell told us? ['No.'] Can the agriculturists consume all the manufactures that are produced? If not, is it not cruel and unjust to refuse to allow them to take them where there is a means of disposing of them? Is there food enough produced at home? I say, no! notoriously not. Is it not monstrous, then, to stand between the people and their necessities, and not allow them to go where they can procure food?

But this being the case, where is the advantage to oppose to so much injustice and cruelty? Can the people increase and not be the worse for it if their employment does not also increase? And if the people get poorer, can the farmer get rich while his customers are declining? [' No.'] And if competition compels him to give the highest price for his land, can he pay his rent if the produce falls in price? [' No, no.'] Where, then, is the advantage to any one in such an unnatural regulation? The Corn Laws have lasted twenty-eight years ; what good have they done you ? You are now called upon to make known your sentiments on the subject. You are summoned here as jurors before your country ; and, after a full and fair trial of these Laws, you are bound to declare your verdict upon them. What do you say ? Are the Corn Laws guilty or not guilty ? [Loud cries of 'Guilty!' and some cries of 'No.'] Well, then, you who think that they ought to be abolished speak out like men—in a manner no longer to be misunderstood ; and never again allow yourselves to be misrepresented as wishing to perpetuate a system fraught with folly and injustice, and unattended with real benefit to any one.

Thanking you sincerely for the attention that you have given me, I will now make way for those who may be waiting to address you.

XVII.

COVENT GARDEN THEATRE, February 8, 1844.

Parliament was prorogued in 1843 without any steps having been taken to remedy the distress in the country. The resolve of the League to raise a fresh fund of 100,000*l.* met with ready support from the banking and manufacturing interests and many distinguished members of the peerage. At one meeting at Manchester upwards of forty manufacturers subscribed on the spot sums varying from 100*l.* to 500*l.* each. The 'Times' announced that the League was 'a great fact,' and that 'a new power had arisen in the State' which owed its existence to 'experience set at naught, advice derided, and warnings neglected.' Mr. Bright's entry into Parliament in July was followed, in October, by the defeat of Mr. Baring and the election of Mr. Pattison for the City of London. When Parliament reassembled on February 3, 1844, the Queen's Speech, whilst it congratulated the Legislature on the improved condition of several important branches of trade and manufacture, and expressed the hope that the increased demand for labour had relieved many classes from sufferings and privations, which at former periods there had been occasion to deplore, made no allusion to the Corn Laws and completely ignored the state of the agricultural districts. On February 8, Mr. Villiers addressed the third metropolitan meeting of the League for the year, at Covent Garden Theatre. Every part of the building was filled to overflowing, and hundreds failed to gain admittance for want of space. At the conclusion of his speech the whole assembly rose, and amidst the waving of hats and handkerchiefs, greeted the Parliamentary leader of Repeal with prolonged acclamations.

When I see in what vast numbers you have assembled in this great building, further to consider and to mark your unshaken interest in the momentous question we are about to discuss, I agree with the Chairman that there is little reason for dismay at the new and would-be-threatening attitude that our opponents have recently assumed. I agree with those who see only advantage to our cause in their proceedings; for if that cause be based on truth, why should we fear the general discussion of it which our opponents are inviting?

I bear our opponents no ill-will; but if I did I should certainly not rejoice the less at their proceedings. If it be true that those who are doomed by heaven are by the same power first made foolish, this recent move is unquestionably evidence of their doom. They are actually doing that which they ought most to avoid; they are disclosing what it is most to their interest to conceal: they are making themselves known to the country; they are revealing to thousands previously ignorant, who and what they are for whom the immense sacrifices of the commerce, the industry, wealth, and greatness of the country have been and are yet being made, and what measure of public spirit, of high feeling and intelligence they possess to entitle them to hold the exclusive privilege of legislation, and enjoy the confidence of those who have submitted to their rule. They seem to have forgotten how much of their power has root in the imagination of men; and how greatly they profit by the confusion that exists in some men's minds between what is great and what is good, and between those who are rich and those who are respectable. Their extreme good fortune, and perhaps some defect of our Constitution, gives them a League ready formed in the two Houses of the Legislature. With this, it seems, they are not satisfied. In humble imitation of the League, that has been formed in self-defence, they have descended, as the Chairman said, into the field of public agitation, and have now fairly entered the lists with those whose course they have hitherto pretended to condemn.

But I doubt much if they have the qualities of success. The drone has not the properties of the other bee, and I doubt their energy in such a struggle. They are strong in rank and strong, it seems, in language, and, unless Monopoly has failed them more than we imagine, they are strong also in pecuniary means; but they are strongest of all in their imagination if they fancy that by mere bluster, by no better weapon than vulgar diction, they can dissipate a power that has arisen from necessity and the sense of wrong, and that receives its strength and spirit from the indomitable love of justice which pervades and, I trust in God, ever will pervade our nation.

It is dangerous to prophesy, still I venture to predict that they will fail. They will, I know, puff themselves inordinately, they will have to pay enormously and they will talk largely, and they may attempt some further wrong upon the people; but still I believe that for want of honesty of object, for want of faithfulness in their agents, for want of unity of purpose, they will first disagree and then disappear. Why is it that they now quit their post in order to agitate? Because they begin to mistrust all around them, and all who—if their cause were decent—one would think, would remain attached to them. They mistrust the Minister whom they have made, they mistrust the Members whom they have named, they have not really any faith in the farmer—though he occupies their land at will, and they do not expect

—as in their hearts, perhaps, they know they do not deserve—excessive gratitude from their much-be-praised, but ill-fed, ill-housed labourer. They feel that the time is come when they themselves must turn out, and their flatterers assure them that if they will but show themselves and speak, the League will vanish, and the tide of public feeling will recede. So now these great men may be seen sitting like the Danish king before the sea, declaring that the waves of the ocean shall not roll on. It is really a diverting scene to see them—these dukes and barons—in their waggons and at their windows, teaching their tenants, what it seems their tenants have still to learn: the good that they have done them; how Parliament has protected them; how many friends they have; how prosperous they are, and what almost incalculable advantage will accrue to them by putting down the men who venture to dispute these things.

It is wonderful that it does not strike these lords as very strange that if men have really been so favoured, they should not have known it before, and that it should require such a special screw (as we know it has required) to make them meet to hear it. But perhaps these lords have heard, what the League certainly discovered: namely, that the tenant farmers are in the predicament that the enemies of Monopoly always said they would be in—that what was foretold of the Corn Laws has actually occurred. It was foretold that after these foolish Laws had injured every other class, they would recoil upon those for whose benefit it was pretended they were passed;

and they have done so. The League has been listened to of late by the farmers because they found that they had been deceived, and they were puzzled to answer the question which was put to them : What good have the Corn Laws done you ? Vainly will these lords preach to them of their profit from the Corn Laws unless they can prove what they say.

The fact is, the landlords found that the whole machinery by which they maintain Monopoly was getting out of sorts, and they deemed it necessary to put it in repair for work before the Session. The part that caused them the most anxiety and excited their gravest suspicions was, it seems, the Steward of the State, the Prime Minister. They would not let him know their mistrust of him, or learn for himself the conditions of his service ; but in every market-town and village they posted him as one not to be confided in for having risked the public good, and they called upon all faithful men to watch him for the future. The Members, too, who are named for the counties by a few great families resident in them, have been summoned before their lords, and cautioned for the future against the corrupting influence of this Minister.

One purpose of these meetings, indeed, has been to lecture the farmers, and to direct them what to do in future. A noble lord in Hertfordshire has desired the farmers to show their teeth ; and in Essex, I think, the labourers are charged in future to speak out. But how the farmers 'showing their teeth' will raise the price of wheat is not apparent ; and whether the labourers might not find some better use for their mouths than that of 'speaking out' is I think, at least, questionable. However, the great object has been to put the whole concern in better trim; and judging by the first night of the Session, it would seem that they have succeeded admirably. There was no hitch; all the cracks through which a little public good could have leaked out appeared to have been stopped effectually, and the landlords pronounce themselves satisfied.

A foreign writer has designated the British Constitution the best taxing machine in Europe. He should have dwelt also on its pre-eminence for Monopoly. And he would, no doubt, had he seen it lately in all its glory; for the enviable position accorded the British Constitution is manifestly due to Monopoly. It is Monopoly that has really elicited the extraordinary powers of the machine. When by the action of Monopoly the people are prevented from paying taxes indirectly to the State, then it is that we are shown what is called the peculiar vigour of the Constitution to extract the deficit directly from their incomes. And if the country just escapes convulsions from the double action of taxes and Monopoly, the Prime Minister has the assurance to congratulate us on its healthy state, and the revival of its business.

But if the people venture to cry out against Monopoly as the cause of their privations and increased taxation, what is there that the Monopolists will not say? I have here, I think, the speech of some squire which was given to me as I entered the theatre.

Yes, here it is. He describes the objects of the League as 'the same as those of the Corresponding Society, of Pitt's time, which was originated by the bloody Jacobins of France.' And 'these men'—meaning the members of the League—he roundly goes on to say, 'are the great grand-children of those bloody fellows. They wish to destroy the landlord, in order to pick the pocket of the tenant, and then to send the labourer to the devil.'

This is moderate, however, to what I have read elsewhere; for at most of their meetings our opponents are reported to have declared the complaints against the Corn Laws to be nothing else than blasphemy. They fall very far short of that simplicity of expression used by the Brahmins in India—apprehensive of a calamity like that now dreaded by the landlords—when Christian missionaries first went among them. The Brahmins were paid by the people in rice, and they foresaw that if the Hindoos became Christians, they would lose their pots of rice. But they did not denounce the missionaries as false teachers or blasphemers, as perhaps they might have been allowed to do, they simply complained to the Government that men had come among them who, if success crowned their efforts, would 'upset their rice-pots'!

The only approach to this simple frankness that I have come across lately is to be found in a circular that has been sent round in Norfolk. The circular invites the nobility, gentry, and clergy to attend a meeting for the purpose of resisting the League, whose doctrine, it says, if successful, will reduce wheat from 18*s*. to 12*s*. a coomb. There lies the blasphemy! But I do not think that they will get many to pray against such doctrines. And I doubt whether they will be able to resist the spread of them in any other way. They are already puzzled with the question whether they can legislate against food without legislating against the discussion of the Corn Laws? Some think not, and consequently twenty-eight petitions were presented from the great men in Lincolnshire praying of Government to stop the League. Others think that they can, and that by their own sweet voices they will be able to charm away the plague. They will succeed about as well as the clergyman in a parish in the West that I heard of the other day, whom the wise people used to call up at night when the wind blew high, to read a chapter from the Bible in order to stay the storm. However, whatever the different views of these folks may be with regard to us, we, I believe, are all of one mind with regard to ourselves. To a man we are determined that the League shall not be put down, and we unanimously meet their resolution not to abandon an atom of their Protection, with our counter-resolution not to surrender an iota of our principle. Our proceedings are perfectly legal; and no Minister yet dare stop free discussion in England.

What we have to do, in consequence of the proceedings against us, is to put forth greater energy, to make greater exertions, and to avail ourselves to the utmost of all the advantages that the landlords have conferred upon us by exciting universal attention to our arguments.

One of the chief things that I have to thank them for, is that of having cleared and narrowed the ground upon which we are respectively to take our stand. I always felt it to be a difficulty in discussions on the Corn Laws, that I never knew exactly what the advocates of them intended to rest their case on. It was sometimes one thing, and sometimes another; but luckily, as they grew more confident, they grew also more clear; and, now that they have got an organ which they recognize as such, it is not difficult to discover their intentions as well as their views. To do so I sometimes turn to the columns of the 'Morning Post'; and yesterday I found an article announcing —as if to remove all doubt on the matter during the coming Session—what it is that the land-owners claim. Now this paper must be considered to be at least of some authority; for at all their meetings they pass a vote of thanks for its past and faithful services. What then do I learn from the article, giving as it were the keynote of the Session? A very interesting lesson: no less, indeed, than the duties and rights of farmers and landlords. In the first place, we are told that the duty of the farmer is to resist the hypothesis that any supply of food from abroad is necessary. This is convenient, doubtless. Then we have the duty of the landlord; and this, too, is quite clear, for they say that it is the duty of the landlord to take care of his own interest. And lastly we come to the right of the agriculturist: the Monopoly of food—

so long as he can supply food—is the inalienable right of the agriculturist. The whole policy of the Sliding Scale is founded on this hypothesis. It is said that in ordinary times the country does not want any food from abroad, and ought not to have any. There is no misunderstanding this. It is all quite clear. It is the bold definition of landlord and agricultural claims, unencumbered with vague verbiage about protecting native industry, or finding means to feed some millions of people who rejoice in something short of good and wholesome food. It is the bare enunciation to the claim of Monopoly, and the mode of maintaining it.

But it would not be just to say they have not considered the consequences that we apprehend from Monopoly, and that we say arise from it. They have considered them, and they have an answer to all objections. If we say that it diminishes the Revenue, they point to the Income Tax as the means of supplying the deficiency in case of need; if we say that it injures Foreign Trade, they say that it is a blessing if it does, for Foreign Trade is overgrown, and ought to be curtailed; if we talk of the ruin that it will bring upon the manufacturing districts, they have an answer to this also, for they say that if the manufacturing districts were engulfed in one common ruin, England would be as great, if not greater, than she ever was before.

They have, moreover, it seems, considered the subject of agricultural improvement, and I must say that the 'Morning Post' always very consistently sneers at this subject. They say that the object of Monopoly is to keep up price, that the effect of improvement would be to increase quantity, and, as that would be followed by a fall of price, the same results which they apprehend from importation would then ensue from improvement. Now, as Monopolists, of course they want to keep up price, and nobody ever has discovered a way of doing so but by limiting quantity; therefore they see no interest to the landlord in anything that would occasion a fall of price.

Then they have often said, which doubtless is true, that improvements require money, that the farmer has got none, and that the landlord has something else to do with his than to lend any to his tenant. Indeed, a Conservative gentleman who made a speech on this subject the other day in Yorkshire, stated that the country gentlemen generally saved their spare money to provide for their younger children, after having provided for the eldest, and that then they had none left for other purposes. Thus it is clear (1) that the object of the Corn Laws is Monopoly in food; (2) that their effects can be felt only by making food scarce and dear; (3) that this is to be accomplished by the Sliding Scale; and (4) that the Ministry the agriculturists will support is the one that will with the greatest subservience support the Sliding Scale.

If I mistake not, they have at last found a Ministry that will suit their purpose. I infer this from the good will that the real organ of the Government now seems to bear them; for only two days ago the

'Morning Herald,' which is in official communication with the Government, suggested to the Monopolists the way by which they could best secure their Monopoly and obtain the adherence of those who might be interested against it: namely, by instantly instituting a rigid system of exclusive dealing. This was suggested only two days ago, remember, and in effect is this: that if any unfortunate tradesman should venture to have and to express an opinion unfavourable to the Sliding Scale, he should have all custom withdrawn from him, and perhaps be ruined. He may be a good man—working hard to rear his family, a good tradesman—punctual in all his payments, a good neighbour, and a good citizen; but notwithstanding all this, if he should venture to think the Scale an injury to commerce, or if, brought in contact with the misery and suffering of the poor, he should dare hold that the Corn Laws are un-Christian laws, this organ of the Government advises that he should be marked for the purposes of persecution in his business.

This is the way in which it is proposed to maintain Monopoly, having such objects and effects as I have described. This is the line of action prescribed by the party who pretend to wish to uphold the morality of the people; who pretend to be more pious than their neighbours; who would build more churches if they could get more money; and who, if it were proposed to give the poor tradesman the protection of the ballot as the means of guarding him against their tyranny, would object to it on the ground that they desire to sustain a manly and independent spirit among the people. If, however, the ballot is proposed, I do trust there will be a cry in favour of it from one end of the country to the other.

The Free Trade party is a powerful one in the country, and they might retaliate ; but I would never recommend that so vile and odious a tyranny should be resorted to. A man has a right to his opinions whatever they may be, and it is a violent invasion of his right to attempt to injure him in his business on account of his opinions. And I only hoped that when our friends heard of the detestable practices to which our opponents are about to resort, such practices would simply have the effect of redoubling their energies in favour of the cause. I would never recommend any other course of influencing opinion save that of fair reasoning. By that means we have already made great progress, and by perseverance in it we shall succeed.

Notwithstanding the twaddle spoken at our opponents' meetings, we have advanced so far that we have at last succeeded in obtaining from every public man of any note in the country the admission that Free Trade is just and wise in principle, and would benefit mankind if universally applied. It now remains for us to conquer the scruples that men honestly and otherwise profess to have to its application. Many of these pretexts have already been exposed, so that they cannot be advanced again. There is one, however, that appears to be specially in favour this year, and it might be well therefore to notice it, though I do not hesitate to say that, above all others, it is the most absurd, and the most ludicrously inconsistent with fact. It is urged that the Debt presents an obstacle to the repeal of the Corn Laws. Now, in the first place, it is notorious that corn has never been taxed for revenue; and pious peers turn up their eyes in the House of Lords, and thank Heaven that it never has been. Well, then, the repeal of the Corn Laws could not injure the Revenue in a direct way. But many other things that people in general consume are taxed for revenue; but as food must be paid for first, their means of consuming articles that are taxed for purposes of revenue depends upon how much people have left after they have paid for their food. So that, in fact, it is just in proportion as food is cheap that other articles may be expected to yield more or less revenue. And this is precisely what Mr. Huskisson meant by warning the landlords in his last speech in the House of Commons, that they could not maintain the Revenue and the Corn Laws together—that the circumstances of the people would not admit of it. He said that the people were exposed to great rivalry abroad; that their wages were reduced; that the cost of living here was very high; and that unless they earned more or paid less for food, they could not consume taxed articles to the same extent that they had consumed them. It seldom happens that the prediction of any public man is so speedily verified as this which fell from Mr. Huskisson. Shortly after he died there was a succession of good and bad harvests which literally substantiated the truth and justice of what he said. I will just call your attention to it, in order that you may see clearly the effect of abundance and scarcity upon the Revenue.

The three years of good harvests were 1835, 1836, 1837 ; and the three years of bad harvests were 1838, 1839, 1840. The price of wheat in the good years was 47*s.*; the price of wheat in the bad years was 67*s.* Now the Revenue collected during the three cheap years was 159,851,000*l.*, and the Revenue collected during the three dear years was, notwithstanding the increase of the population by one million, only 159,240,000*l.* But was the falling off due to diminished consumption? It is proved that it was by the decline in the Customs and Excise. In the cheap years the amount of revenue from these sources was 117,000,000*l.*, in the dear years 116,300,000*l.* It is also shown in the particular articles that were less consumed. For instance, malt, spirits, tea, and sugar yielded in the cheap years 51,800,000*l.*, in the dear years 49,200,000*l.*: thus manifesting a clear connection between the means of consumption and the high price of food.

But let me name another calculation that has been made, and that has not been disputed: the calculation of what the increased population would have given to the Revenue had they consumed in the dear years as much as they consumed in the cheap years. It is shown to have been 2,300,000*l.* Now in connection with these figures the annual deficit to meet which Sir Robert Peel proposed the Income

Tax, is specially worthy of your attention. The Income Tax of 1842 was levied to meet an annual deficit of 2,334,000*l*. So that the deficit was actually only 34,000*l*. more than the deficit occasioned by the diminished consumption of the people in the dear years.

I mention this to show you the justice of what we said at the time, and what we continue to assert: namely, that but for the Corn Laws the Income Tax need not have been imposed; and that it was imposed because, as Mr. Huskisson said, it was impossible to maintain the Corn Laws and the public credit simultaneously, without fresh taxation on income or property.

And I also want you to see what is the connection between the high and the low price of food, and the good or bad condition of a dense and crowded community like our own. That is, I want you to take a wider view than the mere financial view of the question. I want you to observe not only that the Revenue always increases when food is cheap and declines when food is dear; but likewise that pauperism, disease, mortality, and crime all diminish in years of abundance, and increase in years of scarcity. And it is of special importance that you should do so in order fairly to appreciate the advantage of getting rid of the Corn Laws. For what is it that we call for when we ask for their repeal? Why, that there may be a constant good harvest. We want that there shall always be abundance of food; and that all those consequences which we observe to follow from a good harvest may be permanent among us. And is there any doubt that this might be the case? Do our opponents deny it? No; it is their case that it would be so; it is their fear that there would be abundance. They keep their Corn Laws in order to prevent it; they know that there is plenty to be had, and that we have in our manufactures the means of securing it.

I shall never forget my astonishment at hearing a county Member read a letter in the House proving that a most prosperous trade might be carried on between this country and the United States, and detailing facts furnished him by a merchant, that left no doubt in anybody's mind of the fact; and then hearing him apply all this information not as a recommendation to throw open the trade, but as a threat to Sir Robert Peel of what would happen if he persevered in the principle of the tariff. Why, the Chancellor of the Exchequer said last year that whenever the harvest was good, the Treasury was replenished from the Excise. Mr. Gladstone said that if we were to have a trade in food it would give great employment to our people in the production of articles to exchange for it. And Sir Robert Peel said that if we were to reduce the price of provisions the people would not feel the Income Tax. Thus it is that while the evil of a growing population steadily deteriorating in condition is universally recognized, the remedy for the evil is equally well known; but to enrich a section of the community it is refused to be applied. Is it not something like a mockery for the men who acknowledge these things to pretend to have any sympathy with the sufferings of the people, to feign solicitude for their well-being, or to assume that the people need to be cautioned about the obligation of maintaining public faith? When did the people ever want to cheat the public creditor? The people only want to be allowed to pursue unshackled their industry which, by its effects in adding to the resources of the country, is the best security for the public creditor. The people do not want to be dishonest or idle; they want to work, and they implore those who govern them to let them.

At the Sussex meeting held the other day the Duke of Richmond said that when the advocates of Free Trade had succeeded in their object they would seek to defraud the public creditor. The Duke of Richmond had no ground whatever for this assertion: it is a calumny. The public creditor is much more likely to be in danger from persons of the Noble Duke's class than from the honest and industrious classes who call for their trade to be set free. The former are the people whom I should fear most if I were the public creditor. This charge, moreover, comes with a bad grace from the Duke of Richmond, seeing that the only time that the public faith was ever questioned was when a measure of this kind was proposed by the Government of which the Duke was a member. A contract was made with the public creditor, at the time the debt was incurred, that the transfer of stock should never be taxed; but when the Duke of Richmond was in the Cabinet the proposition to tax the transfer was made. I do not say that it was his plan; but at least it was made with his concurrence; and it was considered by men in the City to be a breach of faith. He is the last man, therefore, who should accuse of bad faith those who have never given the least ground for such a charge.

But the manner in which some distinguished people are now talking of the commercial and industrious classes might well provoke an inquiry into the relative importance to the country of the leisured and business classes, and no well-informed man can doubt in whose favour the decision would be given. The greatness of this country is surely owing to the enterprise, skill, and industry of the productive classes, and an attack upon them by those who have inherited their property, who live at ease and do little or nothing to add to the country's wealth and power, is, to say the least of it, most unreasonable. I wish that our landed aristocracy had done more of which the country could be proud to point to during the undisputed Government that they have exercised for a century and a half. But they have engaged the nation in more foolish and fruitless wars than any rulers before them; their schemes of policy have for the most part been shown to be wrong; and they have wasted the resources of the country to a greater extent than all their possessions put together could redeem. At present they are making the most baneful experiments on the temper and endurance of the nation by maintaining this Monopoly in food; they are doing it with their eyes open; the community are perfectly alive to what they are doing; and when difficulties and confusion from want and the necessities of the people again arise, there will be no doubt as to whom the blame must attach. And such difficulties and confusion will arise again, and they will arise when the population has greatly increased and destitution has spread far more widely.

Every five years since the passing of the Corn Laws a crisis has occurred from scarcity of food; and on each succeeding occasion the danger to the peace and order of the country has been greater. We were never nearer confusion than in 1842; and I leave you to judge what will be the effect of the next dearth that arises, when the people will be more numerous, their intelligence greater perhaps, and their impatience for political power much more intense.

Let any man reflect upon these things, and if he has any stake in the country, if he has within his home those for whom he cares, if he has any sense of public duty, I ask him whether a responsibility does not attach to him individually to leave nothing untried, and nothing undone, to procure the removal of such a cause of present evil and future danger as the Corn Laws. If any one mistrusts his own judgment, or the judgment of those who are taking the lead in this matter, let him turn to the authorities by which our opinions against the Corn Laws are fortified. Let him mark the conclusions of the men who have thought most on the condition of this country as regards the danger with which it is threatened, and see if they do not all point to the increasing numbers of the people wanting employment; and then let him say if any sane or sober man can justify any obstruction deliberately cast in the way of the people's getting work, or honestly exchanging the product of their labour for food. The landlords have declared the issue upon which this struggle shall be taken: it is, Monopoly or no Monopoly. I say, and I believe, that the people will win because they are right, and because they are neither powerless nor spiritless.

XVIII.

WOLVERHAMPTON, April 8, 1844.

A deputation of the League, including Mr. Cobden, Mr. Bright, and Colonel Thompson, and accompanied by the two borough Members, Mr. Villiers and Mr. Thornley, visited Wolverhampton on April 8, 1844. So great was the interest manifested in anticipation of the meeting that it became evident that there was no building in the town big enough to contain the numbers desirous of being present at it: a large pavilion was therefore erected in Horsley Fields for the occasion.

ALLOW me to express the great pleasure that I experience in observing the numbers here gathered together; for, assembled as you are to receive and welcome and give your cordial thanks to the distinguished men present, whom I may term the apostles of Freedom of Commerce, such numbers are a sign to the world that the constituency is constant to the cause for which it has so long contended, and that it is found in politics, as in business, ever steady and true.

It would indeed have been lucky for the country had other towns and other places acted and thought as Wolverhampton has. What misery, what ruin, what sacrifice of life might have been spared! For all these calamities are the offspring of scarcity of food and want of employment. And when they prevail, the Corn Laws are fulfilling their purpose. This is no conjecture, no matter of mere opinion; it is the undisputed fact. The Corn Laws were passed to produce scarcity. They are without object or meaning if they do not exist for that purpose. They were passed to prevent food coming into this country which would otherwise come from abroad, in order by scarcity to enhance the price of food grown at home; and the food so shut out would come in for no other reason than because the people have not enough without it.

You were early in the field on this question of the Corn Laws. Quick to perceive their true character, you were prompt in denouncing the Laws as opposed to nature's law, and to every want and interest and policy connected with the well-being of this nation. You were never deceived by the jargon of Monopoly, which sought to prove, if it sought to prove anything, that scarcity is a blessing. Monopolists try to persuade working men that when food is dear the reward of labour is great; or, as they say, that when the price of bread is high, wages are high. Now, the first answer which we can and do give to this assertion is a short one: namely, that it is untrue and that it must be known to be so. And I challenge a denial of the fact that there never has been a period when food was scarce or dear which was not also a period of peculiar suffering and distress to the working classes. I do not say whether it stands to reason or not that it must be so, but that it is the fact that it is so. We have no need to talk about what would or would not be the case under a Corn Law. Experience, unfortunately, has settled that. Twenty-two years are enough to show any one and every one what good and what harm will happen under any given law, and there need be no question, therefore, about the effect of the Corn Laws on wages.

There is, however, a shorter or more pointed answer still to the fallacy, which is, indeed, better than all the rest put together. I once heard a working man give it in this town with great effect. It is this: If scarcity is such a good thing for the working classes, what a blessing no food at all would be! The conclusion is quite logical, and illustrates well the stupidity of the argument. Every one has seen that when food is dear men work harder and longer to obtain the same amount they had of it when cheap; and that the same labour being done by fewer hands, more are thrown out of employment, and wages are thus made to fall.

Neither have the trading classes of this town, any more than the working classes, ever been deluded by what the Monopolists address directly to their understandings: namely, that if the rich are made richer by the Corn Laws they will spend their fortunes upon the shopkeepers, and that their custom, which they call 'Home Trade,' will be better for them than Foreign Trade. The men of Wolverhampton have taken the just view of the matter on this point as well as on the other. They have said: 'Be so good as to leave us alone. Take your hand out of our pockets if you please. We shall get on in our own way, which we understand better than you can understand it for us. We do not see the sense of giving what we have to those who have no right to it, for the mere chance of getting some of it back again.' Fancy a shopkeeper here being told that it was for his advantage that a man should take half the goods out of his shop, and then, being the richer for it, should promise to come some day and buy what was left in the shop! Would not the shopkeeper, think you, hand such a customer over to the police, to transmit him to the gaol, or the asylum? But that is how the Monopolists commonly defend the Corn Laws.

Your complaint against them, however, is that by mischievous meddling with trade they have deprived you of many excellent customers, and have not supplied their place themselves, and that thereby they have caused trade seriously to decline. The effect of what has been done in the case of Foreign Trade in this country is precisely the same as though some four or five wealthy men had wished to spend their fortunes in this town, and the high constable or the chief magistrate of the place had driven them away, saying that he would employ and deal with his own people himself; that he was the natural customer of the people; that if the strangers were allowed to buy your goods, it could be only on very particular terms — terms that he knew, though he carefully abstained from saying so, they could not accept. You would surely think it very cruel, very unjust, when you saw these strangers driven away, if the great man who had expelled them did not fully supply their places, and provide the town on as good terms with the articles that the foreigners had offered in exchange for your goods ?

Nevertheless, this is exactly what has been done ; and if you will suppose the names of the strangers to be Russia, Prussia, and the United States, and put the landlords of this country in place of the magistrate, the illustration will be found exact. Each of these foreign Powers has implored the landlords to be allowed to deal with the people of this country and has given distinct warning that if they are not allowed to, they must go to another shop or manufacture for themselves. The result of our Monopolist policy is that they have done what they threatened ; and, though formerly good customers of ours, they already either manufacture for themselves, or have become our rivals in other countries. On the other hand, the landlords, as you know, have done nothing to supply the place of your former customers, either in trade or by émploying the people. On the contrary, they have made you give double the quantity of goods for the same amount of food.

Nor do they show signs of mending their ways. They are going on with the same pernicious system, and the people, unless they bestir themselves, will suffer much more. We have not yet lost our Brazilian customers ; but, like all the others, they want to pay for the goods they take from England in what they can spare most of from their own country, and in what is most wanted here. They, too, have warned us, like all the others, that they will go to another shop if we do not comply with their just requirements.

And they will go. And a valuable trade will then be lost. The pretext put forward by the Monopolists in this case is a little different from that put forward in the other cases, but that is all: the system pursued is the same. Generally it has been pretended that it was solely for the good of the people that they made food dear and trade less; but in this case all the people who used to support the slave-trade and all the people who used to have slaves, have united to resist the trade with Brazil, not for the sake of the people of this country, and of course not on their own account, but because their hearts bleed so for the poor slave in Brazil! And it would be so shocking for you to eat the slave-made sugar! If they succeed in stopping the trade with Brazil, they will do it after their eyes have been opened. They know that the interest of this country is to allow no obstacle to the imports from other countries. Our imports are the means by which foreigners pay for the goods that we export, and anything that stops imports deprives the hardworking people of this district of their foreign customers.

I will not, however, discuss this further. It is carrying coals to the north to argue the question here. You understand it better than I do. I have myself learnt much about it from you. Moving freely amongst you I have come to understand the importance to the working classes of Foreign Trade more fully than I ever understood it before. I was hardly aware, before I saw its practical working in this district, what numbers of our fellow-subjects depend for the means of life on the continuance, and, I should say, on the extension, of the trade with foreign States. I scarcely realized before how the more or fewer orders from abroad, or the more or less competition with other nations in neutral markets, immediately determines for how much and for how long in the day thousands and tens of thousands here shall toil. I did not fully appreciate the utter ruin to the place and people that would follow the loss of any foreign custom. I have learnt here more than I have learnt elsewhere how competition with foreigners has increased, and how each year the foreign merchants or factors are obliged to get their orders executed at lower and lower prices, or not to accept them at all. And I have learnt, too, how on every occasion the unfortunate people of this district are compelled to work longer and longer for less and less reward. I have often thought how cruel I should esteem it, if I were a working man, that men who do no work themselves, who know nothing of trade, and little of the interests of the productive classes, should pass laws to create and encourage such handicapped competition, and thus deprive me and my family of the means of existence, except on the terms that make life a curse.

It is when I reflect on the privations of the working classes, knowing how much more than any other class they necessarily suffer from such a cruel obstruction to their trade as the Corn Laws, that I am able to treat with contempt and indifference the reproach so often thrown at me, that I am eternally, and exclusively, on their account, demanding the repeal of those Laws. I know that in doing so I am simply asking that the working classes may not be further impoverished and degraded, and so long as the Corn Laws continue I shall continue to make the same demand. I should like to put some of the fine gentlemen who regard all mention of the Corn Laws as a bore, upon short commons themselves for a while, and then, if they should begin to cry out lustily—which they would—for better fare, tell them that there are other things to think of besides their dinner; 'that it is not by bread alone that men live; that they have their immortal souls to care for; that they must cultivate their minds, and improve themselves generally.' And then, after vexing and injuring them in every way, issue a commission to inquire into the cause of their discontent. They would take it very quietly, wouldn't they?

We have no reason to care for the taunts of ignorant, selfish men. We have been right on this question from the first; our opinions are daily gaining ground, and we have reason to be proud that we have done everything that the Constitution allows us to do in order to gain our object.

Near me stands the gentleman who drew up the strong petition from this town against the Corn Law of 1815, which was presented to Parliament. When first the franchise was extended to you, you did not, as some did, select men to rivet the chains by which you were bound, or, which is still more foolish, choose one man to unbind your fetters and another to fix them on again. You sought and returned two of the most determined enemies of Monopoly that the country contained. I allude to Mr. Fryer and Mr. Whitmore. When those gentlemen retired, the borough was famous for its opinions on this great subject. I owe my connection with it to that circumstance. And it is your intelligence and constancy as regards Monopoly that gives Mr. Thornley and myself such satisfaction and pride in being your representatives.

I think that you are acting in perfect consistency with all your former conduct in now giving a cordial hand of fellowship to the League. I believe that there is no way in which any man can support the cause of Free Trade more effectively now than by aiding the League, and I know that you are too honest and too anxious in the matter not to hail their visit with thankfulness and joy.

Ten years ago there were not, perhaps, two boroughs in England so well informed as Wolverhampton on the subject of Free Trade. Now there are at least fifty. I ascribe this chiefly to the information that has been diffused throughout the country by the operations of the League. Let us rescue fifty more from the enemy and we shall succeed. I believe that it can be done. Perseverance in a good cause will do anything. The League is now everywhere. It is a body composed of men drawn from every part of the country. And of men who have the heart and the spirit to be determined that their fellow-subjects shall no longer suffer needlessly; that commerce shall not decay; and that the country shall not decline while they have the smallest means within their power to help to prevent it. Hence you have the fortune to find leaders animated by the right spirit, resolved to vindicate the rights of commerce and the rights of industry, and determined that henceforth you shall not be injured and neglected as you have hitherto been. No revival of trade, no improvement of Revenue, no good harvest ought now to induce you to relax your unceasing hostility to these unrighteous Laws. You should be like your old Member Mr. Fryer, who always said: 'Let us have but one thing to do with the Corn Laws. Let us abolish them.' At the general election of 1837 he requested me to bring forward total Repeal the following year. I assented but remarked that the harvests had been so good that it would deprive the subject of its usual interest. 'Good harvests, Sir,' he rejoined, 'what have they to do with it? A good harvest will not make a bad law a good one.' The Corn Laws are bad Laws, and they will bear bad fruit as long as they last. They will do much more harm yet. Mr. Fryer was a true prophet.

In the year following, 1838, the prices rose, and in consequence of these Laws the whole commerce of the country was disturbed. A period quite unexampled, I believe, of misery and distress to the productive classes ensued for the five following years. And as sure as we are here this day everything will recur that has ever occurred before in connection with the Corn Laws. There is no reason why it should not. Sir Robert Peel's Corn Bill was not proposed to prevent it. Even the squires say the Bill will do no harm, by which they mean that it will do you no good. Would it not be madness to give it what they call a trial, when its principle has been already long tried and has been most justly condemned? There is only one thing to be done, depend upon it: to get rid of every vestige of it. And this will be done at last by agitation. Justice has hitherto, I fear, been secured in this country only by making the ruling classes uneasy. If agitation stops, they say that the people are indifferent. If it perseveres they yield. Then, I reply, there never has been a machine better adapted for the purpose of securing justice than the League; and it is our duty to support it.

I myself speak feelingly on this subject, for if the interest in Repeal is not maintained out of doors it is almost hopeless to move in it with success within. You know that your late Member, Mr. Whitmore, retired from the House in disgust at the impossibility he discovered of making any impression there with the question of Free Trade. He complained of the interest that resisted him within, and the apathy that deprived him of support from without. Had such a body as the League been in existence then the cause might have still retained the service of a valued friend.

The League is now grappling well with its two great opponents, Interest and Ignorance. It is facing those who assert their interest in the Corn Laws, and it tells them that the Laws are as foolish as they are wrong. It seeks to enlighten the ignorant, and to infuse a little spirit into those who dare not call their souls their own. It has drawn the great men of Monopoly from their retirement, it has brought them before the public, it has made them speak out and show cause why these Laws should not be abolished. And a pretty mess the great men have made of their case. The wisdom of their former silence has become striking even to themselves, I should think. When men have nothing to conceal they may talk freely; but not otherwise, especially if they have been found out. We have most of us seen men brought before the Bench; if they had had the luck to be well advised they were silent, lest they should unwittingly commit themselves. Sir Robert Peel, I believe, has admonished his friends that silence is golden; but the League has driven the squires mad, and they will not be advised, they will talk. Formerly they could say many things with impunity in Parliament that now they cannot say with the least safety anywhere. They used to tell the House how prosperous the farmer was, how happy and contented the labourers were, and how they loved their lords. The farmers and labourers never heard what they said, and the Members for Wolverhampton were told, if they ventured to object, that they knew nothing of the farmers and labourers. Lately, however, the squires have been saying these things in the counties, and within earshot of the farmers. And at last the poor farmers all over the country have been roused into thinking for themselves. And they are asking themselves and one another how it is that the Corn Laws can have been so beneficial to them, seeing that no good at all has ever been done them; that for the last twenty-eight years they have been very badly off—never certain of anything, in short, worse off than their neighbours. It is a little more than they can stand, to be told that Laws passed to keep up rents are all for their good, and that the landlord cares nothing about his rent. The farmers have been questioning and thinking about this for the last year; and, at last, as if they can endure it no longer, a thing has happened, the like of which, I suppose, has never happened in this country before: two real live farmers from different parts of the country, not known to each other, but both precisely the kind of farmers said to be benefited by the Corn Laws, came to London, and told Mr. Cobden that, if there were an opportunity, they should be perfectly ready to state the real case of the farmers at Covent Garden Theatre, at one of the great meetings held there by the League. Accordingly, about a fortnight ago, they did so; and a very strange tale they told about the blessings of Corn Laws to them. Such a tale, indeed, that if there is any modesty in the landlords, they will never again as long as they live mention the farmers as an excuse for their Monopoly. It is impossible to do justice now to the narration of all the mischief that the two farmers declared the Corn Laws had inflicted upon them, especially as farmers. But they defied contradiction of anything that they said, and they have not received any. They are noted as good farmers in their counties, and are well known as estimable and able men in other respects.

And even the poor agricultural labourer has found some friends who will not allow his name to be used to support a system that oppresses him. The clergy have actually been roused to speak and write in his behalf. They declare that his condition cannot be worse, and that if the landlords would but pay half the attention to feeding him that they pay to fattening their cattle, they might then venture to speak of him as the subject of their solicitude. At present he is starving, neglected, and degraded, and he feels hostility to all above him. This is the clergymen's statement, remember, not mine.

So much for the blessings of scarcity in the agricultural districts. If the League had no other claim to the gratitude of the country it would deserve it for the revelation of these things. It would deserve it for having raised discussion and spread general interest on the condition of the people. A more important subject could not now be discussed; and by discussion alone will the whole truth be elicited. My friend Mr. Cobden does not despair of convincing even the landlords themselves that they are as foolish with regard to themselves as they are said to be unjust with regard to others. I hope he may succeed. The landlords all know that their rents have increased enormously during the present century, and it is difficult to believe that they can mistake the cause of this increase; and that, forgetting that they have done nothing themselves to produce it, they should overlook, in their measures for injuring commerce and manufacture, the real cause and sources of all their wealth.

That the truth may be elicited in time and justice be done is my fervent prayer, and it is in the hope of this being effected by the efforts of the League that I urge upon all my friends to assist it. I came here to-day out of respect to the borough, and I am sure you will believe me when I say that the same feeling of regard would prevent my advising you to take any course that I did not think right and honourable. Let any one suggest any other course than that which the League is pursuing, and I will attend to it, and adopt it if fitting. But until I hear of something more likely to bring about the repeal of the Corn Laws, I shall do all in my power to support the League.

In conclusion I would beg you to bear in mind that during the three years since I last had the honour of addressing you the population of this country has increased one million; that for forty years past the country has been—as it still is—unable to raise food sufficient to feed the people; and that the Laws in question actually and avowedly prevent the exchange of the labour of the people of this country for the superabundant food of other countries, which is necessary to them. Can such a state of things go on safely? And can any man who believes that it cannot, conscientiously abstain from doing whatever in him lies towards removing an injustice that is leading the country to ruin? Let those who can act, act. Let those who have not the leisure to act for themselves contribute to aid others who can and will act for them, and thus relieve themselves from any participation in the continuance of such an absurd, unjust, mischievous enactment as the Corn Laws.

XIX.

HOUSE OF COMMONS, June 25, 1844.

On June 25, 1844, Mr. Villiers moved for the total and immediate repeal of the Corn Laws. The Whig party made themselves conspicuous by their absence from the debate; of which Sir R. Peel was not slow to avail himself. Immediately on the conclusion of Mr. Cobden's speech the Prime Minister sprang to his feet, and began his reply by saying that the House had been engaged that night for the benefit of the company that usually performed at Covent Garden Theatre. During the greater portion of the performance the front rank of the Opposition benches had been deserted, their usual occupants absent, perhaps, from a lively recollection of the assistance given by the members of the Anti-Corn-Law League the other night 'at my benefit'—alluding to the action of the Free Traders on the Sugar Duties. And afterwards, having treated the solid arguments and principles of his opponents—all carefully based upon or developed from ascertained facts—as mere abstract, philosophical maxims which were utterly unfit for practical application in the existing artificial state of society, though isolated he could not contest them, he spoke of the improvement in the leading branches of manufacturing industry, and emphatically reiterated that the Government did not intend to alter the Corn Laws of 1842, or to diminish the amount of Protection afforded to agriculture. Mr. Gladstone declared that it would be his duty to meet Mr. Villiers's Motion with a direct negative. Lord J. Russell, still adhering to a fixed duty, spoke against, though he refused to vote against, the Motion; and referring to Mr. Gladstone's speech, he said that the Government, instead of being wiser, had only enjoyed much better weather than their predecessors; he questioned whether their Corn Laws would stand two successive bad harvests, and lamented the continued agitation on the question; but could see no end to it so long as the existing laws were maintained. After two nights' discussion the debate closed with a division showing a majority of 204 against the Motion.

The purpose of the Motion of which I have given notice is once again to bring under the consideration of this House the most just and important claim made on the part of the community at large, that the trade in our first great necessary of life, now restricted by an Act of this House, should in future be unfettered and set wholly free; and I can most truly say that if I could persuade myself that the power with which the subject is presented to the House could in any way affect its success I would not again have become the instrument for proposing it. This, however, is notoriously not the case. I have upon two occasions before in this Parliament made a similar Motion and have been supported by other Members of the greatest ability who have left nothing unsaid that could be urged in its favour; and they have done so in vain.

It may then perhaps be asked, upon what ground I again make the appeal. I think I may take credit for not adopting this course without due deliberation, and that I should not have hastily decided upon a line of action that was more likely to injure than advance the cause. Had those who are united with me in opinion on this subject remained silent upon it during the present Session our opponents would not have been slow to infer either that we had been driven from the field by their vast influence and powerful eloquence, or else that we were satisfied with the former decisions of this House. A notion certainly most foreign to the fact; but one in which the public might have concurred, seeing the novel attitude that the country gentlemen have assumed on the question of the Corn Laws during the past year.

These gentlemen, with the hope of influencing public opinion in favour of their Laws, have lately deemed it expedient to descend into the field of public agitation; and to refer their case to the same tribunal as that to which those who in self-defence are now leagued together to oppose the Corn Laws, have found it necessary to appeal. Their meetings appear to have been somewhat select; and the promoters of them seem to me to have agitated themselves rather than to have succeeded in awakening much sympathy in others. Yet, inasmuch as their professions appear somewhat large in print, and as no lack of confidence has been shown on the other side, it would have been curious, when both met together on this common ground, if no occasion had been taken of expressing face to face the conflicting arguments that each are in the habit of using elsewhere.

I, for my part, see no reason for despair in the continued discussion of this question, rather much ground for hope; for I am unable to explain otherwise than from conviction on the part of the Government of the substantial justice of our cause, why they have not allowed any Session, nay, why they do not allow any month of any Session to pass without abandoning some portion of the ground on which the system to which we are opposed is based. I do not say this from any idle purpose to make mischief between the two sections of the opposite party, because I feel no respect for that blindness or that boldness on the part of those opposite which is not ready to defer to the greater experience and greater ability possessed by the Government for deciding how far and when it is necessary to abandon that which they are neither able to keep nor entitled to possess.

It seems to me that we are deriving all the advantage from discussion that a cause based on truth and justice is likely to secure. We are gradually gaining ground in public opinion, whilst those who are opposed to us are rapidly and steadily losing it. Public opinion, fortunately, possesses great influence in this country, and discussion has great influence in forming that opinion; and deference is so far felt to be due to it that any law or institution that is assailed must be defended on public grounds. The difficulty with Hon. Gentlemen opposite in arguing this question is, that they are unable to rest its defence on its true ground, and it is rather awkward to assign any other; for the instant that it is attempted to defend the Corn Laws upon public grounds, the defence becomes the subject of the closest inquiry; it is sifted and tested in every way in order to ascertain whether the plea is hollow or true; and there is no one ground that I have heard proposed since I came into this House that has not now been thoroughly examined and, in my judgment, completely exposed. I am curious, therefore, to hear what fresh ground is to be taken on this occasion.

The ground on which the defence of the Corn Laws was first rested was certainly not without some plausibility before it was tested by experience: namely, that it was dangerous for this country to be dependent on other countries for its supply of food, and that, consequently, our land-owners ought to be protected from foreign competition. This was the plea originally set forth for the enactment of the Corn

Laws: a plea that at the time all thinking men derided, and that has since become contemptible by the practical demonstration of its utter worthlessness. It assumed that we might safely depend upon foreigners for the means of revenue, for the material of our manufactures, and, hence, for the employment of millions of our people whereby they get bread, but that it would be nothing short of imperilling our future safety to depend upon them for the bread itself.

Returns laid before this House during the last twenty years prove that the expectation of being independent of supplies of food from abroad, if ever honestly entertained, has been completely disappointed. Since the Laws were passed we have been largely and constantly dependent on other countries for supplies of corn; this dependence is annually increasing; and during the last five years we have fallen short in our home supply to an amount equal to 17,000,000 quarters. Moreover, the corn that we have imported has not been grown for our market, but for the consumption of other people, and consequently it has been obtained under peculiar disadvantage to us. During the thirteen years of the duration of the Corn Law passed in 1828 no less than 30,000,000 quarters of grain actually necessary for the consumption of the people of this country were imported from foreign countries. The advocates of this Monopoly will then hardly allege a sufficient home supply as an excuse for it—at least not to those who regard the truth. Whether this soil can or cannot produce enough to support its population I do not pretend to say; but the fact stands upon record that it has not produced enough, and that we have been obliged to resort to other countries to the extent that I have stated.

And will any one pretend that the other excuses advanced in defence of the Corn Laws have not been shown to be as futile as the plea of the alleged impolicy of a foreign food supply? When the only profit or gain connected with the Laws has been traced to the owners of the land, the proprietors in Parliament have repudiated the charge; they have denied that they had any interest in the Laws, and declared the single object of such Laws to be the interest of the occupier and the labourer, whose existence and well-being, as they assert, depend on their continuance. But is there now, whatever there may have been before, a single man of honest mind who has given thought to the subject, who for a moment will assent to such a proposition? Will any man this night venture to repeat what is demonstrably untrue? Will a single Member of an agricultural county rise up to-night and say: I can prove that the tenant-farmers have benefited or do profit by these Laws? The interest of the tenant-farmers in the Corn Laws has been fully and fairly inquired into by those leagued together for the purpose of thoroughly testing the whole question; and so far from the Corn Laws being found to be of any service to them nothing appeared to be more identified with the permanent interest of both the farmers and the agricultural labourers than their total repeal. Everybody is now familiar with the fact that the distress of no other class had been more prominently or more frequently obtruded upon the public than that of the farmers. In fact, it is now a matter of notoriety that they have derived no benefit whatever from the Corn Laws. Duped and deceived by them, many a farmer hampered with debt, now finds himself pledged to a rent higher than he could ever afford to pay, and openly and bitterly complains that he holds his land under circumstances the most disadvantageous for its proper cultivation. I will venture to say that not an Hon. Member in this House would repeat again to-night that the Corn Laws were enacted for the benefit of the farmers ; and I defy Hon. Members to repeat that they are upheld for such purpose : the farmers themselves would confute them.

The same has occurred with regard to all the exemptions that have been procured for the farmer in the payment of taxes ; there is not a landlord in the House who does not know that they only contribute to swell the rent given for the land. The Members of this House dare not call a single farmer before them and ask him whether what they have done in his behalf, as they say, has been at all to his benefit. It is the evidence of one of the most competent among agriculturists that whatever relief has been procured for the farmer through Parliament has been for the advantage of land-owners alone.

The assertion that these Laws are for the benefit of the labourer is equally absurd and unfounded. No one would now be bold enough to say that it is for the advantage of the labourer that the price of food should be kept up; and that high prices ensure high wages. There is a volume in this House, produced by the labours of a Commission of the Crown, that effectually disproves that assertion. In the face of that volume, never again can the advantage of the labourer be made the excuse of the Corn Laws. The evidence taken by the Commission is an authority that cannot be disputed; and it proves that no one could be lower in the scale of civilization than the agricultural labourer. Country gentlemen may now study it by the light of incendiary fires in their own neighbourhoods. Scarcely a day passes that the papers are not full of accounts of what are called the crimes of the labouring classes, which must be attributed to their necessitous condition. The Hon. Member for Stockport asked for inquiry upon this subject; he made a Motion to this effect; but the majority, who are proprietors, would not assent to it. The Motion of my Hon. Friend was a perfectly fair one, and one quite in point; but the land-owners refused the test of calling upon the tenantry to give their opinion of the operation of the Corn Laws in raising rents and causing high prices. No! the land-owners will never bring forward either farmers or labourers to tell of their experience of the working of these Laws.

I see in the 'Times' newspaper a statement that in some parts of the country where there have been grave manifestations of discontent and open breaches of the law, whenever the farmers allowed the labourers an opportunity of procuring provisions cheap—thus virtually repealing the Corn Laws—they immediately diminished, and property was safe. How is it, I would ask the land-owners, that the labourers are always found to be contented and well affected after prices have continued low, but that they are always disaffected, and the property of the country endangered, when food is scarce, and prices high? I ask the Hon. Member for Knaresborough, who has thought it decent to give notice of the Amendment that he has placed upon the Votes, to meet and answer this point. I call upon him to give evidence of the good condition of the agricultural labourers—if he can. And here I will read a public letter, yet unanswered, addressed during the last year by Sir Harry Verney—no member of the Anti-Corn-Law League—to the county of Bucks, one of the most purely agricultural districts in the country. The Hon. Baronet wrote as follows :—

My friends, it is with pain that I contemplate the condition of the agricultural classes, especially of the agricultural labourer. See his damp, unwholesome, ill-ventilated, crowded cottage—ride through a village, where groups of men are standing about, unable to obtain work. Remark the downcast look of a man, as honest and upright as the most honest and upright amongst us, who has gone round from farm to farm and cannot obtain labour; follow him home to his family, and see him enter his cottage, where his wife and hungry children await his return, hoping that he may have obtained employment and food; but he has failed. The charity of a farmer, or the kindness of those who divide with each other the widow's mite, of some neighbour less poor only than himself, supports the family for a few days, until the order of admission to the workhouse is obtained. There are few, I hope I may say no deaths from want in our agricultural districts; every poor family that has a crust or a dish of potatoes will divide it with their poorer neighbour who has none; in every village there are farmers and farmer's wives ready to assist a starving family. But are there no diseases brought on by poor living? No constitutions impaired by unwholesome and insufficient diet, want of clothing, and bad dwellings? Are not the minds as well as the bodies of our peasantry often enfeebled by their sufferings, and unfitted for the very exertions that would better their condition? You know as well as I do the reply to such questions.

This is the letter of a Baronet of Buckinghamshire, a magistrate of the county, and one who has property in the county; and this is his description of the state of the labourer after thirty years of Protection.

I will now read the evidence of a farmer as to the state of the labourers as well as the farmers, and the benefit that they expect from the continuance of Monopoly. This witness, Mr. Josiah Hunt of Almondsbury, a practical tenant-farmer of great experience, spoke in the presence of other farmers at a public meeting in the county of Gloucester. [An Hon. Member here made a remark about the Poor Laws.] I will notice the reference of an Hon. Member to the subject of the Poor Laws presently. Mr. Hunt said :—

I believe that with Free Trade the cultivation of the land would be improved, the produce of the land would be increased, the independence of the tenant secured, and his prosperity greatly augmented. I can fully bear out what Mr. Cobden has said about the agricultural labourers: their wages are miserably low, and yet the farmers cannot pay more. In my own parish hundreds of families live on 7*s*. per week; their fare is worse than that of the pauper. Whole families of grown-up children sleep in one room to the total disregard of the decencies of life, and to the total destruction of feelings of propriety and morality. It has been said the land has to bear peculiar burdens: it should also be said that the farmer has peculiar exemptions; but that though his windows are untaxed, and his riding horse and his dogs are free of duty, it is not to benefit him, but to enable him to pay higher rent to his landlord. I cordially second the resolution, believing that a repeal of the Corn Laws would improve the prospects of the tenant-farmer, and promote the physical, moral, and social condition of the labourer.

In the same speech, also, he expresses a distinct opinion on these Laws, and says:—

The Corn Laws I am fully convinced are no benefit but an injury to the tenants; they were designed to raise rents, and to place the tenantry subservient to the political domination of the landlord; and if I needed something more to fortify my opinion on the Corn Laws I have it in the fact that the best practical agriculturists in the kingdom entertain the same views upon the subject; the whole system is not to benefit the farmer, but to raise the land-owner's rent.

The Hon. Member opposite referred just now to the effects of the Poor Laws: what does he suppose is the average weekly cost of supporting a man with his wife and six children in the workhouse in the country? He would find it to be 17*s.* 6*d.* a week, whilst the wages of the labourer are only 7*s.* 6*d.* a week. The working labourer, therefore, is far worse off than the pauper; and he is forced into the workhouse in self-defence. Let the Hon. Gentleman opposite stand forward and avow himself the friend of the land-owners if he pleases; let him court the dominant class in the State if he thinks it convenient or proper to do so; but before he stands forward as the friend of the poor labourer, I call upon him to answer the statements that I have just read to the House.

These statements, along with a host of others to the like effect, fully bear out my position that neither the farmers nor the labourers are interested in the continuance of the Corn Laws; and it is but justice to add that it is to the exertions of the Anti-Corn-Law League that the disclosure of these important truths is owing. Let Hon. Gentlemen, then, apply themselves to these facts: disprove them—if they can; prove the contrary—if it is in their power. In this way they will satisfy the public far better that they are right and honest in their professions than by any amount of vulgar abuse of the Anti-Corn-Law League. Knowing that they cannot refute them, I am at a loss to anticipate what popular or public ground they will attempt to occupy on the present occasion.

The Right Hon. the Vice-President of the Board of Trade, who did not like to repeat all the foolish things that were said by his supporters, started, when this subject was last discussed, an argument of his own which I confess I do not think much wiser than the arguments of his friend. The Right Hon. Gentleman said that he would not urge the objection of danger from not obtaining a sufficient supply of corn from abroad when wanted, as he believed that the supply of corn would be regulated pretty much upon the same principles as that of any other commodity, and that we should not be liable to more interruption in the trade of corn than in any other trade. But he did urge that a depression of price, consequent on an increased importation of corn, would displace a large amount of agricultural labour; though he gave the House none of the data upon which his opinion is founded. I suppose that the Right Hon. Gentleman calculated on the displacement of agricultural labour as the consequence of a great deal of land being thrown out of cultivation by the increased importation and low price of agricultural produce that would follow the repeal of the Corn Laws. But looking at what has been said by agriculturists themselves, I am at a loss to understand that the necessary result of a reduction of prices would be to throw any considerable quantity of land out of cultivation. The fact, I believe, is, that if a little science and economy were applied to the cultivation of land, a low price would be compatible with paying the labour of cultivation and obtaining a good profit.

Lord Ducie, a nobleman distinguished for his knowledge of agriculture, has declared publicly that all apprehension upon this score is a fallacy, and that, exclusive of rent, wheat could be produced on almost any land at lower prices than those quoted at any foreign port. Now it is obvious that before land could be thrown out of cultivation it must have given up paying rent; and before it ceased to support the labourer it must go to waste. The Right Hon. Gentleman ought, therefore, to have shown at what prices land could not be cultivated with any advantage; and he would also have to show that it would not be worth the mere application of labour required for cultivation, before he declared that the lowering of prices in the market would be followed by the displacement of labour. I do not think it probable that the Right Hon. Gentleman will repeat this argument again to-night. Since he used it, he has possibly profited by the study of what has been written by men well acquainted with the subject.

But there is another argument that the Right Hon. Gentleman has advanced since; it is to this effect: that we should be careful how far we risk the reduction of rent, lest owners of land should themselves become farmers. The Right Hon. Gentleman is afraid that the farmers themselves might be ousted from their tenancies, and that the land-owners, by attending to the cultivation of the land, might effectively supply their place. I do not think that the Right Hon. Gentleman need labour under any very serious apprehension on this score. I do not think that the firstborn of the land will be very likely to take to so laborious a pursuit as long as they can be more agreeably employed. Let him not be alarmed; let him rest satisfied that during his time at least those who were born to inherit the land will continue to be trained as they have been heretofore, and that they will be better pleased to consume the fruits of the earth than to produce them.

But instead of dreading the displacement of agricultural labourers, let the Right Hon. Gentleman reflect upon the alternative in the consequences of fettering trade, necessarily resulting in the displacement of manufacturing labour. It appears that between the Census of 1831 and that of 1841, upwards of 360,000 agricultural labourers left their villages and went to the manufacturing districts to seek a means of living. Does not the Right Hon. Gentleman perceive that by the return of any considerable portion of that number to the agricultural districts, in consequence of the want of employment in manufactures, there would be a far more certain depression of agricultural labour than he apprehends would result from the introduction of foreign corn and the consequent lowering of prices?

But the most intelligent land-owners themselves are now convinced that increased production and low prices do not displace labour; on the contrary, they instruct their farmers that the principle to proceed upon is that of employing more labour and increased skill, and improvements generally, in order to produce the largest possible quantity at the lowest possible price. Indeed, if the argument against low prices is good, it is equally applicable against improvement as against Free Trade; increased supply and reduced price is the result to be expected from each. The productiveness of the land cannot be increased without the effect of the additional quantity being felt in the market; and the Right Hon. Gentleman argues from the effect of low prices that land would go out of cultivation.

Another argument to show the necessity of great caution in any change is drawn from the numerical importance of the agricultural classes in the scale of society. An analysis of the late Census recently published gives us information on this matter. It appears from these calculations that the agricultural classes about which so much has been written, and which are said to constitute seven-ninths of the whole population of the country, are only 7 per cent., and a little more, of our population. With what show of right or justice, then, can any one claim to exclude the whole mass of the people of this country from their natural right to buy their food as abundantly and as cheaply as possible, out of regard to the supposed exclusive interests of such a fraction of the community? No right can be allowed to any portion of the public to impose taxes or restrictions on the rest; and I contend that those who would continue the Corn Laws are bound to prove that they are the means of giving the most abundant supply of food to the people at the cheapest possible rate.

And this ought to be the real question with the supporters of the Corn Laws; if they fail to prove that the Corn Laws are the means of giving the most abundant supply of food to the people at the cheapest possible rate, then I say that the maintenance of them is the maintenance of tyranny and the cause of enormous evil. And I stand here, not on the part of this or that interest—manufacturing or otherwise—but on the part of the people at large, to assert that it is their right, and for their unquestionable advantage, and for the good of the whole country, that they should procure and have access to their food as cheaply, as abundantly, and as conveniently as by means of capital, commerce, industry, or any other human contrivance they possibly can.

Do the Corn Laws effect this ? If not, where is that public necessity that Lord Grenville says so truly ought to be imperative to justify any tampering with the means of the people's subsistence?—For, as he further remarks, to confine ourselves to our own soil is to mar the provision of heaven, which by varying the climes and seasons of the earth has relieved a nation like our own from exclusive dependence on itself.

To legislate for limiting the sources of supply is, in point of fact, to encourage scarcity ; and it is monstrous to confer upon any body of men who are irresponsible, and whose interest in this respect might conflict with that of the community, the right to enact laws for regulating the supply of food. It is giving them absolute power over the people. He who determines the amount of food can make slaves of the people ; and the attention of the country cannot be too quickly directed to the immense importance, in all its bearings on the condition of the community, of abundance of food and of the purpose and effect of the Corn Laws to restrict that abundance. The time is most convenient for doing so. Our information on the subject was never greater ; never was our experience of the effect of more or less food upon the moral as well as physical condition of the people more complete ; never have we approached the subject at a moment more calm or free from excitement ; never has there been a period in all respects so adapted from the knowledge of the past to legislate for the future.

There are, moreover, Hon. Gentlemen on the opposite side of the House now occupying themselves much in the praiseworthy endeavour to discover the cause of the bad physical condition of the people—who, wishing, as they say, to overlook pecuniary and selfish considerations, are anxious to legislate on principles of humanity alone. I invite those Hon. Gentlemen to go into the question of the main cause of the misery and sufferings of a great portion of the labouring people: the dearness and insufficiency of wholesome food. I ask them to investigate the cause of that severe and pressing competition which they themselves say compels the people to toil too long, and to work too hard. I wish them to examine the connection of this circumstance with the limited amount of food, which by inducing high prices absorbs all the earnings of the workman in the payment of the bare necessaries of life, deprives him of the power of educating his children, compels him to neglect the domestic duties of life, and thus sinks him in the scale of civilization.

It is said by some of them that people are now made slaves by circumstances. I ask them, then, to examine the circumstances that cause this evil with a view to their removal. I ask those Hon. Gentlemen who are actuated by such philanthropic motives whether the competition which leads to such lamentable results is not influenced by a deficiency of food for an increasing population, and by laws that limit the supply of food, while none can exist to check the increase of the people? Can there be any doubt upon the point? The truth of this proposition is sometimes admitted by Hon. Gentlemen opposite themselves. They are always anxious for a good harvest—they pray for it in their churches; and why? Because a good harvest renders food more plentiful. These Hon. Gentlemen have certain associations in their minds as to the effects of a good or a bad harvest; and amongst such associations is the idea that with a good harvest the people have more employment, that they are improved in their condition, and are not liable to the extreme sufferings that a bad harvest and the consequent scarcity of food and high prices entail upon them. Then why quarrel with those who seek to obtain by other means—by the freedom of trade, the same results that they only look forward to as the consequences of an abundant harvest? The object of both parties is the same: the desire of Hon. Gentlemen opposite for good harvests and our desire for Free Trade each proceeds from the same motive. When they pray for good harvests we do not accuse them of a wish to reduce wages and to benefit themselves only: let them give us credit, then, for being actuated by the same motives that they are in our efforts to increase the supply of food by other means. Is there any difference, in point of fact, whether food is rendered scarce for the people by a bad harvest or by limiting the supply in any other way?

If they care to know what would follow from Free Trade, let them ascertain what follows a good harvest:

whether wages fall; whether the Home Trade is bad; whether labour is displaced. And if they wish to know what would be the effect of restricting the supply of food to the growth of this island, let them consider what they expect would follow from confining the supply of this town or the county in which it stands to the growth of its spare soil. Apply the system of the Sliding Scale to London, and attempt to make the squares, or Grosvenor Square alone, supply corn for the whole town; and what would be the effect? If the people increased and the food did not increase in proportion, would not the price of food rise and competition for food increase? Would not wages be reduced and the people be compelled to work harder for less money and less food? And would it not be said of those who refused to admit corn from without for the purpose of keeping up the rents of the square, that they were guilty of the grossest selfishness and the grossest injustice? And what is the difference, whether the principle is applied to a single town or to a whole kingdom?

The population of the country is increasing rapidly; the produce of our own soil, it is notorious, is not keeping pace with that increase; and yet we refuse to admit an adequate supply from other countries. Let in food from abroad, and customers enough would be found for it, otherwise it would not come in. If there is nothing to apprehend from the admission of corn, why not allow it? If there are fears of the results of a change, on what do they rest? Can it be denied that they arise lest food should become very cheap, and this blessing very widely diffused? But can this be justified on any principle of justice or humanity? And what ought to be said of any man who being a party to this injustice, who supporting this system for the interest of his order, should go forth to sympathize with his victims and get credit for seeking to heal the wounds he has inflicted? Would you not charge him with the grossest ignorance or the grossest hypocrisy?

This is a question that does not affect the operatives of the mill and factory alone: it affects the whole working population; and we have no excuse for not inquiring into it.

The means of judging of the result of years of scarcity and plenty upon the moral and physical condition of the people have lately been forced upon us. Within ten years we have had four years of scarcity and four years of plenty. From 1832 to 1836 was one continued period of abundance; from 1838 to 1842 was a period of scarcity. I will first compare the effects of scarcity and abundance by figures. I find that in the four years of abundance, from 1832 to 1836, the price of wheat averaged 46*s.* a quarter; and in four years of scarcity the average price was 66*s.*—a difference of 20*s.* a quarter in the price of wheat. Here then, clearly, is an opportunity for judging of the sacrifices that the people have been called upon to make during these dear years.

One of the first consequences of a period of scarcity is that the people have less to consume and more to pay than during a time of abundance, when they have less to pay and more to consume than in a period of scarcity. This was the case in the years that I have referred to. The difference of consumption is usually one-tenth more when food is cheap than when it is dear; this is shown by the sales and deliveries in the markets. The average consumption of wheat in this country is calculated at 16,000,000 quarters. In cheap years there would be an addition of one-tenth to this amount, making the consumption of wheat in those years 17,600,000 quarters; and in dear years one-tenth must be subtracted from the average, leaving the consumption in years of scarcity at 14,400,000. Now, for the 17,600,000 quarters, the people paid 149,000,000*l.* during the four cheap years; and for the 14,400,000, 184,000,000*l.* during the four dear years. Mr. M'Culloch has calculated that 195,000,000*l.* is the annual value of the agricultural produce of this country; and it appears that the increase in price of all other produce besides corn during these years was one-sixth higher than it had been during the cheap years. These calculations are based upon Returns made to the House, and the contract prices at Greenwich Hospital. I believe that their correctness will not be disputed; and with this data it will be found that the people of this country are called upon to pay 33,000,000*l.* a year more for their food in dear years than in cheap years, while the amount of that food is diminished in the proportion I have stated.

This is one of the effects of the deficient supply of food consequent on the dependence on our own seasons instead of on regular commerce; and of itself it is sufficient, by diminishing the consumption of other things than food, to occasion stagnation of trade and depression of prices.

Then, on these occasions of scarcity, a great sacrifice is always entailed at first by the necessary exportation of bullion, to the prejudice and derangement of all the monetary affairs of the country, in order to procure supplies from abroad; which, by limiting credit, tends still further to depress prices, lower profits, and create that which is called over-production or glut in our markets.

These are some of the consequences that have hitherto followed from an insufficient supply of corn in this country. From the same cause results an increase of pauperism and Poor Rates, an increase of crime and emigration. In making these statements I am not merely asserting my own opinion, or simply expressing the bare speculations of those who agree with me; the acts of the Government and the utterances of Ministers, to which I will now refer, show that these effects result from this cause, and that to remove or diminish the evil the cause must first be dealt with.

I will first call the attention of the House to the several remedies that have been proposed by the Government and recognized by all the leading Members of the House as efficient for the purpose of removing the evils in question, which show that in their opinion all the sufferings and misfortunes of the people result from a deficient supply of food.

In 1841, eighteen months after the period of scarcity and depression to which I have alluded, Her Majesty in the Speech from the Throne referred to the deficient supply of food and the consequent sufferings of the people, and recommended remedial measures to the consideration of Parliament. What was the remedy that the Ministry of that day—those who were responsible for the good order and welfare of the country—proposed? The then Government came forward and said that they had no remedy to propose but an alteration in the laws that restricted the supply and enhanced the price of the great necessaries of life. Mark well this fact: the deficiency began at the end of 1838 and continued till 1841; and at the beginning of that year Ministers came forward and said that they had nothing else to propose to relieve the distresses to which Her Majesty had called the attention of Parliament than an alteration in the duties upon the import of corn and sugar. My noble friend the Member for London on that occasion expressed his regret that the people of this country were in a worse condition than the negroes of the West Indies; that they were subject to greater privations; and that the mass of the labouring population were fast falling into a state of pauperism and becoming recipients of public relief. The Noble Lord referred to this condition of the people in introducing a measure to relieve their distresses by altering the Corn and Sugar Duties and those other laws that tended to enhance the price of food to the people. The House well knows the fate of that proposition. They know the results to the Government that brought it forward. Those who were interested in keeping up the price of corn, united and combined with those interested in keeping up other monopolies and ejected the Ministry. But did this cause the distress to subside? What was done in the year following? Her Majesty in opening the Parliament was again obliged to refer to the sufferings and privations of the people. She said:—

I have observed, with deep regret, the continued distress in the manufacturing districts of the country.

After bearing testimony to its being no fault of the people themselves, she added:—

The sufferings and privations of the people which have resulted from it have been borne with exemplary patience and fortitude.

And the Mover of the Address in this House on that occasion said:—

Six months ago the House had heard statements made of the awful distress under which that part of the country with which he was connected was then suffering. He regretted to say that the distress was now frightfully aggravated. He would refer to the returns of workhouses to show that applications for relief were greatly increasing, and were, in many instances, made by persons who had been formerly in a state of comparative prosperity. He would refer to the charity and visiting societies, to prove that many were now applicants to that charity for relief who had, not long ago, been themselves dispensers of charity. He regretted to be obliged to state that in his opinion pauperism was advancing in this country.

The admission of the distress, however, did not relieve it; and we find the Archbishop of Canterbury shortly afterwards writing a letter to the clergy, exhorting the ministers of every parish to promote subscriptions amongst their parishioners for the succour of the poverty-stricken people. But finally, after making many other attempts to talk down the distress and prove that it would pass away of itself, what happened? The Right Hon. Baronet at the head of the Government came down to Parliament and told them that taxes upon the necessaries of life had exceeded their limit and that as a means of relieving the sufferings of the people and to enable them to consume other taxable articles they must reduce the cost of living. And by the reduction of duties that he proposed and carried, he admitted what we had so long been contending to prove: that the cost of living in this country had been rendered extravagantly high.

This, however, was not enough: the Right Hon. Baronet at last felt that he was obliged to alter the Corn Laws; and he declared that he introduced his measure to do so amidst the greatest suffering of the people. Those Corn Laws that the Hon. Member for Knaresborough[1] looked upon as essential to the protection of industry and the contentment of the poor, the Right Hon. Baronet at the head of the Government altered himself, alleging as his reason that as it was absolutely necessary that the price of food to the people should be reduced, those Laws the tendency of which was to keep up prices must in mercy to the people be altered.

[1] Mr. Ferrand.

At last there came a time when we found the Queen congratulating the country on its improved condition. And when was this? When the harvest had been ascertained to be good, when supplies from abroad had been introduced, and when the food of the people promised to be cheap and abundant. And when was it that the Secretary of State announced to the country that he was happy to say that the rate of mortality was diminishing? It was in 1843, when food was more plentiful; when importation had increased the supply and reduced the price. Great God! the rate of mortality was diminishing! Then the people had been actually dying of want, starving to death under the influence of our legislation! For this is what the admission of the Right Hon. Gentleman amounted to.

The suffering of the people did not depend upon a mere surmise; we have unfortunately official evidence of it to which I am anxious to call the attention of the House. I will in the first place refer to the progress of pauperism. In 1837 the rates levied in England and Wales for the relief of the poor amounted to 4,044,741*l.*; in 1843 they amounted to 5,200,000*l.* The number of paupers chargeable upon the rates when the period of distress commenced was 1,000,000; and when the Minister announced that there were indications that the distress was subsiding, the number was 1,500,000. What was the number of able-bodied adult paupers unable to obtain employment and depending on the Poor Rates for relief at the same period? When the distress commenced, that is in 1836, the number was under 200,000 : in 1842 the number was 407,570.

Then observe in particular places the increase in the amount expended in relieving the poor in dear years as compared with cheap years. I find that the amount expended :—

	In 1836	In 1841	Increase
	£	£	per cent.
At Stockport . . .	2,628	7,120	134
" Manchester . . .	25,669	38,938	52
" Bolton . . .	1,558	6,268	304
" Oldham . . .	3,968	7,682	159
" Hinckley . . .	2,040	4,200	97
" Sheffield . . .	11,400	23,800	109

Throughout the manufacturing districts there was great increase more or less in these proportions ; but it was not confined to these districts. The increase was hardly less in the agricultural districts. In the fifteen chief agricultural counties the increase in the amount of Poor Rates between 1836 and 1842 was 21 per cent. ; while in the twelve principal manufacturing counties the increase had been 30½ per cent. This surely is sufficient to show the injurious effect of high prices of food on the labouring population—the universality of the effect of scarce food upon the nation.

And what was the effect upon the Revenue? This I am aware is a large subject, but there is not one more deserving of the attention of the House and the country ; and although I feel that it would be inconvenient for me to go into it fully I trust that some Hon. Gentleman more competent than myself will draw the attention of the House to it. If there is anything that is operated upon more directly than another by the scarcity of food it is the state of the Revenue; and as I find that this excites more interest in the minds of some persons than the sufferings and privations of the working classes it is on this ground alone an important matter for consideration.

I will just refer to the state of the Excise Revenue as affording more especially a striking evidence of national distress. It appears from Parliamentary Returns printed May 30, 1842, that although the augmentation of the taxes made in 1840 was estimated to yield 784,000*l.* to the Excise, the Excise showed an increase of only 58,170*l.* that year; and in the year following it showed an actual decrease of 182,747*l.* In the year ended October 10, 1842, the net Revenue from Excise was 733,448*l.* less than in the year ended October 10, 1841. Such was the state of things in the fourth year of the deficient supply of food.

And what is the effect of scarcity on the moral condition of the people? What is the increase of crime in periods of scarcity as compared with the periods of abundance? In 1834 the number of commitments in England and Wales was 22,451; in 1836, a year of low prices and plenty, the number was 20,000, showing a decrease of 2,451. In 1843 the number had gradually increased under the influence of scarcity and high prices to 31,000, being an increase over the year of low prices of 11,000.

I now come to the effect of dear years and limited supplies in increasing emigration. From 1832 to

1837 (that is in cheap years) the average number of emigrants was 70,000. In 1841, under the influence of distress and the high price of food, the number was 116,000; and in 1842 it had increased to 128,000. In 1838 bankruptcies numbered 800; in 1842 they rose to 1,500.

This is the experience that we have of the effect of scarcity and high prices on the condition of the country; and I repeat again emphatically (and there is no single instance to the contrary) that when food was abundant and cheap the working population both in the manufacturing and agricultural districts were better off than when food was scarce and prices were higher. I could quote an authority upon this point that perhaps the House might be induced to receive with respect. I allude to the late Lord Liverpool. In 1822 the harvest was extremely good and prices were exceedingly low; the proprietors of land came to Parliament complaining as usual of great distress and begging for relief; in that same year when the price of corn was so low the Noble Lord, speaking in the House of Lords in reply to Earl Stanhope, said:—

When the Noble Earl [Earl Stanhope] says that the low prices incident to the distress which agriculture suffers benefit no man, I answer, that although I sincerely wish the distress did not exist, I cannot be blind to the fact that they certainly do benefit a great majority of the people. Do they not benefit those who were during the war the principal and almost the only sufferers? In all large towns they have occasioned considerable benefit by the fall of the Poor Rates. I have been at some trouble, my Lords, to ascertain the real state of the case, and can pledge myself to the accuracy of this statement. In this metropolis, in which your Lordships are now sitting, never were the lower orders of people in a better condition than they are at the present moment.

This was at the beginning of a year in which the agriculturists, clamouring for a rise of prices and scarcity in food, were complaining of distress as the consequence of abundance and plenty; and when, according to Lord Liverpool, the working classes generally were in a condition than which they had never enjoyed a better.

What was the opinion of Mr. Tooke upon the same point? Writing of the period from 1819 to 1822, this gentleman said:—

That the great mass of the community was greatly benefited by the transition from dearth to abundance there is not, there cannot be, any reasonable doubt. What but the privations and sufferings of the great bulk of the community led to the popular discontents and commotions which prevailed, and were with difficulty repressed, in the great dearths at the close of the last and the beginning of the present century, and again in 1812, in 1817, and 1819?—dearths which, after their natural cessation, these legislators would, as far as in them lay, have artificially perpetuated; while, on the other hand, the contented state of the working classes in 1821 and 1822, and not to mention the great increase of the Revenue in those years, attests the comparative well-being of the bulk of the community in periods of what those who are interested in high prices and high rents are pleased to characterize as agricultural distress.

There had been Committees on agricultural distress appointed by the House of Commons in the cheap year of 1833; and Mr. Tooke remarking on the evidence said:—

There is one point which the whole tenor of the evidence before the Committee of 1833 tended to establish beyond doubt, and that is, the improved condition of the agricultural labourer; and the fact is thus noticed in the Report: 'Amidst the numerous difficulties to which the agriculture of this country is exposed, and amidst the distress which unhappily exists, it is a consolation to your Committee to find that the general condition of the agricultural labourer in full employment is better now than at any former period, his money-wages giving him a greater command over the necessaries and conveniences of life.'

I must now ask the attention of the House to some evidence of the effects of the scarcity of food upon the health and life of the people. I am induced to refer to some details on this matter from observing the willingness of the House to listen to similar evidence on another question; indeed I am fortunate in being able in this case to refer to testimony that was relied upon in the other, I allude to the factory question; and the evidence that I am about to cite shows that nothing tends so much to shorten life and injure the health of the people as a scarcity or a constantly varying price of corn; which means, in fact, a varying amount of food. If I remember rightly, the Noble Lord[1] during the debate on the factory question alluded to the authority of Dr. Hawkins and M. Villermé. The former of these authorities stated his own opinion as well as that of Villermé and Quetelet in the following passage:—

The price of corn has a most remarkable influence on the movements of population and of disease. We have not a sufficient number of data to enable us to estimate the exact amount of its influence, but we shall assuredly not be mistaken in classing it among the most energetic causes which press upon the operations of life. This influence extends not only upon deaths

[1] Lord Ashley.

but upon births. It affects also the number of marriages, of diseases, and even of crimes.

It is the opinion, then, of these eminent medical writers that upon the supply of food depends in a great measure the physical welfare of the people.

In Milne's work on Life Annuities it is stated that that which is the case in England with respect to the influence of food on disease holds equally true with regard to other nations. A table is given in this work 'exhibiting the number of deaths, the proportionate mortality, and the character of the crop of each year in Sweden and Finland from 1750 to 1803,' which shows that throughout this whole series of fifty-three years there is not one exception to the rule, that every increase in the scarcity of food is accompanied by a corresponding increase in the mortality of the people. In every year following a scanty or failing crop the number of deaths was increased, and in some instances to a most appalling amount: for example, in 1760, after an abundant harvest, 60,323 persons died; and in the next three years, the crops being successively middling, scanty, and a failure, the deaths were respectively 63,188, 74,931, and 85,093. From 1770 to 1773 the deaths rose from 69,895 to 117,509, owing to the same cause: failing crops. And not only is every failure of the crop marked by a rise in the ratio of mortality but conversely there is no marked decrease of mortality throughout the whole series of fifty-three years that is not preceded by a plentiful crop. In fact, the evidence on this subject is more uniform than that on almost any other matter of medical observation. All authorities are agreed that the greater or less mortality is influenced by adequacy or deficiency in the supply of food.

Taking the Returns furnished by the Manchester Dispensary and comparing six dear with six cheap years, I find that 196 persons more died annually in the dear years than in the cheap years. From extensive Returns obtained from sick clubs in various parts of the country—from Blackburn, Stockport, Maidstone, the Potteries, and many other places—it appears that during the six cheaper years the mortality among the members was 3 per cent.; during the dearer years it was 4 per cent., being an increase of 1 per cent. from dear food and bad trade.

An important work was lately published, entitled, 'An Address to the Clergy of the Established Church of England on the effects of a Scarcity of Food, showing the tendency of Starvation to engender Epidemic Disease.' In this work it is shown by quotations from the Reports of physicians writing for purposes quite independent of any agitation, that each of the three remarkable periods of scarcity by which this country has been visited, viz. 1798, 1816, and 1840, were quickly followed by epidemic fever; and this fever was attributed by the medical men of the respective times to want as its principal cause.

The evidence of Dr. Fitzgerald regarding a late epidemic in Clonmel, the part of Ireland in which he practised, shows that in his opinion the primary cause of the disease was insufficiency of food. He said :—

Let me take this opportunity of guarding myself against misapprehension. It is by no means my intention to affirm that epidemic typhus always owes its origin to deficient and deteriorated food, and to that cause alone. I fully admit the influence of contagion, dirt, cold, damp, insufficient clothing, want of employment, depression of spirits, and the other causes of the disease alleged by physicians; but I would observe that these causes must in this climate coexist with scarcity and some of them, at least, be occasioned by it. They may be more or less obviated by the particular circumstances of the country at the moment, and hence the pestilence will be found more or less general; but the great truth which I have laid before you will remain unaffected, that typhus fever is the inseparable companion of great and continued scarcity after bad harvests.

Take evidence from another country. There is a most important Report by Dr. Alison in which it is stated that 23,000 persons exist in Edinburgh in an entirely destitute state, absolutely dependent upon casual charity. Dr. Alison says :—

As the botanist can tell the quality of the soil from the flowers that spontaneously arise upon it, the physician knows the state of a people from the epidemics that mow it down. It is not asserted that destitution is a cause adequate to the production of fever (although in some circumstances I believe it may become such), nor that it is the sole cause of its extension. What we are sure of is, that it is a cause of the rapid diffusion of contagious fever, and one of such peculiar power and efficacy that its existence may always be presumed when we see fever prevailing in a large community to an unusual extent. The manner in which deficient nourishment, want of employment, and privations of all kinds, favour the diffusion of fever, may be matter of dispute; but that they have that effect in a much greater degree than any cause external to the human body itself, is a fact confirmed by the experience of all physicians who have seen much of the disease.

Then again there is the evidence of Dr. Grattan, of Ireland, whom I find writing as follows :—

Next to contagion, I consider a distressed state of the general population of any particular district the most common and extensive source of typhoid fever. The present epidemic (that of Ireland) is principally to be referred to the miserable condition of the poorer classes in this kingdom ; and so long as their state shall continue unimproved, so long fever will prevail, probably not to its present extent, but certainly to an extent sufficient to render it at all times a national affliction.

Lately I applied to a medical gentleman practising in a populous district of London—Dr. Hunter of Bloomsbury, whose experience quite confirms all the other information that I have received upon the point. This gentleman wrote to me as follows :—

An extensive practice for more than twenty years, almost in the very focus of typhus localities, has given me an opportunity of seeing that disease in all its various degrees of malignity. There are numerous predisposing causes, such as impure air, crowded neighbourhoods, want of cleanliness, and so on ; but all these sink into insignificance and unimportance when compared with the great monster predisposing agent—I mean a scarcity of nutritious food ; and it may be said, if other causes have slain their thousands, this alone has slain its tens of thousands. My experience justifies and warrants me in affirming that where the people have insufficient nourishment, there typhus fever manifests itself with all the horrors of a depopulating plague. Witness Ireland. No sooner does a year of scarcity appear but this fell destroyer of the human race shows itself, carrying off thousands ; and this affirmation will, I am sure, be confirmed by any medical practitioner who has had the misfortune to see, as I have, whole families carried to their weary bourne by this scourge of the human family, brought into existence and activity by the physical wants of the people. I happened to know a family of nine persons, seven of whom died in one short month, and all by the fell destroyer, typhus, and this too in an agricultural district, where the air was as pure as the morning breath of Heaven, and where contagion was impossible, as the farmhouses were at a considerable distance from each other. But in the same district, where the families had sufficient food, and of a good quality, fever was wholly unknown.

I have a great amount of evidence of the same kind relating to France, Belgium, and Germany. All medical men seem to have come to the unanimous conclusion that the well-being of the people varies with the quantity of food with which they are supplied.

Now I may be asked what all this has to do with the Corn Laws. These Laws it will be said are intended to avert such evils; to increase the supply of food and to protect native industry; at least I see that something of this kind is implied by the Amendment of the Member for Knaresborough. This brings us directly to the question, What is the purpose of the Corn Laws? And I want to have it answered. What is the object of those Laws if it is not to limit and restrict the supply and thereby produce scarcity? I wish to know what other purpose they have, and if any, why it has never been shown? I want to know if any person who speaks in defence of the Corn Laws has ever argued for anything but for preventing cheapness by preventing plenty? If their object is to produce plenty, why are those who maintain the Corn Laws dissatisfied whenever there is abundance in the country? How is it that when the people are well fed and well off it is precisely at that moment the proprietors come forward with complaints? We have it in evidence that it is always the case that when the people are in a comparatively comfortable state the complaints of the agriculturists are loudest. If plenty is the object of the Corn Laws, the supporters of them should be most satisfied at this moment. If plenty has been the object of the Corn Laws how is it that it has not continually been a question how prices could be most effectually raised with regard to various other products besides corn?

Moreover, what do we find stated before every Committee on agricultural distress but that the great evil has been the excess of produce, and that the remedy for the evil is to sow and to raise less? In 1836 when, as I said, the people were well off; when they were well employed; when the Poor Rates were diminishing and crime was decreasing; then the agriculturists were asking what could be done to mitigate or modify the cause of these things. In 1833 and 1836, when by the evidence of all competent persons the condition of the people was comfortable, the agriculturists both of this House and the other were asking how they could best lessen the supply of food with the view to what they would call improving the prices. If the purpose of the Corn Laws is to prevent scarcity and to secure abundance how is this to be accounted for? How comes it that when the Laws were first introduced no one had any idea that they would produce plenty? How is it that those who introduced and defended them never did so on any other grounds than their tendency to make food scarcer than it would otherwise be; to produce, in fine, the scarcity that I have shown is invariably attended with want, disease, crime, and death? How is it if the Corn Laws have not this object, that those who have been most prominent in opposing them have always charged the supporters of them with wishing for and aiming at the production of scarcity? On what did Lord Grenville rest his opposition to the Corn Laws but the ground that they would produce scarcity and uncertainty in the supply of food? This object of the Corn Laws, this view of the framers of them, are not denied: it is even sought to justify them. There was a Member of the House at the time these Laws were enacted, a distinguished man, the respected father of the present Prime Minister, who protested against them, and stigmatized them as cruel and oppressive towards the people. He said:—

Those who have profited by the war prices, are the landowners. They have reaped a rich harvest from the misfortunes of the people, and they now propose the Corn Law to keep up war prices, which is to perpetuate national misfortune. They are about to perpetuate the effects of war by acts of legislation. The effects of war, owing to the interruption of commerce which it occasioned, are high prices; and the object of the Corn Law is to perpetuate these prices. But while I say this, I warn the land-owners that eventually they themselves will be the sufferers of their selfish legislation. They will raise rivals in manufacture, and thus injure their best customers, and bring fresh burdens on the country; although by the enactment of a Corn Law they hope to promote their own interests, they will in the end be most cruelly deceived.

These were in effect the words of the late Sir Robert Peel; and they have been most fully verified. How came the popular opposition to the Corn Laws at the time of their introduction if their object was conceived to be any other than to produce scarcity?

What was the cause of the riots in this town at that period? Did the people then think that the promoters of the Corn Laws wished to protect their industry (a phrase unheard of at that time) or to improve their condition? If the agriculturists could then have defended their measure why did they not use argument instead of artillery? They used no argument: they used cannon instead. The people were answered by fire and shot and not by reason. It was the only available argument.

Can we gather from what has been said and done in more recent times either, that any other result than that of scarcity was aimed at by the Corn Laws? Two years ago amidst great national distress the Hon. Member for Somersetshire was objecting to the tariff proposed for the purpose of relieving the distress by lowering price; representing the agricultural interest and supporting the Corn Laws the Hon. Member objected to the tariff not because it would diminish the supply of food but because he apprehended precisely the opposite result. The Hon. Gentleman read a statement which he considered to be entitled to the utmost confidence, to the effect that if we were to open the trade with the United States there could be no doubt but that a most extensive traffic would ensue; that food would be poured into this country in abundance; that our manufactures would be largely exported to make payment in exchange; and that the effect would be the lowering of price on articles of general consumption. This the Hon. Gentleman looked upon as a great evil. The

Hon. Gentleman now shakes his head ; but his speech recorded in 'Hansard' is to be found in the library, and according to that speech he regarded the tariff as a means of making food cheap and opposed it upon that ground. Are we, then, in the face of such facts to be told that the Corn Laws had plenty and cheapness in view?

I lately took the trouble to look at the speeches made at the meetings of Protection Societies ; and though I carefully went through them I was not able to find that any of the speakers at those meetings wished to increase the supply of food. Indeed at one of these assemblies met in the county of Surrey, a great proprietor present, with more candour if not with more wisdom than the greater number of his brethren, confessed frankly and broadly that they were met upon that occasion to advance their own interests, and to render food dear. He acknowledged that to render food dear was their interest, and that the purpose of their meeting was to concert how they could best accomplish that end. And he told his audience that if any resolution should be proposed that did not take that view of the case he had an amendment in his pocket which he should propose and which embodied his opinions.

Now many of the great landed proprietors of Surrey were present at this meeting. It was a meeting of the nobility, gentry, and clergy ; and although it is quite true that in any meeting there may be found some wild man, some enthusiast whose views are not generally shared by those present, yet on the occasion to which I am alluding not a syllable was uttered with the purpose of contradicting opinions so candidly and boldly put forward. It went forth therefore to the world that the meeting had no other object than that of promoting their own interests, and that these interests were to make food dear. Manifestly then, if this was the original object of the Corn Laws, the original object is still adhered to. When we hear of settlements, mortgages, personal interests, and that the objection of land-owners to the repeal of the Corn Laws is that the prices that these Laws enable them to obtain for their produce enable them in turn to provide for the interest of these mortgages, how is it possible to come to any other conclusion than that the purpose of the Laws was to raise price, and this by diminishing quantity? I shall not be satisfied that this is not the case until some county Member gets up and says that his object was to lower the prices of produce as much as possible, in order to make food as accessible to the people as they could, and without any regard to the advantage from the price to land-owners. I shall watch for such a sentiment with attention, and I hope that the public will observe whether any such falls from any defender of the Corn Laws.

But the Hon. Member for Berkshire [1] will perhaps say that Protection is necessary for the development of agriculture, and that food would be rendered abundant and cheap by adopting improvements in husbandry. Now I beg to ask what it is that the

[1] Mr. Pusey.

experience of this system of Protection during the last thirty years proves in this respect? What is the present state of agriculture? Has its advance satisfied the supporters of Protection if that is their object, or the wants of the people if that is its defence; and if not, is the promise of other results in future any better?

I do not know exactly for what reason (perhaps from fears of an impending change in the system of Protection) there has lately been so much bustle among Agricultural Societies. A good deal has been said and a good deal promised. But in looking over the Reports of their meetings what strikes me most forcibly is the universal admission on the part of the people of all stations that nothing could be more deplorable or more imperfect than the present condition of agriculture. They all said that these are not the times for agriculturists to stand with crossed arms—as if that was their accustomed attitude; that the state of their respective localities is shameful; that something must be done; that they could not afford to follow the example of their forefathers. This is a sort of confession that is now heard on every side.

The Right Hon. Baronet at the head of the Government and the Noble Lord the Member for North Lancashire took it into their heads during the recess to deliver lectures upon the state of agriculture in their respective neighbourhoods. The Right Hon. Baronet attended a Tamworth dinner last autumn. He began by stating that they had met there not for the *Protection* but for the *promotion* of agriculture.

A very important distinction, by the by, and one that should not be forgotten. He went on to say :—

It becomes us seriously to consider what we can do to promote agriculture. It is impossible to travel ten miles in this district without seeing that mere reliance on personal experience will not ensure success as a farmer.

In short that they must conduct their business in a different way from what they had hitherto done. At all these meetings I observe that after the evil has been mentioned the cure is always pointed out by somebody. At the Tamworth dinner for instance, after having referred to the defective state of agriculture in his neighbourhood and following Dr. Buckland, who said that he had never before seen such a deplorable state of things as was presented by the farming about Tamworth, where there were more thistles in one field than he believed grew in the whole of Lincolnshire, the Right Hon. Baronet adverted to some of the modes by which this state of things could be improved; and alluding to one of them he said :—

On a late occasion, in a neighbouring city, I took an opportunity of saying something about leases. I said then that the habit of this county was adverse to the practice of granting leases, but still, that if any tenants of mine felt that their position would be raised, their confidence in the security of their tenure increased, and they were to apply to me for an extension of the terms now generally granted, in order to have additional security as to the application of their capital—I said, then, that I should be disposed to give to any such application my favourable consideration. I remain of the same opinion. I repeat the same declaration in presence of many who occupy my land.

He then pointed to another grievance of a most

serious kind much felt by the farmer: the ravages committed by the game. With respect to hares the Right Hon. Baronet informed his auditory :—

I will forego the gratification of mere sport; and if any tenant informs me that the hares upon his farm are so numerous that they are doing him serious damage, I shall at once give orders for their immediate destruction to that extent that shall satisfy him that he can in future sustain no loss in that way.

This was all very well, and a very good example to set; and very important for the proof it afforded of the party really in fault for all this bad farming. But I should like to ask the Right Hon. Baronet whether he supposes that either in Warwickshire or in Staffordshire the hares of any other landlord have been killed or leases granted at the request of farmers in consequence of his Tamworth speech; and if not whether this grievance of the cultivator does not continue.

Then in the same autumn, the Noble Lord the Member for North Lancashire paid an agricultural visit to his own county and told the people there what improvements he and his family had recently effected upon their land :—

But every month [said the Noble Lord] that passes over my head convinces me that, so far from having done all that could be done, we have only made a beginning, and are only doing that which it is our bounden duty, but still more our abundant interest, to do.

But why is this discovery made only now? I am afraid that the efforts of the League are answerable for the clearness with which land-owners now see that something must be done. Were the League to cease its efforts, or to relax them, what would be heard about improvements in agriculture or about liberal offers from landlords to kill all the hares and rabbits upon their estates? His Lordship went on to allude to tiling and draining:—

> Over and over again I have heard from tenants that their land has been doubled in value by draining and tiling with slate soles which have a great advantage over tile soles, being lighter and less liable to break in the carriage. You will tell me, perhaps, that these are very expensive operations, and that the farmer could not afford them.

To which the meeting vociferously responded, 'Hear, hear, hear!' And what said his Lordship? Why, precisely what the Free Traders have been saying for years past. He said (I am reading from the report of a Liverpool paper):—

> Well, perhaps they could not, unless they had perfect confidence in their landlords, or unless they had the security of a long lease. [Loud, repeated, and marked applause, the object being apparently to elicit something further on the subject of leases from his Lordship.]

Nothing, however, was elicited for his Lordship went on as follows:—

> There are many other topics that I might press upon your attention. This is no time for the farmer to stand with his hands behind his back, going on half asleep, just as his father and his grandfather had gone before him.

But at all these meetings there seems to have been some practical man ready to comment on the advice given by the landlords: on this occasion Mr. Neilson was present. Let the House attend to his observations. They were as follows :—

His Lordship has said that a material improvement in the agriculture of the country has been seen, but as far as my observations go, these improvements have principally taken place on farms where the landlord has come forward with a liberal hand: I do not hesitate to say, however, that with some exceptions, the landlords are more deserving of blame for want of improvement than the tenants themselves. Look at the state of the land when the tenants first get possession of it. Look also at the terms on which it is let to them. They are asked rent without legalized terms of possession, or they have a lease abounding in clauses for the protection of the landlord, but none for the tenant. In many instances these are totally restrictive of cultivation; tying them down from ploughing a certain part of their land, or restricting their cultivation to one-ninth of fresh land each year. These terms are not likely to induce a farmer to expend his money on property not his own. Far be it from me to make any depreciatory remarks on that noble system of mutual confidence which enables estates to be handed down from generation to generation of tenants under the same family; but looking at the uncertainty of human affairs, and the fluctuations of property, this is not a general system—one under which a man is justified, with a proper consideration of his family, in expending his money. Seven years are not a sufficient time to enable a man to repay the outlay of improvement, without doing injustice to the land during the latter period of his lease. Give him a long lease, and he would freely stretch out his hand, with a certainty of getting it back again.

These remarks were made by a farmer in the presence of the Noble Lord. They were received with marked applause, and not a word was uttered in repudiation of the sentiments expressed.

There is moreover an extraordinary unanimity of opinion as to the causes of defective agriculture (which means as regards the community a defective supply of food throughout the country) wherever there is independence enough combined with experience to give it expression. I have here the sentiments expressed by Sir Harry Verney on the subject of tenure at a public meeting of the Bedfordshire and Buckinghamshire Agricultural Association. The Hon. Baronet after alluding to the generally defective state of farming stated that :—

There is a remedy, and one which, aided by your landlords, it is in your power to adopt, viz. an improved system of farming. This would at once afford employment to the labourers, and the money which you now expend in Poor Rates for the maintenance of their families would render them industrious and happy, and would yield to you a profitable return. In order to carry out such a system, you would require your farm-buildings to be adapted to increased produce from your land. You ought to have well-arranged farm-yards, with the needful barns, and cow-houses and stables, and with cesspools, into which all your cattle-sheds and yards should drain. You ought to have encouragement and assistance in effecting such improvements, such as draining, &c.; and, having obtained these things, which it is as much your landlord's interest as his duty to provide, you ought to have the assurance of such permanence of tenure as will enable you to reap the fruit of any capital that you may embark in the cultivation of the soil.

The Hon. Baronet went on to say :—

One of the essentials to the prosperous pursuit of agriculture is a good farm-yard, and I will boldly state what I believe to be another—you all have stated your opinions freely, and my opinion is, that unless you get leases, long leases, agriculture will never prosper in England as it ought to.

On this same occasion, the editor of the 'Mark Lane Express'—the avowed organ of the farmer, expressed his unqualified approval of the opinions of Sir Harry Verney and said that :—

He was happy to be present at this meeting, and to hear such sound observations from those who must give the start in agricultural improvements—the landlords. He felt confident that if the capital invested in the United States and other stocks were invested in that best of securities—farming, they might bid defiance to the world.

The Hon. Member for Bridgewater was also present at this meeting, and his opinions on the matter, and indeed on the question before the House, were expressed with still greater distinctness. I have seen them reported as follows :—

The more I see of, and practice agriculture, the more firmly am I convinced that the whole unemployed labour of the country could under a better system of husbandry be advantageously put into operation; and, moreover, that the Corn Laws have been one of the principal causes of the present system of bad farming and consequent pauperism. Nothing short of their entire removal will ever induce the average farmer to rely upon anything else than the Legislature for the payment of his rent, his belief being that all rent is paid by corn, and nothing else than corn, and that the Legislature can, by enacting Corn Laws, create a price which will make his rent easy. The day of their (the Corn Laws) entire abolition ought to be a day of jubilee and rejoicing to every man interested in land.

Farmers' Clubs and Agricultural Societies all seem impressed with the idea that the cultivation of the soil ought to proceed in a more efficient manner; that its capabilities are still great; but that the conditions under which land is occupied preclude their full development. For instance at the Herefordshire Agricultural Society I find that Colonel Powell, who was described as 'a friend of the farmers, a friend of the landlords, a friend of the poor, and a friend of man,' said :—

I can see no prospect of any benefit till rents become more equalized with, and parallel to, the value of the produce of the land. Many meetings connected with agriculture have of late taken place, and various plans at these meetings have been adduced to meet the pressure of the times; but, gentlemen, although good in themselves, they do not hit upon the right remedy. One says, drain, drain! You are all to be drained. Another tells you to keep up your orchards—nothing equal to Herefordshire orchards. Others say guano. This new manure will produce such immense crops that you yourselves will not fail to receive the bulk; this will be a remedy for all evils. Another says, if you are eaten up with hares and rabbits I will have them all killed—by-the-by, a proposition not to be entirely despised. Nothing more is wanted than that. But still there is only one thing that can be done to alter your position at the present time; it must come to this, that rents must be adjusted to the prices of the produce, and leases must be granted.

And again :—

There must be fresh rents and corn rents. Draining, manuring, &c., are subjects worthy to be attended to, certainly; but these, if we may judge from the tone of the addresses that have taken place at some of our meetings lately held, are to be a specific remedy. There is a new dictionary just published, which contains a vast number of words—many new ones—and a most excellent work it is, and some critics speak most highly of it; but it has an omission of one little word—one little word is left out—that word, gentlemen, is 'rent.' To some this is a most perplexing little word, and to many it proves so; at all meetings that take place the speakers use excessive caution about repeating this little word, and I observe invariably, the word 'rent' rarely comes out—this bolus, gentlemen, they cannot articulate, much less digest.

Colonel Powell thus concludes his able and honest speech :—

I say, gentlemen, that one thing only can benefit us so as to do us any lasting good, that is, fresh rents, corn rents, long leases. These form a just and equitable guide between landlord and tenant. The farmer would then know what to depend upon. This would be only fair between man and man.

The gallant Colonel sat down amidst loud and general applause.

Again, Sir R. Pigott, as chairman at a recent meeting of the Worcestershire Agricultural Association, said :—

It is through the medium of such societies as these, and these alone, that we can hope to throw off the weight that oppresses us, and promote the regeneration of agriculture.

The Hon. Baronet so describes agriculture after thirty years of Protection that something must be done to regenerate it, and he goes on to say :—

I trust there is no one so blind in this way as not to see that a sort of public interdict has gone forth against the return of high prices throughout the world, and apart from all political influences—though no doubt it is very agreeable to us to be able to talk over those days when sowing and gathering were mere mechanical operations, and when the profits were sufficient to cover any deficiency either of produce, industry, or skill—depend upon it those days will never return.

That is, the happy days when the high price that the people could be made to pay for their food would cover the consequence of ignorance and neglect among the producers. And here also the practical man had a word to say. Mr. Collis, a farmer, speaking after Sir R. Pigott, is reported to have said :—

The president has said that the landlord would be glad to meet the wishes of the tenant; but, at the same time, I do think that if the tenant had a more fixed tenure in the land [Here the speaker was interrupted by the cheers of the farmers], the landlord would get as good rents—better perhaps—and more regularly paid; and that it would be to his advantage, as well as to the advantage of the tenant. [Loud cheers.] There is no other means of accounting for the prosperity of the Scotch farmer, except that he has a better tenure than we have. [Cheers.] I read with great pleasure a speech of Lord Hatherton, in which he said that light and poor lands were not only better cultivated where the tenant had got a lease, but the tenant was able to pay much higher for them. [Cheers.] We must also recollect the very able paper by Earl Spencer on Lord Leicester's farm—very light soil, which has been reclaimed, but which now grows excellent crops. It is quite impossible a tenant can do this unless he has a fixed tenure [Loud cheering.], because, whatever may be his faith in his landlord, circumstances over which he has no control might occur—the tenant might die as well as the landlord, and then his family would not have any return for the money which he had spent upon the soil. [Loud cheers.] Besides, great advantage must arise to the landlord as well as the tenant, because the land would be very much benefited, and thus become more valuable. I lately read a speech of the Earl of Stair, in Worcester—and I find the farmers are framing it—in which he says he will grant his tenants leases on terms; the tenant to lay out money as well as the landlord; and the only advantage to the tenant—and a great one it is—will be, that he is to have a lease.

I have many more reports of what has been said lately all showing that it is the opinion of the most experienced men that agriculture is behindhand, that it ought to be improved, and that the conditions under which land is now held prevent that improvement. I have particularly adverted to this point because I expect to find some Member rising on the other side and saying that by chemical processes and other improvements the deficiency of past times is likely to be supplied; and though admitting what perhaps it would be difficult to dispute—that the country is under-supplied with food—yet alleging at the same time that if the skill of the agriculturist is encouraged he will be able to meet the demand. I have adverted to these several meetings not for the purpose of disputing this position, but to show that such encouragement depends upon sacrifices made on the part of the landlords that are little likely to be made. The sacrifice required from the landlord is a sacrifice of power, patronage, and pleasure.

First, they are asked to convert tenants-at-will into tenants under lease; I need not tell Hon. Members what a sacrifice that is. Instead of the farmers going to the hustings like serfs, they probably would, because they could, exercise an independent judgment in the choice of their representatives. It cannot be denied that ever since the passing of the Reform Bill the custom of giving leases has rather discontinued and the practice of taking tenants-at-will has become more general. There is not the least likelihood then of tenants getting leases. The fact is, the competition for land makes landlords comparatively safe in not granting them. I saw lately that fifty-six applications had been made for one farm in the county of Hereford. Under such circumstances does any man think that landlords will not look for and will not get the highest possible price for their land?

Then they are secure of their rent, for being the law makers they have of course not forgotten themselves, and by the somewhat arbitrary law of distress they obtain priority over all other creditors and such power over the tenants' property as makes them sure of what rent is due.

Again, as regards the prospect of money being laid out in improvements it must be remembered that the proprietors of land are generally but tenants for life themselves, as the occupiers are holders-at-will, and they have therefore but a slight motive to lay out much money for a distant advantage. From the customary mode of settling property in this kingdom when our hereditary proprietors come to an age to look to the improvement of their estates, in nine cases out of ten they find themselves in a position for saving rather than spending money; and knowing that their properties must descend to their eldest sons they feel bound to make provision out of their personal property for their youngest children. This is not my observation only, the same opinion has been expressed by those who have turned their attention to the circumstances under which the improvement of agriculture might be expected.

Again, is it likely that the landlords will sacrifice the pleasure appertaining to the preservation of game? Nothing harasses or perplexes the farmer more than the preservation of game. The game destroys his crops, without its being possible in many cases to make him any indemnity. It is impossible to estimate the discouraging effect upon him in his calculations for improving the land, of being obliged to preserve or not being allowed to destroy game; yet when we read of the quantity of game killed at a battue of a landholder, is it to be expected that he should forego such a source of patronage and pleasure?

The fact is, we shall never be able to induce the landlords to make the sacrifices required by the interests of the community until they see that it would be for their advantage to have the greatest amount of produce at the lowest price. When that time comes then they will be induced to seek out men of capital and skill to confer a lease on them. Under such a system we might hope to see landlords seeking out farmers who would farm the land well, happy to give them leases at the rent they would agree to pay. I should like to see landlords competing for tenants instead of fifty tenants competing for one landlord. I am however bound to admit that from inquiries made by myself, there is at present great reluctance on the part of some farmers to accept leases if the landlords would grant them. But why? From the uncertainty of the present state of things. They have been severally promised 80*s.*, 64*s.*, and 56*s.* a quarter for their corn. They have at different times got 40*s.* instead of 80*s.*; 39*s.* instead of 64*s.*; 46*s.* instead of 56*s.*; the farmers have been promised the higher price but they have been deceived after they had acted upon the faith of getting it; they now see that there is no assurance for their price, and they never know from year to year what the Legislature may think proper to do. No intelligent farmer would say he could suffer as much by Free Trade with certainty of tenure as he now does as a tenant-at-will harassed by competition and deluded by a Protection that is never realized.

I consider that I have now established these several positions: that the supply of food provided from the soil of this country has been deficient; that great inconvenience and misery have resulted from it; that the Protective System leads to and favours a bad and slovenly system of cultivation; that we have no hope of a sufficient supply from our own soil without great improvement in agriculture; that vast numbers of the people are daily suffering from want; and that the people are rapidly multiplying.

Under these circumstances I maintain that we are bound to consider whether the evils of a deficient supply cannot be averted in future. I ask whether such evils are inevitable? Why should they be? Why should commerce subject to and regulated by competition be mistrusted in this case more than in any other? The Right Hon. Baronet said that we could and ought to trust to this principle in every case except in the issue of money. We generally trust to the operation of mutual self-interest among members of a community for satisfying their respective wants. Is there any reason to expect that it will fail in this case? Why should it? And if any doubt honestly exists on this subject why do we not inquire if it is well founded? Why do we not question at this Bar or in our Committees those who would naturally engage in the trade? Why are not our merchants and ship-owners and others who conduct our Foreign Trade examined and asked whether they have reason for doubting that under the ordinary operations of commerce a regular and abundant supply of food at the lowest cost at which it can be procured, could not be furnished to our markets should the produce of our lands at home prove inadequate for the wants of our vast and augmenting population? If this inquiry is not made, does anybody really doubt that it proceeds from the certainty that is felt of the reply that would be given, and of the confidence with which it would be asserted that the objection or doubt is totally and without question unfounded?

Happily, some of the foolish things that have been said before to create doubts on the matter can scarcely be repeated after the experience that we have recently had. For instance, we should hardly hear this evening that nothing but bullion would be taken in exchange for grain if the trade in grain were free. We have been importing for five years past large quantities to the amount, as I said before, of 17,000,000 quarters, and the greater part of it we know has been paid for by manufactures exported to the countries from which this grain has been brought; and notwithstanding the apprehension that the bullion would disappear altogether if the trade in grain were free there never has been so large an amount in the coffers of the Bank of England as there is now and as there has been for upwards of the last three years.

A short time since a very able article on this subject appeared in the 'Economist' newspaper, from which I will quote figures showing that during this time while our exports to other parts of the world were falling off, to the grain-growing countries from which we have been importing largely, it increased:—

	1837.	1842.
	£	£
Exports to Continental Corn Countries .	11,581,242	16,860,416
Exports to all other Countries . .	41,787,830	30,520,607

Will anybody, then, pretend to doubt that if under all the disadvantage and uncertainty with which the trade in food with other countries is carried on at present the exchange is still effected by means of manufactures, it would not do so with more certainty and profit if the trade were regular and unrestricted? These things, indeed, can hardly be questioned with honesty in future; and it rests now with those who cannot deny that under the present circumstances of our country and the mode in which our agriculture is conducted we are insufficiently supplied with food, to justify by reasons that we have not yet heard the continuance for their own benefit of restrictions so replete with danger and disaster to the people.

I have already to apologize for having occupied the time of the House so long; but I must for one moment advert to the objection usually taken to the Resolution I now propose: that it is extreme and unreasonable. I should wish to ask in the first place who it is that has a right to make this objection? Who is it that has a right to complain that the demand I make is too large? Is it those who say that they will under all circumstances stand by the existing Protection and have nothing to do with those who assent to the abatement of an iota of it? Ought those who use this language to deter me from demanding on the part of the community what is right in principle and what in justice they are entitled to? No! surely. Yet they, it is said, constitute the majority in the Legislature. What chance should I have had with them if I had proposed a moderate fixed duty, which I am told is the reasonable thing to move, instead of my Resolution? Is there the smallest reason to say that a moderate fixed duty would be received with more favour than what I propose? Or if there were any real ground of alarm or complaint at the extent of change that would be effected by totally abolishing the Corn Laws, would not the danger be as great according to the apprehension of interested opponents if the principle of the Laws were altered and what is called a small, or moderate, or low fixed duty were proposed instead of the Sliding Scale? If there are vested interests involved in this system of making food scarce by means of inferior lands being kept in cultivation would not these (granting the position to be true) be said to be as much in jeopardy by this change as by a total repeal? What is it that is said by the advocates of the Sliding Scale in private? Why that its great merit is that it prevents the trade in corn being regular; that it prevents the market being calculated upon by foreign growers; and that if the trade were to be regular they would sooner have Free Trade and the question settled than a pretended or delusive Protection in a small fixed duty. Indeed the intelligent men of this kind say that if the trade is to be regular they would sooner have the price at home low than high; for they know well that it is the high price and not the low price that makes this a good market for foreigners. Under the operation of the Scale there is never much to come in from abroad when it is wanted most; it is only the surplus of what is grown for other countries; but if the trade were made regular the price at home would probably fall, and while this would lead to economy and improvement at home it would make the market less good to the foreigner.

Whenever, therefore, Gentlemen opposite are induced to admit that they have no right to legislate against the community to benefit themselves they will be as ready for Free Trade as for a fixed duty. But so long as they have the power to refuse this admission they will not fail to determine the amount and form of Protection that suits them best.

With regard to the adoption of the immediate change that I propose, I may say that I have the best authorities in its favour: all men who have had experience in these matters say that when commercial changes are to be made they ought to be made completely and promptly. We had the authority of the President of the Board of Trade only the other night in favour of this view. Nothing could be wiser than his declaration. He said: Commerce will always adapt itself to circumstances, and to keep great questions of trade in suspense is the way to contract commercial enterprise and produce the evils that are apprehended. Upon this ground the Wool Duties were totally, immediately, and unconditionally repealed. And what said the Right Hon. Gentleman at the head of the Government only a few nights ago to console his friends, who were complaining of the measure? No less than that the sudden transition from restriction to freedom had improved the prices in the market.

In looking back to the period when the policy of an open trade between England and Ireland was in question, we find that every argument that is now used against Free Trade with the rest of the world was then used against the trade with Ireland being made free: the cheapness of Irish labour, peculiar burdens of England, vested interests, the apprehension that land here would be thrown out of tillage —in short, everything now relied upon as pretexts for continuing the Corn Laws was then dwelt upon. The trade, however, was opened; and what was the result? Large importations of wheat doubtless took place; but the trade between the two countries greatly increased also; and while through the increasing demand of the people here the price of food was maintained in the market, nothing but advantage accrued to the two countries.

Such pretexts, indeed, seldom succeed when the interest is weak; the Beer Duties for instance were repealed without delay, in spite of large capitals having been invested in the licensed ale houses and arrangements having been made all upon the faith of the Act that regulated the old system. The complaints of brewers and publicans were disregarded and the principle of minor or particular interests yielding to the general interests was acted upon.

Again, with regard to machinery it was plausibly argued that by allowing its free exportation an advantage is given to foreign manufacturers in rivalry with our own. The interest affected in the matter was comparatively weak, remonstrance was unheeded, and now our best machinery is exported freely to the world. [Mr. Gladstone: 'The change was eighteen years in progress.'] Well, the changes in the Corn Laws have been going on for the last thirty years, there have been about seven alterations in them since 1815, and one undeviating struggle against them on principle.

Again, a case quite as strong in point of effect and hardship might be made out in favour of those who lent their money on Turnpike Trusts: they had an Act of Parliament to depend upon and they considered the security a safe one; but the projectors of railroads obtained an Act to enable them to carry out their project. The paramount interest of great public advantage in the better mode of travelling demanded that every facility for its adoption should be given, and no time was allowed to the mortgagees to change their security.

But a still more important change was effected of late years, and without any of the considerations that are assumed to operate in this last case: I mean the change in the Poor Law. The analogy in this case is close; for though the old Poor Law was very prejudicial to the poor themselves they did not think so. They had expectations raised under it however mischievous the expectations might be; they were influenced by it in their conduct and in their domestic relations; their character indeed may be said to have been formed under it; and perhaps if ever there was a case in which the feelings of the people ought to have been considered, though opposed to an enlightened view of their own interest, it was in this one. Nevertheless there was the sudden introduction of a somewhat rigid system without any deference to what might be termed the feelings or immediate wishes of the poor. [Mr. Borthwick : 'Hear.'] The Hon. Member appears to be sensitive on this point; I should like to ask for whom he is going to vote to-night? [Mr. Borthwick : 'For the poor.'] The Hon. Gentleman is going to vote against this Motion, and he will doubtless tell us that in doing so he is swayed by the old arguments of existing interests, peculiar burdens, and the necessity of consulting the feelings and prejudices of those whose interests would be immediately affected. But he knows that he cannot repeal the new Poor Law, which in truth should only have been passed after the repeal of the Corn Laws, and knowing that he cannot alter it as he is supposed to wish to do, knowing that its rigour proceeds from the extent of pauperism in the country, the Hon. Member is going to vote for the continuance of the Laws that limit the employment of the poor and render food dear to those who are, God knows, but ill requited for their labour. He is going to add to the wealth of the rich by raising the price of the poor labourer's food; but he is not going to do anything to raise the wages of the unfortunate man; and then he says that he is going to vote for the poor! He knows that he can do nothing so pleasing to the dominant class as to vote against this Motion, and nothing more offensive than to support it: to conciliate their favour or to obtain their patronage he must oppose my Motion ; and if he can be offensive to those who support it, the more will he be applauded.

This same anxiety for procrastination was shown with regard to the question of the Slave Trade when slavery was allowed by the British Government and a few persevering persons sought to abolish it : the identical arguments that I am combating as to existing interests and the danger of suddenly changing a system so long established were urged at that time in favour of perpetuating the abomination. Mr. Pitt himself was unable to shake the interested influence in this House on the matter ; and it called forth one of his most indignant rebukes when he was charged with disregarding the vested rights of the planters. He said :

I do not understand complimenting away the lives of so many human beings. I do not understand the principle on which a few individuals are to be complimented, and their minds set at rest, at the expense and total sacrifice of the interest, the security, the happiness, of a whole quarter of the world, which, from our foul practices, has, for a vast length of time, been a scene of misery and horror. I say, because I feel, that every hour you continue this trade, you are guilty of an offence beyond your power to atone for; and, by your indulgence to the planters, thousands of human beings are to be miserable for ever. I feel its infamy so heavily, I am so clearly convinced of its impolicy, that I am ashamed I have not been able to prevail upon the House to abandon it altogether at an instant—to pronounce with one voice, 'immediate and total abolition.' There is no excuse for us, seeing this infernal traffic as we do. It is the very death of justice to utter a syllable in support of it. Sir, I know I state this subject with warmth. I feel it impossible for me not to do so; or, if it were, I should detest myself for the exercise of moderation.

Now considering the irreparable mischief that has been inflicted on millions of our people by the operation of the Corn Laws; considering the moral as well as pecuniary ruin that by their effect on our commerce they have at different times brought upon the industrious classes, and the certainty that their continuance holds out of a recurrence of these evils, I cannot and will not for the sake of conciliating a few men of rank abandon a great principle that in its application has in view to redress an enormous wrong and to confer a vast advantage upon the people at large. I therefore now beg leave to move the Resolutions of which I have given notice.

The Motion embracing the Resolutions was:—

That this House do resolve itself into a Committee for the purpose of considering the following resolutions:—

That it appears by a recent Census that the people of this country are rapidly increasing in number.

That it is in evidence before this House that a large proportion of Her Majesty's subjects are insufficiently provided with the first necessaries of life.

That, nevertheless, a Corn Law is in force which restricts the supply of food, and thereby lessens its abundance.

That any such restriction having for its object to impede the free purchase of an article upon which depends the subsistence of the community, is indefensible in principle, injurious in operation, and ought to be abolished.

That it is therefore expedient that the Act 5 and 6 Vic. c. 14 shall be repealed forthwith.

REPLY.

I hear some Hon. Members reminding me of the length of my previous address: I am not going to repeat that infliction, so there is no need to interrupt me. I have a special reason to be short: I have nothing to reply to: the question has been shirked. I am not surprised at this, I expected that Hon. Members opposite would not venture to discuss the question this year. ['Oh!'] I do not mean to say that Hon. Members dare not speak, but that consistently with a regard for truth they dare not contradict the statements on which the case for the abolition of Monopoly in food is grounded. I called upon them distinctly either to prove the good that the Corn Laws have done to the community, or to disprove the evils that are asserted and shown to have followed from them. They could do neither; and to that just challenge they have remained mute. The evils of the Corn Laws are obvious: Hon. Members have not ventured this year to say that those are benefited for whose interest they have been pretending to support it.

The debate is now concluded because the important speech of the occasion has been made. I mean that of the Right Hon. Baronet; and its importance has been admitted to me by one opposed to my views, on a ground of which the Right Hon. Baronet could hardly be ignorant himself: namely, that until he delivered that speech neither his friends nor his opponents knew of what character it would be. I was told by an opponent this evening that if the Right Hon. Baronet made a thorough Protection Speech with no wanderings into the labyrinth of Free Trade and no fresh admission of the justice of that principle that he would then unite his real friends again, and that he would receive cordial support upon all the questions on which they had separated from him: let him in fine only say that he would support the present Corn Laws without reference to anything or anybody else and he would hear no more of Ten Hours' Bills, or Poor Law Bills, or any more cant about the suffering of the poor.

Well, this famous speech has been made; a speech it seems to satisfy dissatisfied supporters; an out-and-out Protection Speech; a fresh pledge to those who considered themselves to have been deceived. I see that Hon. Gentlemen are satisfied. Were any of those who appear to be so in this House in 1839 I wonder! If so, do they remember certain assurances given on that occasion? The speech of to-night was the counterpart of that made in 1839. It was characterized by the same features: great levity, apparent disregard of the privation endured by the people, and a solemn pledge given to the agriculturists to adhere firmly to the present Laws. I do not recollect a single assurance intended to be given by the speech we have just heard that was not given more solemnly in 1839. Where are Hon. Members' grounds of confidence in these Laws being maintained? Upon the faith of such pledges Hon. Gentlemen got together a majority to turn out the late Government because it had proposed to deal with Monopoly: when the power was acquired they know what happened.

I do not blame the Right Hon. Baronet for having broken faith with his friends; he would, under the circumstances, have been much more to blame had he not done so. The fact is he cannot resist or escape from things that are inevitable; and he may say now as he said before—just what he pleases or just what pleases his friends; but he must also—as he did before—throw his friends and his pledges and his principles overboard, when an overwhelming necessity springing out of the wants and privations of the people renders it necessary. If the things said in defence of the Corn Laws by its friends are true this will not be necessary; but they are notoriously otherwise; and when men are starving something else than talking or saying what is untrue is required to satisfy them.

These Laws throw upon its upholders the responsibility of providing the people adequately with food; this they undertook to do, but regularly at given periods they fail to do it. The people would be able by free and regular commerce to feed themselves: these Laws prevent them from doing so; the Legislature, therefore, is bound to accomplish the necessary supply of food in some other way.

Whenever the harvest is bad, the people by being made dependent on the accident of a season are subject to great want and suffering; and the Minister whoever he may be is obliged (for he would not venture to do otherwise) to relax the Laws enacted for the purpose of cutting off a vast source of supply to this country.

Now, I maintain that while the Corn Laws continue the same reasons exist for the recurrence of the evils that have already followed from them. Gentlemen opposite may be satisfied with the Right Hon. Baronet's promises if they like ; but under present circumstances the promises are made only to be broken, as they will discover ere long. They are certain of their majority now ; but let them recollect that it was only the other day that the Right Hon. Baronet told them that the Revenue could not be collected if the cost of living were not reduced. [Cries of 'Question.'] The Hon. Member who is attempting to put me down (the brother of the President of the Board of Trade I believe) will not succeed. I am speaking to the question. I am speaking to the point when I read extracts from Hon. Members' speeches made during the Recess, notwithstanding the remark of the Right Hon. Baronet. I read those extracts to show that while the alternative for liberating the trade in food would be to apply the highest improvements to agriculture, to the cultivation of the land with a view to great production and adequate supply, the effect of the present system has hitherto been to retard those improvements, and is calculated to prevent them in future ; and that all the knowledge that we possess as to the better modes of culture are useless unless a more liberal system is pursued towards the occupiers, which can only be expected under the influence of competition. When Hon. Gentlemen are setting up the necessity of Monopoly for the agriculture of the country I maintain that it is in point to examine the truth of such a plea in the light of evidence afforded by the Hon. Gentlemen themselves. And I am now determined that it shall be distinctly known to the country under what circumstances the Vote is about to be given. I have proved to demonstration that the people are inadequately supplied with food from the soil of this country; that they have suffered intensely from this circumstance and that numbers are still suffering; that there is no prospect at present that their wants will with their increasing numbers be adequately supplied by the growth at home; and that the population is rapidly and daily increasing. Indeed, since I have been in the habit of initiating discussion on this matter there have been 2,000,000 added to the number of the people. And now when this increase of population presses home with increased force the fact that the poor must work hard and long for the bare necessaries of life, gentlemen come forward with long faces, groaning over their fate and urging everything to excite feeling and passion among the people themselves at what they call their wretched state; and yet when a great primary cause of the evil is pointed out to these philanthropists, and they are implored to assist in removing it, for some very good reasons of their own which it would not be difficult to explain, they are going to perpetuate that cause of suffering, and treat the request to remove it almost with derision.

I challenge anybody upon examining this debate to discover one solid reason why the Corn Laws or any like policy should be continued under the circumstances of the country.

I cannot wonder at the feeling of the people towards this House, when they witness such disregard of the public and general interests. A working-man came to me only this morning and detailed what he and his family have suffered during the last four years from want of employment and the high price of living relatively to his earnings. He said: 'I wish you may succeed, Sir, in moving the feelings of that House on this subject; I wish you may turn their hearts to do what is just to the people at large in abolishing so wicked a law; but I fear you never will.' I told him not to despair; but the man was convinced that while 6,000,000 out of 7,000,000 of the male adult population of the country remained wholly and entirely without a voice in the Legislature, their chance of justice would be very small. It is for the House to consider how far they will justify this opinion by the Vote they are about to give.

XX.

COVENT GARDEN THEATRE, July 3, 1844.

The result of the debate on Mr. Villiers's Motion in 1844 was viewed rather in the light of a success than of a defeat outside the House: a hostile majority had tacitly confessed that they were maintaining abuses that could not be defended, while the Cabinet virtually declared that its legislation was provisional, and depended upon contingencies that could not be foreseen. The weekly meetings of the League at Covent Garden showed no diminution in numbers or enthusiasm; and the week following the defeat of his Motion Mr. Villiers addressed an enormous assembly there. Mr. Cobden took occasion, amidst the applause of all present, to speak of Mr. Villiers's unfaltering assistance and consistent advocacy of the question 'in spite of all sinister influences and in defiance of all those associations which he, as a member of the aristocracy, must have had brought to bear upon him,' ever since he took possession of it in the Legislature six years previously.

Your Chairman has told you that of which you were doubtless already apprised: namely, that since our last meeting here for the purpose of considering the Corn Laws, I have been to the House where those Laws were enacted for the purpose of making my annual inquiry of the authors of them whether there are any grounds of justice, or wisdom, or humanity on which their existence can be defended; and whether there is any fresh experience, or new circumstance, or policy of any kind that can be alleged as a set-off against the mass of mischief and misery which yearly flows, and ever must flow, from the Corn Laws so long as they are in force.

I have now come, in compliance with a request

made by our friend the Chairman, and notwithstanding the contemptuous reference made to these meetings by Sir Robert Peel—I have come, out of respect to those who attend here for the purpose of marking their sympathy with the people and to manifest their interest in this question, to convey to you my impression of the result of the recent discussion and Division in the House of Commons. And I may say at once that, for the reasons just given by my friend in the Chair, I never in my life felt less discouraged about the cause, and that the result of the Division has exceeded my most sanguine expectations. My Motion was brought forward under every circumstance of disadvantage, and I was quite unprepared for the influence that public opinion has exercised over the constituencies, shown in the numerous fresh votes in favour of Repeal.

It is, I know, asserted by our opponents, in Parliament and in the Press, that the result generally has been most satisfactory to them and disastrous to us. But on this point I have something to say. The friends of scarcity in the House of Commons derive their satisfaction from the speech made by the President of the Board of Trade, Mr. Gladstone. They hailed that speech with joy and surprise because—they said—of its honesty. The honesty of it seems to have taken them by surprise; and it consisted, as far as we could gather, in his pledge to stick to the Sliding Scale to the utmost of his power for the rest of his days! And they believed him, which is not always the case when the present Ministers pledge their faith. Whenever Sir Robert Peel is more than usually solemn in his assurance of fidelity and of his adherence to the Protective System, some caustic friend is always heard to say: 'Then he is going to attack us again!' or: 'Now it is certain that he has another Corn Bill in his pocket!' But on what ground the pledge of the President of the Board of Trade found such favour in their sight, I do not know; for, as far as my experience goes, this young statesman is not exactly made of the stuff of which martyrs are composed, and clinging to the Scale through life certainly savours of martyrdom.

In the House of Peers great consolation is drawn from the result of the Division; and the organ of Monopoly there, his Grace of Richmond, announces to the country and tells his friends the tenants-at-will that now they may renew their engagements and hire their land at the Act-of-Parliament price, for the majorities in Parliament in favour of the Scale are constantly increasing. I dare say that some poor farmers here and there have, from the faith they feel in persons of such high degree, been induced to offer higher prices for their land than they would otherwise have done. But what is the broad fact? My Hon. Friend has just stated it: so far from the majority having increased, it has decreased, and no less than twenty-eight members who never voted before for total Repeal did so upon the occasion of this last Division.

But the great organ of these luminaries in the

Press, the 'Morning Herald,' is so convinced by the avowed contentment of its clients, that it will not occupy itself with the truth or wisdom of what they have said; and the morning after the Division it entered at once upon a curious inquiry—occupying two columns of its space—into what it was that had killed the League, and the reason why the people so dearly love Protection. The League is dead, then, and its opponents have nothing more to do with it but to inquire how its death was brought about! I own that I was ignorant of the cause as well as of the event itself; but the 'Morning Herald' was equally ready with the one and the other; and has discovered that the death of the League was entirely owing to the measures of Sir Robert Peel. His measures have been of that comprehensive character that they have settled everything. The agriculturists are now at rest; they enjoy peace at last: they know that the question of the Corn Laws is settled, and they are content.

I venture to differ from even so venerable an authority as the important organ from which I have just quoted. The matter seems to me still to admit of some doubt. What are the grounds for supposing that this great agricultural difficulty is settled? What are the grounds for telling the farmers they may now set about their business in peace? Simply that Sir Robert Peel has told them that he will stick to the Sliding Scale! But it is not enough for him to declare that he will stick to the Scale. There is another condition necessary to assure the agriculturists; and that is, that the public will stick to Sir Robert Peel; because, unless they do, his sticking to the Scale will not do either the Scale or himself any good. And it is possible, nay, probable, that some day—not far distant—they will both sink as well as stick together.

Now what is the truth about the Sliding Scale? Let us for the sake of the farmers examine the subject. We do not in these days find the public very apt to agree about many things; but is it not true that if one thing does unite them more than another it is hostility to the Sliding Scale? The commercial classes are not apt to be very united upon any point; yet upon this one they agree unanimously. The Liberal party in Parliament are not very apt to be united, yet upon this matter they are of one mind. Even Lord John Russell, who is not in love with the League—and who, the other night, was very cross about corn, because he had been crossed himself the week before about sugar—says that, if he should get into power again, and should be obliged to show favour to the agriculturists, it would never be in the form of a Sliding Scale. And he also says that as long as the Sliding Scale exists all and every agitation against it is, in his opinion, not only justifiable but commendable. There is not a single man of those likely to compose the next Government who is not opposed to the Sliding Scale. And the state of the present Government is not quite so strong as it was, I think. If you ask the man in the street what he thinks of it, he says,

'It is going, Sir!' Everybody says that it is very shaky, that it is tottering, and may go any day.

It is important to consider why this is the case. The fact is, that owing very much to these and other meetings of the kind, and owing very much to the dissemination of your opinions throughout the country, public feeling generally is up against Monopoly. All may not be agreed as to the mode or as to the time of abolishing it; but public opinion is nevertheless opposed to Monopoly.

The present Ministry entirely depend upon Monopolists for support. The consequence is that while they do not dare to outrage public opinion by openly upholding Monopoly they cannot retain the goodwill of their friends without doing so: they cannot get popularity without attacking Monopoly, and they cannot keep their troops together if they do so.

For this reason I think we may expect a pretty constant recurrence of those 'family jars' which very nearly upset them the other day: the disturbance was all about Monopoly, nothing else.

Never before was the Sliding Scale in such jeopardy as it is now. Never before were the Corn Laws so thoroughly unsettled. And any man connected with agriculture would, in my opinion, be an arrant fool if on the faith of the continuance of the present system he invested a single shilling in any improvement or laid out a halfpenny on the faith of any expected or promised advantage secured to him by the Corn Laws.

And how does this state of things suit the agriculturists? Why, they say, and say truly, that they are now in the very worst position they can possibly be in. They say: 'Give us total Repeal; give us Free Trade; give us anything that will be final; let us have anything but this uncertainty.' And whose fault is it that they are in such a plight? It is the fault, it is the natural result, of bad laws, of laws that cannot be defended by those who maintain them; that are an outrage on all that is just and right; and that must irritate as well as injure the people and promote agitation till they are abolished. The Monopolist peers and their friends in the House of Commons may pretend that the Corn Laws are settled; but the fact is, that greater uncertainty about them never existed; and they know well that this very uncertainty, this very unsettlement indicated by everything that has lately taken place, is a strong reason for us to continue our exertions, and a sign to us that we must succeed if we persevere.

The poor agriculturists see how they have been duped; and they know that any day the Government may be turned out and their professed friends turned round. The Government might have fallen the other day; but at any time when a Government has the wisdom to make a judicious distribution of 'stars,' and 'ribands,' and 'places,' the farmers' friends can be reconciled to extraordinary changes.

The real reason, however, why our opponents in the Lords and Commons are so anxious to shake hands with Sir Robert Peel and to say that, after all, he is their true friend, and that in future he shall be their leader, is that recent discussions in both Houses of Parliament have shown them their utter impotence, have proved to them that they can do nothing, and that, compared with former times, they are numerically weak, without a spokesman to support them within, and without public opinion to back them without. On the flimsiest pretext, therefore, they go back to Sir Robert Peel, eat 'humble pie,' and offer to do just what he pleases. This, however, fixes upon Sir Robert Peel a heavy responsibility for the future. He has humbled his party; he has supreme power; he can do what he likes; and if he does not do what is right he is solely, wholly to blame.

If anybody thinks that the prospects of progress for Free Trade are based only on the speculations of an individual, I would ask him to consider for one moment the progress which the cause has been making uninterruptedly for years past. Observe the altered tone of the supporters of Monopoly as compared with that of a few years back when Mr. Canning was in office. There were then, as there are now, three parties on the subject of the Corn Laws in the House of Commons: in the first place there were those who were for the entire prohibition of all food entering this country; secondly, there were those who favoured a Sliding Scale; and lastly there were those who opposed Monopoly in every shape.

I will just give you a specimen of the respective opinions and manners of the Free Traders and Monopolists, when Mr. Canning, in 1827, proposed the Sliding Scale. Mr. Wolryche Whitmore, who represented the Free Trade party, and who sat for the same district which I now have the honour to represent, wanted to expose the Sliding Scale; he predicted its mischievous effects, and said that he rose for the purpose of expressing his doubts as to the advantages which were promised to accrue from it. I find in 'Hansard' the following description of the way in which he was treated:—

The Hon. Member was proceeding to state his objections when he was interrupted by loud and general coughing. Having waited till the noise had subsided, he said, had he proposed counter-resolutions, he should not have been surprised; but he felt at a loss to account for this interruption. He conceived that the evils of the present system could not be alleviated by the new measure. [Renewed coughing.] He hoped that they would not stifle the opinions of members who wished to give a free opinion on the subject. The Hon. Gentleman in vain attempted to proceed, and the interruption continuing, he sat down.

That is the way in which the people were treated a few years ago, when the Sliding Scale was proposed, and when an independent gentleman ventured to express his doubts with reference to its merits. Mr. Whitmore was immediately followed by a person with whose name you are now familiar—a man of importance, indeed, as far as position goes, I mean Sir Edward Knatchbull. Sir Edward Knatchbull, I should be disposed to think, would not be one of those who would have suppressed his cough, had he been afflicted with irritation when Mr. Whitmore tried to make himself heard. The commencement of his speech is amusing. He said that—

He entertained a very different opinion from that of the Hon. Gentleman who had just sat down. [A laugh.] This was an important question. It was, whether the House should legislate on the principle of Prohibition, or admit corn on payment of a certain duty. He thought himself bound to state that he was in favour of Prohibition in preference to a duty. That was his deliberate and confirmed opinion, and he took the opportunity of stating it distinctly to the House. He had heard with horror and distrust what had fallen from the Right Hon. Gentleman [Mr. Canning]: he had said that he inclined to Free Trade. He cautioned the House, then, against this dangerous measure.

This dangerous measure was the Sliding Scale. Well, it did get through the House of Commons; but it was thrown out in the House of Lords. There the Prohibition party was headed by the Duke of Wellington, and they were triumphant. We know what was their fury against Canning for having in one Session attacked their Monopoly both in corn and Church—for he pressed the Catholic Emancipation upon them as he did Free Trade: they fairly worried the life out of him, and the Session hardly passed before he died. They then came into office and carried the famous Sliding Scale, of which we have heard, and from which we have suffered so much.

And let me just mention to you what happened, in order to show what advantage there is in proposing moderate instead of extreme measures, and to see what one gets for compromising great principles in the House. Mr. Whitmore, who was coughed down for making observations opposed to the Sliding Scale, was more tolerated as the Bill advanced, and he ventured to propose an Amendment. What do you think that Amendment was? It was but a slight Amendment, as he called it fourteen years ago, but it was the very change that Sir R. Peel proposed only the other day. They went to a Division. I am told that my minority was so small in consequence of the extreme Motion that I made: I asked for total Repeal. Mr. Whitmore asked for a slight diminution of the Sliding Scale—the very safe, reasonable, moderate thing as it is called, that Sir R. Peel proposed himself two years ago: 385 voted against it, only 50 for it. There is encouragement for moderation! And, mind you, the Amendment was repudiated by all the county gentlemen, with all the usual arguments of being highly injurious to agriculture, anarchical in its character, and certain to cause confusion. In fact, everything that was said the other night against total Repeal was urged against that and every other modification.

Well, after the excitement of the Reform Bill was over in 1833 and 1834, Mr. Fryer, Mr. Whitmore, and others proposed various alterations—some great, some small—in the Sliding Scale; but they were treated exactly alike: they were all voted as revolutionary and injurious to the best interests of society. In 1837, Sir William Clay proposed a fixed duty, and had an enormous majority against him, and his minority was rather less than mine the next year, when I brought forward my Motion. In 1838, seeing that there was no use in attempting to reason with these men, seeing that their hearts were really bent on prohibiting all food coming into the country, and that they cared for nothing but swelling their rents without reference to any other interest, I proposed what I considered to be simply justice to the people; what

I was prepared to defend upon principle; and what was at once intelligible to all: I proposed total Repeal.

I now will call your attention to what is the effect of constant agitation upon these questions when pushed earnestly and urgently, however bitter the opposition to them may be. In 1838 there was a majority of 300 against my Motion. I had framed it so as to admit of its acceptance by any person who though not agreeing with me in the justice of total Repeal might nevertheless agree with me as to the necessity of going into a Committee: I argued for total Repeal, but I only moved that the House should resolve itself into a Committee, and yet there was a 300 majority against me. In 1839, I proposed the same measure, and the majority was reduced to 147. In 1840, I brought it forward again, and the majority was reduced to 123. I may mention that our friends of the Anti-Corn-Law League were then in active operation. They were doing everything to diffuse information on the subject of the Corn Laws throughout the country, and it was greatly the result of their efforts and energy in the matter that the majority was so signally reduced that from 300 in 1838 it fell to 123 in 1840.

In 1841, such had been the evidence disclosed, such was the suffering of the people, and so clearly was the connection of the Corn Laws with all that the people were enduring to be traced, that the Ministry of that day said that they could no longer resist, that, in fact, they were bound to propose an alteration in the Corn Laws as well as in other monopolies; and that they could not retain their supporters or continue in office without proposing a change. In 1841, therefore, they proceeded to deal with the Monopoly in corn; and then it was, as we know, that the present Government and the present supporters of this Government resorted to every means calculated to lower Lord Melbourne's Cabinet in the eyes of the country. There was nothing that they did not urge against it; there was no calumny, no misstatement, no fallacy that they did not circulate throughout the country to make people believe that this Monopoly could be maintained, that it ought to be maintained, that it was for the interest of the country that it should be maintained, and that if they were brought into power they would maintain it. In vain we may look through English history for such an instance of wholesale imposture as was resorted to for this purpose, and for the purpose of encouraging the people to believe that it was possible to put down the Free Trade party, and to uphold the Monopolists. At the latter end of 1841 they came into power, and before the spring of 1842, we all know what happened.

There was Sir Robert Peel, first of all, proposing his tariff, which more or less attacked every Protective duty except that of corn. Then he was compelled to turn to the Corn Laws, the necessities of the people leaving him no choice. And he admitted every principle that his party had repudiated, and explicitly acknowledged the truth of the Free Trade principle, that you should 'buy in the cheapest market and sell in the dearest.' In fact, he made a full and complete acknowledgment that he and his party were wrong before, and that we had been right all the time.

Well, it was in that year, that seeing how the people were suffering; hearing how in our manufacturing districts there was hardly security for property on account of the despair of the people who were actually starving; knowing as we all did know how disease and mortality were spreading in a dreadful way owing to privation and the want of the necessaries of life; seeing and hearing and knowing all this, then it was that I said: It is time to propose total Repeal to the House. Now that the principle of Free Trade is acknowledged, now that these people avow they have been in error, and have surrendered the ground they formerly occupied, it is time to propose the total and immediate repeal of the Corn Laws, and to propose it in a way that shall admit of no mistake in the vote that is given. The Laws, I contended, were murderous Laws, for they were Laws that could be proved to be producing death, and, therefore, they ought at once to be repealed.

This was in 1842, so that it was in 1842 that I first proposed that all duties on food imported from abroad to supply a sufficiency for home consumption should cease and that trade in food should be free.

I beg to call attention now to the progress that this particular Motion is making and has made during the last few years. On the first Division that took place in 1842, on the Motion for the total and unconditional repeal of the Corn Laws, the majority against it was 303. In 1843, I repeated the Motion, and the majority was reduced from 303 to 256. And last week when I again repeated it the majority was reduced from 256 to 204. I ask, What is this but progress? What does it show but the influence of public opinion? What does it mean but that conviction has reached the electoral body of the people that the Corn Laws are atrocious Laws and that they ought forthwith to be abolished? I find that in the last Division there was not one single Liberal Member returned for any borough, with the exception of the City of Carlisle, who voted against the Motion. Every Member returned on Liberal principles voted for it. Those, therefore, who were not returned on Liberal principles were Monopolists, and, consequently, have to vindicate their conduct to the people at large, for whom they profess to hold the franchise in trust.

To justify yet further my opinion of our advance, I would refer to the argument by which my Motion was met last week, and the way in which it was received. I was determined that what we mean when we call for total and immediate repeal of the Corn Laws should be brought clearly and explicitly before the House, and I therefore framed Resolutions for this purpose. I did not want to dogmatize or to dictate to the House, or to impose a test or formula which people were to subscribe without knowing what it meant. I did not want to thrust total and immediate Repeal down their throats without showing valid reasons for it. I framed my Resolutions with a distinct view of showing the necessity of removing a great obstruction to the welfare of the people, and the urgency of the necessity which made an immediate consideration of the Laws imperative. These Resolutions declared that large numbers of the people of this country had been reported to the House as being deprived of the necessaries of life; that the numbers were increasing; and that the Corn Laws existed for the express purpose of cutting off a supply of the necessaries of life. Moreover, I extracted from the famous protest of Lord Grenville, made in 1815 in the House of Lords, the just sentiments it contained, to the effect that it was unwise and unjust to tamper with the subsistence of the people, and that Laws having for their object to cut off the supply of food were unjust in principle and injurious in operation, and, as such, ought not to exist.

That was the nature of the Resolutions that I proposed to the House. I wanted to know if they could be controverted. I wanted the majority to say whether the people were well off in this country, and whether the mass of the people were not deprived of the necessaries of life; and I wanted to hear from those who passed and maintained them, whether these Laws did not limit the supply of food. I placed the question distinctly before them, in order that the whole world should be satisfied whether the Monopolists are right or whether we are right; and now I want to know whether anybody who has looked through the debate can point to a single word in it uttered in proof that the contents of my Resolutions were not true. Did anybody dispute the fact that the people were ill off, as I described them to be? I confined myself in my opening statement strictly to the Resolutions that I proposed. I resorted to no declamation; I did not appeal to feelings. I am no orator. I simply stated facts in support of my Resolutions—facts resting on official authority, facts drawn from the Reports of their own Commissioners, disclosing the distress of the people and their lamentably insufficient supply of the necessaries of life. And I asked for an answer; I asked for a proof that the Corn Laws were not an injury to the people. I inquired of the agricultural gentlemen whether their labourers were well off, or whether their farmers prospered; I begged of them—I defied them to adduce a tittle of evidence to show either the one or the other. And then I asked, if they did not and could not do so, to resolve with me that any Laws that presumed or even purported to benefit labourers or farmers and had failed, should be repealed.

How was I met? Do you think that if they could have proved that the labourers were well off that they would not have done so? Do you think that if the farmers could have been shown to have benefited in one single respect, or if advantages resulted to anybody but themselves from these Laws, that we should not have heard of it? No! certainly no. But what did they do? They began to talk about the Anti-Corn-Law League. There was a long yarn about what the Anti-Corn-Law League had done or said a year before. There was not one to deny that large numbers of the people were suffering from physical want; not one to deny the effects, the odious effects of the Corn Laws in adding to disease and destroying the health of our people. I showed them over and over again that the sole object and the avowed intention of the Laws were to limit the supply of food, and to increase its price; and I begged of them that they would take that opportunity, if it were otherwise, of announcing to the world that this was not the purpose of the Corn Laws. Not a Member rose to say that it was not. It was only too clear from what they did say that the case was as I stated. We listened and strained our ears in vain to hear anything to justify, anything to excuse the Corn Laws. And when at last Sir Robert Peel rose, it was only to utter what we were meant to accept as an apology for their continuance. He said that the Corn Laws are part of a Protective System. He did not say that the people are not starving; he did not say that the Laws are just, or that they are not what Lord Howick properly described them to be: 'a robbery.' But he said that they are part of a system; which we could have told him before. They certainly are part of a system; and a very pretty system it is! The system is this: that the people are not to be adequately fed—they are to suffer because it is the interest of A, B, C, D, to injure them. The peoples' suffering, and the power of A, B, C, D, to make them suffer, constitute 'the system.'

Sir Robert Peel next pointed to the peculiar burdens that the landlords bear; and what do you think was the special burden he named for which food is to be made scarce and dear? Of all the burdens that have been or can be named, would you imagine that the one he would select would be the Poor Rate? But what is the Poor Rate? Why, the fund that is actually raised to relieve the poverty caused by these very Corn Laws. I have stated, and other gentlemen have stated it also, that there has not been in the history of the condition of the poor, one single exception to the rule that they are worse off when bread is scarce and dear, and that they are better off when it is abundant and cheap. And it has been found invariably, both in agricultural districts and in towns, that when bread is cheap the Poor Rates fall, whilst when bread is dear the Poor Rates rise. Well, Sir Robert Peel says: 'Think of the Poor Rates which the landlords have to pay!' Even supposing that they had a greater share to pay than other people, yet that would be answered by what one of them said to me privately the other day; and when they speak privately it is perfectly astonishing what different sentiments they express to those to which they give utterance in public. He said: 'All this poverty is very shocking, certainly; but, to tell you the truth, the poverty is not so mischievous to us as it is to other people. If the people could not consume food, it would be very bad for us; but, by means of the Poor Rate, a fund is raised from the people in towns—tradesmen and others—to buy food to feed the paupers.' So that literally, you see, they are the last people who suffer from the Poor Rates, or from the poverty that the Poor Rates entail, because even by the purchase of food to supply the workhouses, landlords are benefited.

Now, what other thing did Sir Robert Peel say? He said: 'Think of poor Ireland.' Think of Ireland! Only conceive of his thinking of Ireland! This is one of the consequences of shutting up Mr. O'Connell: they can take liberties with Ireland. For if Mr. O'Connell had been in the House on that occasion, you know, from what you have heard from him here, that he would never have permitted that Ireland should be pleaded as a reason for the Corn Laws. Mr. O'Connell said in this place, as he said elsewhere—and I must say that there is no man who has voted more constantly for the repeal of the Corn Laws than Mr. O'Connell—he said, 'I stand before you as the representative of one of the most agricultural counties of all Ireland, I stand here better acquainted with the wants and the means of the people of Ireland than any other man who can stand before you, and I tell you that the agriculturists not only have no interest in the continuance of this Law, but they share in the misery, and privation, and suffering which it brings upon the people of the whole country.' They cannot be worse off than they are. And Mr. O'Connell mentioned also—I don't know whether it was in this place, but, if not here, certainly at some other public meeting—that the landlords had attempted to get up a meeting in favour of the Corn Laws in two counties in Ireland, and that they were beaten hollow by the peasantry and the farmers themselves. There is not a single man who really loves that country, there is not a native of that country who has been prominently before the world as its friend, who is not eager and anxious to repeal the Corn Laws as one of the causes of its misery. Aye, the words were scarcely out of Sir Robert Peel's mouth, when we found Mr. O'Connell, Mr. Sharman Crawford, the son of Mr. O'Connell, the nephew of Mr. O'Connell, Mr. Sheil, and others, all voting for their repeal.

Well, I have told you literally all that Sir Robert Peel had to say by way of reason and argument; but he had recourse to something else—to something that people generally resort to when they have nothing else, no other mode of defence left—and that is personality. It is a weapon, I believe, constantly made use of against Sir Robert by his own friends. He said that he positively did not believe that any *ten sane men* could be found, either in the commercial classes or in any other section of the community, who would really advocate the total and immediate repeal of the Corn Laws. That is the old, stale form of offensiveness which is used by everybody against anybody who does not at any time agree with them in opinion. Why, Sir Robert Peel has been twenty times called mad for one or another of his measures! There is his Currency measure of 1819: people have said, over and over again, that he must have been mad or he never would have introduced it. But I want to know what right he has to call persons insane because they are warm and strong advocates of the repeal of the Corn Laws? Upon what experience of agriculture does he presume to tell either Lord Spencer, or Lord Ducie, who took the chair here upon one occasion, that he is a madman?

A man ought to know something of agriculture to assert that this measure is unwise. Sir Robert Peel unhesitatingly says that no man of sense can for a moment think of totally repealing the Corn Laws with a view to the improvement of agriculture. Yet we have heard men acknowledged on all hands to be the best practical farmers, men most intelligent, some of them being landlords, proclaim from this platform that the total repeal of the Corn Laws is as essential to agriculture as it is important to the interests of the whole community. As to the safety of total Repeal, what business has Sir Robert Peel to tell such men as Mr. Jones Loyd or the Marquis of Westminster that they have not a sufficient stake in the country to judge of the importance of this matter? They have a *little* property, those two. And they have come to the years of discretion, and have some claim to be trusted, I should think. You may all of you be supposed to be mad, and Sir Robert says you are mad; but surely those men who are reckoned to be the wealthiest in the empire; who have considered this subject in reference to their own interests as well as with regard to the interests of others; and who come forward in the most public manner to declare that the repeal of the Corn Laws is not only a wise, but a just and necessary measure, and by contributing largely to the funds of the League to give the proof that men when they are sincere do give in this country of their attachment to our cause, surely such men might be considered something short of maniacs because of the conclusion they have come to. It is indeed the strong part of our case, that there never was any question brought before the public which was fortified by the support of so many and such high authorities as is this which we now advocate. We have on our side some of the most thoughtful men in the country; we have some of the wealthiest men in the empire—men respected by all for their character and their station. And does Sir Robert Peel think that a contemptuous reference to the state of their mind, because they differ from him, can be any ground for you to stultify your own proceedings and to admit that hitherto you have been wrong?

Their organs in the Press, moreover, echoing what Protectionists say in the House, tell us that to bring this question before the House is a sad waste of the public time. Let any one reflect for a moment on the questions that do occupy the public time in the House of Commons, and are not supposed to waste it, and he will find that they generally are those that are of the least public importance. If there are any of graver importance you will find that as a rule they are but branches of this all-important question, and only attempts to tinker or patch up some of the evils that spring from Monopoly.

Look at the Factory Bill. That has occupied considerable time in the House. And what is it but a mode of preventing the people from working hard and long, which by necessity they are compelled to do? Is it not far more rational to remove their necessity for overworking themselves by improving their circumstances?

What is the Poor Law Bill? That is thought of great importance, and probably will occupy a month in discussion. It is actually a measure to mitigate the existing Law because the people are so much distressed, and because poverty has so much increased of late, that some alteration in it is required.

The great question of the country is the condition of the working people, and that is what you are here to consider. Our object in meeting is to secure by the repeal of the Corn Laws the best mode of improving the circumstances and of elevating the social condition of the working classes. Is it not ridiculous, then, to treat such a question as unimportant, when small branches of it, when small remedies for some of its evils, are constantly engaging the whole interest and time of the House?

Again, there is the recent Currency Bill. That is an important question; and, by-the-by, the measure is supposed to have been recommended to Sir Robert by the man that he considers to be insane; by the very man that he considers to be stark, staring mad, because he advocates the repeal of the Corn Laws. Everybody says that the Currency Bill is Mr. Loyd's measure. And the great benefit of the measure is, Sir Robert Peel says, that it will prevent the grave revulsions in commerce which from time to time have occurred in the history of this country. But every one who knows the consequences of the Corn Laws knows that whilst the Corn Laws continue revulsions in commerce must constantly occur. Gold will go out of the country as before, and, in the event of a deficient supply of food, the people will find themselves in precisely the same difficulties under the new Bank Charter Bill as they were in previous to its enactment.

I mention these things simply to show that so far from wasting the public time, we are calling attention to *the* great question of the country, the due consideration of which would allow the House of Commons to suspend its labours on many other matters of secondary importance involved in it. The country is generally speaking in a healthy state as far as its wealth, its influence, and its relations with foreign countries are concerned; but attention is needed, and imperatively called for, to the condition of the people, who suffer great want, and are daily increasing in numbers, in misery, and knowledge — a condition which we hardly can regard as consistent with the security either of our institutions or of society.

We have, then, ample excuse and abundant reason for persisting in our course. I have been anxious to show you that we have no ground to despair of the cause, if we persevere in expressing and making known and explaining our opinions. You contribute much, by assembling here, to form and direct public opinion;

and as long as public opinion is allowed fair and free expression in this country, it must have great weight with the Legislature.

There is no instance of a measure sound in itself and founded on truth and justice, that has not succeeded in this country. And I entreat you, do not regard either the cowardice, or the baseness, or the desertion of other people ; but, for the satisfaction of your own conscience and the good of your country, do your duty. Go on in the course that you have commenced. Persevere in your determined resistance to the Corn Laws and to all Monopoly by every legitimate means, and our opponents will ultimately yield absolutely as they have already yielded partially. Precedents abound to justify your perseverance, for it is by such earnestness, energy, and independence as ours that every great measure of liberty has been carried in this country.

I referred the other night to what had been done with respect to the Slave Trade, and I have since been informed that Mr. Pitt, when he proposed in the House of Commons not 40 years ago the total and immediate abolition of the Slave Trade, was defeated by a majority of 80—the majority declaring that the abolition ought to be moderate, slow, and gradual, and that the peculiar interests of the planters ought to be considered. How would you deal with that question now? How would the House of Commons itself deal with it? Would they not immediately and totally abolish a system so fraught with misery and degradation to their fellow-beings, whatever the 'peculiar claim' for continuing such cruelty might be? We have abundant proof of the monstrous evils that the Corn Laws produce—evils certain to be aggravated with a constant increase of population: your benevolence, then, cannot be better exercised than by continuing to call for their total and immediate repeal.

XXI.

HOUSE OF COMMONS, August 9, 1844.

Previous to the prorogation of Parliament on August 9, the last day of the Session of 1844, Lord J. Russell raised a debate on the condition of the country. In plain language he pointed out that the labouring classes had not advanced in comfort and well-being in proportion to the progress made by the other orders of the community; that, while the upper classes had advanced immensely in luxury, and the middle classes in the enjoyment of all sorts of advantages and conveniences, if they looked to the men who either tilled the soil or laboured in the factories, if they looked to the quantity of necessaries that their wages would buy in the middle of the last century, and that which they could buy then, he believed that the House would be convinced that the labouring classes had not participated in an equal degree in the benefits that civilization and improved knowledge had conferred upon themselves. He thought that it would be necessary to revise the whole subject of the import duties in order to ascertain how small an amount of duty should be paid upon articles of food and general consumption; but he had no intention of depriving agriculture of Protection: he still maintained that it would be unwise to abolish all laws restricting the importation of corn without taking into consideration the special burdens on land. Mr. Villiers rose to protest against the assumption that there were burdens specially imposed on land, and once more vigorously exposed the old fallacy.

If the Hon. Member for Bridport[1] is sincere in his wish to better the condition of the poor and thinks that increasing their employment is the way to effect it, I wonder at his complaint of the speech of the Right Hon. Baronet. If I rightly apprehend that part of the speech that refers to this matter, the Right Hon. Baronet finds cause for congratulation in the improvement that has taken place.

The Right Hon. Baronet points to the im-

[1] Mr. Baillie Cochrane.

provement of the Revenue, the prosperity of trade, and the better employment of the poor, that has resulted from his policy. As that policy consists in relaxing the restrictions on trade, lowering the protective duties, and thereby increasing the demand for labour, I cannot but wonder that the Hon. Gentleman is always found in opposition to it.

The Right Hon. Baronet is right in saying that trade has improved and that the poor are better off; and, as the Hon. Gentleman's remedy—abolishing the new Poor Law—has not effected this, he would do well to inquire whether it has not resulted from the causes of pauperism having been somewhat mitigated. I would also recommend him instead of confining his whole attention to the means of providing for pauperism as it occurs to study the means by which pauperism might be prevented, as an object worthy of his consideration. I would recommend him to employ the Recess in considering what is the effect of restricting trade, checking the employment of capital and narrowing the resources for consumption, upon the condition of that class which is the professed object of his solicitude. If he applies his mind honestly to such consideration I expect that next Session he will not be found in constant hostility to every measure that has for its end the extension of trade and the augmentation of the resources of the nation. Let me advise the Hon. Member to give a little time to this subject, and if he does I do not doubt that he will take some higher view of the wants and condition of the working class than that which ranks them with those of beggars and paupers.

I have not, however, risen to enter upon a discussion of these topics, or to refer generally to those matters that have been touched upon by the leaders of the two great parties, and on which they appear to differ ; but only to refer to that point on which they seem to agree but on which I so entirely differ from them that I never could hear what has fallen from them without rising to express my utter and unqualified dissent. I refer to the assertion made to-night, that agriculture bears peculiar burdens, and thereby affords an excuse for Monopoly. I do not hesitate to say that this is not borne out by facts ; I give it an unqualified and most emphatic denial. I defy those who assert it to prove it. Inquiry into this point has time after time been demanded by the House, and been refused, and now without a shred of proof the plea of peculiar burdens literally stands before the country a bare, unsupported assertion, used only as a pretext for the continuance of the Corn Laws.

I repeat, as I have often repeated before, there is not one single charge on the land that can be termed peculiar or exclusive. Whatever local taxes are imposed are borne in due proportion by property other than land. In some parishes and in some counties the property other than land bears a much larger share of the taxes than the land itself.

My Noble Friend has alluded to those taxes that he thinks the heaviest—the County Rate and the Malt Tax, and his remarks were assented to by the

Right Hon. Baronet. I really wonder how they could keep their countenances in urging such an argument. The County Rate an excuse for the Corn Laws! Look at its amount, in the first place, compared with what the Corn Laws cost! And next look at the property liable to it, the owners of which suffer quite as much from the Corn Laws as any other body or class! Look again to the fact that within a very few years a very considerable portion of that which used to exist before the Corn Laws were passed has since been placed on the Consolidated Fund! Can this be gravely believed to be a reason for limiting the supply of food to the whole community?

Then, again, the Malt Tax which is a tax on the beer of the community, and which if it injures the agriculturist at all does it, of course, by first injuring the consumers in limiting their powers of consumption. And after this injury has been inflicted on them they are to be told that on account of it they must be visited by a tax on their food! Because through poverty the people cannot consume beer enough to suit the agriculturist, they are to be made to indemnify him by a further tax on their bread! This, certainly, is very just and rational; and it is the ground for continuing the Corn Laws. [Mr. Cochrane: 'The Poor Rate?'] The Poor Rate! Why, really, I thought that this ridiculous notion had at last been abandoned, both from its not having been already mentioned to-night, and from its utter unreasonableness. What! make food scarce, make employment difficult, reduce the working-man to pauperism, and then complain of the cost of relieving him, and call this self-inflicted burden a peculiar charge for which you are to have indemnity? Very just, very consistent, indeed! No, these things cannot be said in earnest; and most certainly they will not be treated as such out of doors.

I am glad, however, that they are mentioned at the close of the Session when so many persons are giving thought to the subject, for they will doubtless be well sifted and considered during the Recess, and they ought to be fully prepared for discussion next Session.

I am obliged to the Noble Lord[1] for having raised the question on this occasion. I thank him for saying that he is dissatisfied with the present system, and that he, though others be not, will always be forward to disturb it. I am sure that when the Noble Lord, with all the authority of his character and station, at the head of a powerful party in the country, declares that he considers that the present Corn Laws are a vast evil and could not too soon be changed, nobody out of the House will consider the question settled, or that the little change that was made two years ago can be said to approach a final settlement.

It is important that this should have been said just now. There was, I know, a fancy on the opposite side that the present Laws were to have a trial, and were considered satisfactory for the time. The Noble Lord has dispelled that illusion to-night;

[1] Lord J. Russell.

and his speech will go forth in season to the country; for to my certain knowledge the farmers generally are greatly dissatisfied with the operation of the Corn Laws. At this moment, their produce is yielding 6*s.* per quarter less than they had been taught to expect, and it is precisely on this account that they complain of being constantly meddled with and deceived.

What they want is that there should be a final settlement, and an appropriate adjustment with those with whom they have to contract for the land. The farmers want stability in things, they want you to give up legislating for agriculture, to do, in fact, what you promise, or to do nothing.

The farmer never will be well off, he never can do justice to his labourer, if he is to be giving rent for his land under a delusion which makes him a victim and renders him spiritless and timid in the conduct of his business.

Rent is, I know, an affair between landlord and tenant, and this House in the ordinary course of things has nothing to do with it; but it is forced upon our attention when landlords come here and ask for laws to keep up the price of produce, which instead of making produce plentiful results only in maintaining high rents. Under these circumstances we are compelled to examine into the state of the farmers and the influence that the Corn Laws have upon them; and at this moment their condition is one of loss, and suffering, and discontent. [Colonel Sibthorpe: 'No.'] The Hon. Member for Lincoln says that the farmers are not dissatisfied with the present state of things. I tell him here and in the face of the country, that they are; that they see nothing but the prospect of prices falling and rents being maintained; and that this is simply a prospect of distress and ruin to them.

I say, further, that there is no hope for any improvement in such a state of things while the Corn Laws, which it is impossible to place on any just or rational ground, last. These Laws cannot be tolerated in this free and densely-peopled country under the present circumstances, and the farmers cannot be well off till they are repealed. Settlement of the question is worth any price to the agriculturist, and this can be effected only in one way.

I would again thank the Noble Lord for the assurance he has given the country to-night that the present arrangement shall not, as far as he can prevent it, be final; and the more this is impressed upon the parties interested the sooner they will prepare their minds for the total abolition of the Corn Laws which is alike required by policy and justice.

XXII.

HOUSE OF COMMONS, May 26, 1845.

The Session of 1845 opened happily for the Ministers, notwithstanding the Duke of Richmond's complaint that the Queen's Speech had taken no heed of the bad case of the farmers and the distress of the tenantry of the country. And notwithstanding the activity of the Anti-Corn-Law League, whose electoral tactics promised Free Trade majorities in North Cheshire, South Lancashire, and the West Riding of York, and large accessions to their ranks in Middlesex, North Lancashire, and several other populous counties; and whose annual Report showed that 87,735*l.* of the 100,000*l.* fund had been collected and 3½ millions of their publications disseminated throughout the country during the past year. The improvement in the Revenue had foreshadowed a surplus of 5,000,000*l.*, and therefore disregarding Lord J. Russell's (Lord John by the way still clung to a fixed duty) warnings that Protection was not the support but the bane of agriculture, that a constant recurrence of bounteous harvests could not be reckoned upon, that if they did not legislate on the Corn Laws calmly and considerately in a season of prosperity with the dignity becoming legislators, they would have to do so hurriedly and inconsiderately under the pressure of popular uproar — disregarding all this, Sir R. Peel proceeded to deal with all sorts of comparatively unimportant duties, thus laying himself open to the charge of a host of inconsistencies: that is to say his new tariff the express object of which was declared to be to cheapen the necessaries of life, maintained Corn and Provision Laws whose sole object was to make them dear; professing to relieve trade and commerce for the sake of which a Property Tax was imposed, it showed still greater concern to uphold the rent of land, for the sake of which trade and commerce were loaded with a Bread Tax, and so on. Mr. Disraeli waited his time, and then, when Mr. Miles brought forward his Motion claiming special consideration for the agricultural interest in the application of the surplus Revenue after the Government had voted against Mr. Cobden's Motion for a Select Committee to inquire into the causes of the alleged agricultural distress, he bared with unsparing bitterness the inconsistencies of the Prime Minister to the House, and wound up by declaring his satisfaction at an opportunity of publicly expressing his belief that 'a Conservative Government was an organized hypocrisy.' On May 26, Lord J. Russell moved a series of Resolutions on the condition of the people pledging the House to take measures in the existing state of political tranquillity and revival of trade for the permanent improvement of the labouring classes, and condemning all Protective Duties, especially those on corn.

I HAVE been attending to the debate for some hours, and listening with some anxiety to the statements made on both sides of the House. I have done so in order to learn if possible, whether, either from the proposition suggested on this side, or the opinions expressed on the other, I might not be spared from again making the Motion that I have been in the habit of annually proposing to the House.

The question of the Corn Laws is, I think, distinctly raised by the Resolutions of the Noble Lord; and the Noble Lord regards it in precisely the same light that I myself do.

Many things are embraced in these Resolutions; but I think that any one who has listened to the statement of the Noble Lord must have seen that the real question upon which the discussion necessarily turns is the policy of what is termed the Protective System, and the mode of dealing with a system that, according to his own account, has a very important bearing on the subject that he has submitted to the House.

The Noble Lord brings before the House the condition of the people, and the mode by which that condition can be improved. In doing this he refers to many things that doubtless have been, of late years, productive of great evil to the people; but for which he finds either that any remedy would be too late, or that Parliament has no power of interference. Other things, however, likewise of pernicious effect, he points out that are capable of remedy and within the control of the House; and to these he specially directs our attention.

Amongst the foremost of them the Noble Lord very properly places the system by which the price of the necessaries of life is artificially raised for the purpose of favouring a particular interest that preponderates in the House. He traces it in its connection with the whole well-being of the labouring classes, and he finds it productive of enormous, almost boundless evil.

The object of the Noble Lord being, then, to direct attention to the wants of the people, and the policy and propriety of doing something to elevate their condition, the interest of the House is naturally drawn to what he regards as the prime cause of evil, which he properly alleges has been occasioned and is maintained by this House. I wish that my Noble Friend had been more distinct in the mode by which he proposes to deal with it. If he had his case would have been more complete. I should like to have heard it proposed that an evil so clearly established, and so deadly in its character, should be completely abolished.

The admissions made to-night of all the grounds on which I have always rested this proposition have doubtless been most satisfactory. The Right Hon. Baronet[1] opposite has really laboured to prove the great advantage to the community, and to the labouring classes in particular, that has resulted from reducing the duties imposed for the purpose of Protection. He has also, however, endeavoured to show that some restrictions that have not been yet

[1] Sir James Graham.

removed are beneficial to the people. But such arguments, I think, may be viewed in the light of those that the Hon. Baronet the Member for Essex called this evening productions intended for the consumption of this House alone. Nevertheless, the Right Hon. Baronet's admission and evidence as to facts upon the subject of Protective Duties are most valuable; he in fact establishes the case that the failure of Protective Duties, resulting as it does in plenty and cheapness, is of the first advantage to the people. I hardly know where, had I so wished, I could have procured more satisfactory evidence upon this point. If the House had decided, as it was once requested, to hear evidence at the Bar on this subject, I know not where a witness could have been found whose testimony would have been more full and conclusive than that of the Right Hon. Baronet's.

The opponents of the present Corn Laws have been constant in their endeavours to show in the most conclusive way what would be the incalculable advantage to the people of Free Trade: namely, a low price of food—the special evil always anticipated by Protectionists. The price of food of late has been low from plenty; and the Right Hon. Baronet has come forward to tell us what, as far as he has been enabled by his official position to observe its effect, has resulted from this circumstance. He told us that he was happy to be able to announce that the people have been generally very well off under it; that they have been well employed; and that there have been fewer of those evils and mischiefs consequent on poverty and discontent than have been observed before. He contrasted most satisfactorily the present period—with the price of food low—with the years 1840 and 1841, when the price was high; and having reminded the House of the frightful amount of misery and suffering that existed in those years, he proceeded to show the coincidence of low prices with the diminution of pauperism, crime, and destitution, and the marked extension of comfort and well-being among the poor.

The Right Hon. Baronet, from his official position,[1] is a great authority upon the influences that affect the extent of crime in the country. He observes its invariable increase with the increase of poverty; and he states that of late crime has diminished concurrently with the cheapening of food.

The Right Hon. Baronet seems to have made a particularly careful inquiry into the general condition of the people under the influence of cheap and abundant food. He has ascertained what the rate of wages has been of late compared with the period when food was dear; and not only has he told us that it has risen universally in the manufacturing districts, but he also had the satisfaction of informing us that it has likewise improved in the agricultural districts; that the condition of the labourer in those parts, tested by any or all of the evidences of the fact, is found to be better, compared with his condition in years when food was dear. There is not so

[1] Sir James Graham was then Home Secretary.

much expended in parochial relief, fewer are out of employment, less privation and misery prevail than in those very years when, food being dear, the chief purpose of what is termed Protection to agriculture had succeeded.

In short, the Right Hon. Baronet in his review of the condition of the working classes during the two periods, past and present, has presented to us a contrast the most striking and conclusive in favour of the period when those much dreaded results of abolishing the impediments to trade—and, above all, to the trade in food—have been signally manifested.

But the Right Hon. Baronet, very properly, is not satisfied with merely noting the recent improvement in the condition of the people; he deems it likewise to be his duty to express his opinion as to its cause, and he has not hesitated to declare that it is due to the great reduction in the price of all the prime articles of necessary consumption. He detailed to the House the prices of these different articles during the two periods of the good and bad condition of the people, which he has so closely investigated; he reminded the House of the particular prices of wheat, of flour, of meat, of sugar, and of other articles now considered necessary, during the dear years, showing the precise reduction in each; and he himself ascribed the improvement in the people, to which he has so agreeably invited our attention, to that reduction.

In fine, the Right Hon. Baronet, convinced as he obviously is of its justice, appears determined to establish the case of the opponents of protective duties. He has shown how the results of abolishing the system that made the necessaries of life dear will operate for the advantage of the people; and he has fully exposed the fallacy of the notion that the removal of those duties would deteriorate the condition of the people. Indeed, he has left no doubt of the blessing of cheapness and plenty to the community, however procured; and that this blessing, as regards food, has chiefly resulted now from an unusually abundant harvest last year.

But what is still more to the point, inasmuch as it shows that it is in the power of this House to secure such blessings permanently to the people, the Right Hon. Baronet has proved that in many respects this our present abundance and cheapness have been produced by the measures of the Government that had for their object the diminution of those duties and taxes that were imposed to enhance the price of articles of general demand. He has this evening engaged the attention of the House by showing on what the condition of the working classes depends, and how much we have it in our power, by legislation or by changing the system, to improve that condition. It is impossible, therefore, to over-rate the importance of his statements and opinions upon this matter, speaking as he does with the authority of his official position, and representing as he does the Government, who have still the support of a large majority in this House.

The Noble Lord who has brought this subject

before the House, expressed his opinion last year that the working classes have not of late years advanced relatively with the wealth and prosperity of the country; that while the wealth of individuals and the accumulation of capital have been extended in a wonderful manner, a corresponding progress in the condition of the people generally has not been observed; that they have, in fact, declined, in comparison with their former condition and with reference to the condition of those above them; and that this has been occasioned by, and can be traced to, the partial and impolitic system that, for the purposes before mentioned, is maintained by the Legislature.

This opinion of the Noble Lord is corroborated by the important statement made by the Right Hon. Baronet opposite, who has discovered that the people improve as that system is mitigated.

These views are certainly propounded at a momentous time: a general uneasiness, a sort of consciousness that something is wrong, that something ought to be done in the matter, appears to prevail. There never was a time when certain people made a more liberal display of sympathy with the poor, or when, actuated either by fear or benevolence, they were more ready to suggest particular remedies for particular distress, or to administer partial relief to the necessitous classes at large than we witness now—the specifics, however, all having unfortunately one feature in common: they all fall short of the requisite sacrifice of self-interest to accomplish the desired object.

These philanthropists are always for anything but the abandonment of the system which is the real root of the evil they would cure, but which it is their interest to uphold.

It is at such a time that the Noble Lord comes forward and says: 'True, the condition of the people is not what it ought to be; but away with all your pretended sympathy with the poor, unless you relieve yourselves from the charge that for the purpose of promoting your own interests you are yourselves the cause of their deterioration!' The Noble Lord tells the majority in this House that the system which has been proved to be so prejudicial to the people is upheld by them to serve their own interests; and he has this evening charged the Legislature itself with being the cause of the deterioration, or at least an impediment to the progress of the people, by having enacted and by still maintaining laws for the avowed purpose of artificially rendering scarce the necessaries of life.

So far I entirely agree with the Noble Lord, and I thank him for giving his authority to the views so often taken by myself and those around me on this subject; but, as far as I can collect his opinions regarding the remedy to be immediately applied, I cannot agree in his conclusion that we should stop short of abolishing altogether, and at once, a system proved to be fraught with great, unqualified, and enormous evil.

I fail to understand how, after this evening, there can be any hesitation as to the course to be pursued;

for the case that I and many others have laboured to establish, in order to show the justice and propriety of the remedy that we have proposed, has been admitted and confirmed on both sides.

The Noble Lord's view of their state embraces what is required to raise the people morally as well as in their material condition; and he very properly admits that the privations that the Legislature imposes upon them by what is termed protecting particular interests, impedes their moral progress—that they are debarred from the means of educating themselves and their families, and that their minds are almost wholly unfitted for instruction or moral culture of any kind whilst they are struggling to obtain a bare subsistence. In this view he has been fully supported by the Right Hon. Baronet, who pointed to the results of dearness of food. If any man wishes in future to know the effect of high prices upon the people, he will only have to refer to the speech made to-night by the Right Hon. Baronet.

The condition of high prices would, according to him, be a return to the years 1840 and 1841; and let any one who wishes to know what were the results of that system that had in view to make the necessaries of life scarce and dear study the state of the people during those years.

We have obtained then, this evening, something like an authoritative agreement as to the cause of great evils that influence and affect the condition of the people. The question now arises: Why is such a cause of mischief to be allowed to continue, if there is an honest desire to raise and improve the people? We are to hear, I suppose, that these low prices have occasioned great discontent among a very influential class, and that the Government has lost the confidence of many friends for the changes that they have already made. But these Hon. Gentlemen must remember the novel position in which they are now placed. While it was contended by their leaders that high prices were of advantage, and benefited the people, that was a ground on which they could rest their defence of the system by which those high prices were produced; but now the matter is altered, and I shall be curious to see how Gentlemen opposite will in future settle this question among themselves.

One party among them calls for high prices and Protection; the other party shows them what are the consequences of high prices. 'Get what you want,' says the Right Hon. Baronet, 'and you will bring the country back to the state of 1840 and 1841—a state that I almost tremble to contemplate, so terrible to the poor, so alarming to the State.'

This is the position in which they are now placed. They complain of the present state of things. The price for their wheat being 10*s.* a quarter below what they expected is really the grievance of which Gentlemen opposite complain. Because wheat is low they mistrust the Government. It is only 46*s.*: it ought, according to expectation, to be 56*s.*

But it turns out, and it is so declared on their own side, that what occasions their disappointment occasions at the same time the well-being of the people at large. When Hon. Gentlemen, then, complain of the Government, and call for high prices, they are in fact complaining that there is not more crime, more misery, more disease, more death, more of all those evils the mitigation of which the Right Hon. Baronet has traced to cheapness and to the reduction and modification of the Protective System.

I contend that, at this moment, this is a fair statement of the case; for, as I said before, nobody stands up now for there being any advantage to the people and the poor in high prices, though some, it appears, still call for them.

I concluded when the Hon. Baronet the Member for Sussex rose to follow the Right Hon. Baronet that he was going to show the fallacy of his views and to prove, from what he himself had witnessed around him in the country, the calamities that befall the poor from what his party terms agricultural distress—in other words, a low price of food. I thought that he was going to show what he and others had always predicted of low prices: namely, the land thrown out of cultivation and the poor deprived of their employment. But what was our astonishment when we heard the Hon. Baronet, in vindication of his particular county and in answer to the Noble Lord, assert, as within his own knowledge, that the labourers around him were never better employed, and were never receiving higher wages! He said that he paid no less than seventy of his own every week, for every one of whom he found profitable employment; and he spoke also generally for the county that he represents in the same strain: a happy state of things which, it appears, is quite compatible with the price of wheat that for years past it has been asserted would produce ruin and suffering, and in consequence of which the Member for Essex is about to withdraw his confidence from the Government!

Does any man doubt what is the ground on which the Hon. Baronet withholds his trust in the Ministry? He expected more shillings a quarter for wheat than he has got; he thinks that the Ministers ought to have secured a better price for him, and not have raised his expectations in vain. He is angry that the Protective System has not been maintained; but he forgets that its failure has proved a blessing to the nation. And, though he may still call for its continuance, I want to know why it is to be continued; why, if what has been said to-night is true it should not be abolished; and why with such unequivocal proof of its mischief to all parties it should not be abolished immediately? This is the point that I want to come to: the mischief and error of the system being established, why not remove it?

I know the usual things said upon such occasions, about carefulness, and the uncertainty of the experiment, and all that sort of thing; but I contend that the Noble Lord is not satisfied with simply showing the enormous mischiefs of the system, but that he also shows that whenever any part of it has been abolished, whether immediately or gradually, senseless alarms have been raised which subsequent experiment proved to be idle and unfounded.

The Noble Lord referred to several cases. He mentioned the foolish things he had heard said and expected upon those occasions; and in every case nothing but advantage to the community and the interest itself affected had resulted from such treatment of the system.

The Noble Lord alluded to the case of wool, in which the duty has been totally repealed, and pointed triumphantly to the result. He referred likewise to the case of silk, in order to show the folly of the alarmists in that business, and the success of the change.

The Noble Lord has no fear of totally and immediately removing all duties on manufactures, feeling satisfied that nothing is so beneficial to those interests as the influence of competition. What, then, are his fears about agriculture? At the beginning of the Session he spoke of the effect of Protection to that interest, and since then he has left no doubt as to his opinion of the mischief of it to the public.

No instance can be named of any other interest that has suffered so much and so frequently from Protection as the agricultural interest. The agricultural interest is complaining now, though the rest of the country is contented and prospering. I have no doubt that the farmers have reason to complain. They have been deceived, I know; but their grievance is, in truth, one that they can and ought to settle with their landlords. The landlords assured them that they would get a price sufficient to pay them a high rent: let the landlords redress the wrong they have inflicted. If the farmers have been disappointed, they have no cause to complain of the House or of the Ministry, who are bound to consider the interests of the community at large.

Agriculture is protected at this moment at the rate of 50 per cent., while no other interest receives more Protection than at the rate of 20 per cent.; yet agriculture is said never to have been so depressed.

The fact is, there is not a pretence for the continuance of this Protection after all the evils admitted to follow from it, without any advantage whatever that can be named: unless it be that panic might seize those who would be affected by the change, and so produce evil that has no necessary affinity with Free Trade.

But I ask the Noble Lord whether he really believes that the mode in which he proposes to prevent this would be attended with any advantage? He is afraid of the shock of too great a change; yet can he really suppose that any ignorant, or timid, or interested agriculturist will have his fears or feelings allayed by a proposition such as he now makes, which would pass at once from the Sliding Scale to a 4*s.* fixed duty, with the prospect of ultimate abolition?

I think that this plan cannot be received with much favour by any party. No reason can be assigned for the continuance of any tax on food with the view to raise its price, after the admission of its baneful influence upon agriculture itself, and when its injustice and inhumanity to the people will be more obvious than ever.

I think that the Noble Lord has done much good by raising the discussion, and that he deserves much credit for the courage that he has shown in facing the general opinion of the House against his Resolutions. He has also elicited very valuable statements from the other side; but, in doing so, I can only thank him for having prepared the way for the Motion that I must make for the complete relief of agriculture and for the unqualified advantage to the community at large that the Noble Lord himself is bound to consider will follow from the repeal of the Corn Laws.

XXIII.

HOUSE OF COMMONS, June 10, 1845.

The sun was shining brilliantly with alternating refreshing showers at the beginning of June 1845, and speculation said that there was little chance of success for the Motion to abolish all restrictions on corn of which Mr. Villiers had given notice, unless a clouded sky should come to make the Government tremble for the prosperity they had reaped from fine weather. The clouds did not come, and amidst glorious sunshine Mr. Villiers, opposed by a Tory Cabinet dependent on the contingencies of the weather and a hostile Whig party pledged to a fixed duty, brought forward his eighth Annual Motion. After one night's debate, in which Lord J. Russell, Lord Howick, Mr. Cobden, Mr. Bright, Sir James Graham, and Sir R. Peel all took part, the House divided. The numbers were 122 for the Motion to 250 against it; 10 had paired, and 56 members were absent. This showed a decrease of 76 in the Protectionist majority since 1842.

In rising to bring under the consideration of the House the Motion of which I have given notice, I am happy to feel that amidst the many disadvantages under which I labour, there is one circumstance that I cannot view otherwise than as favourable: there is a sort of general admission of the propriety of my Motion. At least it is acknowledged that such is the importance of its object and that such is the necessity for some settlement of the question it involves, that it is proper and expedient that the opinion of the House should each year be tested upon it.

Hitherto this has been unworthily done by myself; and the reference to my resuming the task has been so frequent that I really believe many Hon. Members on the opposite side would for the first time be disappointed if I failed to bring forward my Annual Motion.

The Noble Lord the Member for London said the other night (and I agree with him) that there could not be a more favourable moment to legislate on the subject than the present; and I am happy to learn that many members on the opposite side now agree with the gallant Member for Brecon [1] that the next time it is thought expedient to alter the Corn Laws, it will be far wiser to abolish them altogether.

I have some reason, therefore, to trust that on this occasion I shall escape the charge of bringing forward an extravagant measure at an inconvenient time, which has not seldom been urged against me: no party, it seems, is satisfied with the present Corn Laws, and most men believe that they neither ought nor can endure much longer.

It is also an encouragement to me to observe that Her Majesty's Ministers are each year getting more confidence in the principles for which I am contending; and that they now see that nothing is gained by a timid and partial application of them. The interests assailed are not less offended by the compromise of a restricted disturbance, while the satisfaction of the public is less than it would be if complete measures were adopted.

I think that I see in the House, likewise, a preference for measures that settle great questions rather than for small disturbances of them. My Hon. Friend the Member for Gateshead hoped to con-

[1] Colonel Wood.

ciliate the House the other day by a very moderate measure on the subject of bringing corn from Australia; but I did not see that he was treated with more respect or that he had more success than he would have met with had he proposed the measure now before the House. And my Noble Friend the Member for London has not received much encouragement to reproduce the measure by which he hoped to reconcile conflicting interests; and most people will, I think, say that he not only will be justified, but that he will also be most wise, if on this account he never moves it again.

I observed, too, that whenever the Government has acted with boldness in dealing with other measures they have received the support of the House. Even the Member for Essex has given his approbation to a total and immediate repeal of the duty on cotton; and though he objects to the same principle being applied to the more important article of corn, others in the House will support it. Indeed before a Corn Law debate is over I now hardly know with whom I am differing on principle. Wherever any responsibility is felt for the consequence of these Laws, or any disinterestedness of opinion exists, there, I observe, that either some apology is made for their continuance, or altogether unqualified condemnation is bestowed on them.

In the course of this Session, two or three Noble Lords who before supported the Corn Laws, have avowed in their places—one that he wished that they had never existed, another that he was sorry they were now necessary, and a third that he was not afraid of their repeal. Indeed, I really believe that if the leading members of the present Government, those of the last Government and the leaders of the League, were to retire into a Committee to consult on the matter, they would find that they differ very little; and that if they reported the result of their deliberations to the House, the report, if not in the language, yet in substance, would be the same as what I now ask the House to agree to: namely, that the Corn Laws are wholly unsuited to the present circumstances of the country; that they never had a laudable object in view; that they have been very injurious to the working classes; and that the sooner they are abolished the better.

If there were such a thing as the mind of the House, I should say that this would be the impression found upon it; but unfortunately it is well known that it is the vote and not the mind of the House that determines its legislation; and doubtless there will yet be great difficulty in repealing the Corn Laws.

It was only last night, indeed, that I heard that the Society for the Protection of Native Agriculture is yet living; and we know that the interests and opinions which that Society represents preponderate in both Houses of Parliament. The majority in Parliament are doubtless in favour of the object of the Corn Laws, and they are yet uncertain, perhaps, as to whether the Laws have failed, and whether they can still be safely maintained.

With regard to this latter point, it is the purpose of that very useful body, the Anti-Corn-Law League, to relieve their minds. What the purpose and object of these Laws is I believe to be now generally understood. They may be shortly and completely expressed as intending to make and to keep land dear. Such was the original object, and all subsequent legislation has had this object in view; and it is curious to observe the decided character of the legislation respecting it from the time that the proprietors of land became dominant in the State.

I refer that period to the Revolution in 1688. In that very year, when William III. accepted the Constitution and was at the mercy of the proprietors, they boldly began to deal with the subject. In the month of May of 1688, a Committee in Parliament was appointed for the simple purpose of inquiring into 'the cause of a fall in rents;' and before the Committee could even make their Report a tax was imposed upon the people to enable them to pay the costs of conveying the produce of land to other countries, thereby raising the price at home. This was called a bounty upon exports; and the scheme lasted until the latter part of the last century, when, from the increase of population and the general discredit of the export tax, the most effectual way of raising the price was supposed to be a tax imposed upon food coming into the country: this policy has continued until the present hour, the same object of raising the value of land being always in view.

Fortunately, however, though the Constitution is

the same, men's minds are not politically constituted as they were when the Corn Laws were first passed. The people in relation to their rulers are numerically and intellectually far stronger than they were; and I do not believe that, when their opinion is firmly and clearly expressed against any grievance, it will long be maintained.

A certain deference to public opinion has, indeed, already been shown by the landlords on this subject; for they have spared no pains to influence the people and to delude them on it; and I am bound to say that they have done so with considerable success. They have addressed themselves particularly to two classes, hoping by their concurrence to maintain the system: the one class consists of the tenants of the soil, and the other embraces the working classes generally. They endeavoured to persuade these classes that the Corn Laws are necessary for their interest, and that those who uphold them have generous and national objects in view. To some extent their efforts have, I admit, succeeded; but though their task may not have been very difficult hitherto, it will be far from easy in future.

We have heard this year, from the gallant Member for Sussex, a description of the farmers of the country. He told us that they are men whose vision is so contracted that they can hardly see more than one object at a time; that their whole attention is engrossed with the cattle they rear or the vegetables they grow; and that they are apt to measure the world's affairs by the market they get for their produce. And he said that he could not submit to learn from them how this country is to be governed.

Now, if this is a true picture of these men, it is not wonderful that they should be easily deceived by others; or that they should have been deluded into confusing the effect of price with that of profit; or that when they are assured that they will be secured a high price for their produce that they should believe it to be the same thing as a high profit upon their capital; or that, having their eye upon only one thing, they should forget that if there is to be a large profit obtained from the land, there will be many who will desire to have the land, and that consequently the land will fetch a high price. This they overlook in their bargains for the use of the land. They listen to men who call themselves their friends and who tell them that if they will send them to Parliament they will uphold the Laws that will give them a good price for their produce; and that they will resist the men who tell them that if they trust to such Laws they will be deceived—that they will pay more for the land in proportion to this promise of price and be ruined if the price fails them. The farmers believe these professed friends; and Members are sitting in this House now upon no other pledge than that of maintaining Laws that will keep up the price, and thereby secure the agriculturist a high profit on his capital.

I am in a position to-night to call the attention of the farmers to this circumstance; and to ask them to consider who are their friends and who are their enemies, and how far their supposed enemies have been wrong in advising them not to trust to the Corn Laws because otherwise they would be induced to give a high rent for the land without having any security for a high price for their produce or a high profit on their outlay.

The Member for Somersetshire says that, thanks to the League, the farmers see things much clearer than they did before. I trust that such is the case, for it will assist me in one of the objects that I have in view in bringing forward my Motion : namely, to procure for the farmer from the leaders of the Protection Society some explanation of his present condition, some explanation as to how with so many friends he comes to be in his present plight.

I see the Member for North Northamptonshire in his place. He, I believe, has charge of the Library of the Protection Society, and probably knows all that is to be known upon the matter : perhaps, therefore, he will be good enough to explain matters a little to us. I hope that he will tell us what the real relation of the farmer is to the landlord, and how it comes to pass that it is to his interest for the farmer to pay dearly for the raw material out of which he is to get his profit, while the rest of mankind consider it an advantage to pay as little as possible for the things they want. Will the Hon. Member tell us how it is for the interest of the farmer to pay a high rent for land and for the Hon. Member himself to pay a low interest for money ? I cannot see the difference myself. If the land is to the farmer the material on which he employs his capital, it will appear at first that his object must be to get it as cheap as possible, as requiring less outlay. Money is a thing that any capitalist may require, and all men, I believe, consider that they are fortunate when they pay a low rate for its use.

I assure the Hon. Gentleman that it is a farmer himself who has particularly requested me to endeavour to get the gentlemen of the Protection Society to explain this matter to the House; for, as we know, the Protection Society cares only for the farmer and has closely studied his interest.

I will, however, venture to put the Hon. Member on his guard on two points: he is precluded from alleging that the farmer's position is occasioned by the late measures of the Government, and that the landlords are in the same boat with the farmers—that they are suffering as well as the farmers. The first they cannot say because the farmer's friends in the House all supported the measures of the Government; and, which is more important, because this condition of the farmer is no novelty: he has frequently been in the same state, and this has happened under each of three laws passed for his particular protection, as it is called. And moreover it is remarkable that he has been worse off when the land has been most protected. His condition was worse in 1836 than it is in the present year; and though he was told then that it was owing to the Whigs being in power, he remembered that he was worse off still under the Corn Law of 1815, when the Tories were in power in 1822 than he had ever been at any other time. The farmer therefore begins to think that there must be something wrong in the principle itself of the Corn Laws.

The other thing that the Hon. Member must not say is, that the landlords as well as the farmers are badly off; for those who are called the landed aristocracy were never better off; they never made more display of their wealth; they never were spending more money than they are now spending in London; and I am quite sure that the Protection Society cannot prove that they have put down a single dog or horse, or turned off a groom or a footman, in consequence of the unparalleled distress, as they call it, of agriculture.

It really will be a great advantage if the Protection leaders will explain the case of the farmer, and tell him and tell the House what is the matter with him, and how it comes to pass that he has been so often indisposed in the same way; and whether it may not be that there is something that the landlord himself can do for him.

Judging from the reports of different meetings in the country, I cannot help thinking that the Agricultural interest, as it is called, is not altogether agreed upon in this matter. I wish particularly to call the attention of the Hon. Member opposite to this subject. I have observed in my endeavour to understand the case, that there are two kinds of meetings: one called meetings for the 'Protection of Agriculture,' and headed 'Agricultural Distress,' and the other called 'Farmers' Meetings,' and held at the farmers' clubs, where their interests are discussed.

Now I observe that at these two kinds of meetings there are two very different sorts of topics broached. At the first, where the nobility, gentry, and clergy assemble, I observe plenty of abuse of the Ministry, great complaints of diminished Protection, threats of withdrawing confidence, and strong expressions in favour of the repeal of the Canada Act and the new Corn Laws, with a view to the re-enactment of the old Laws of restriction.

But when I turn to the farmers' meetings I find something quite different: they seem to be talking of quite another thing that would set them all straight again. Their notion appears to be—they seem to be certain that they could do very well if rents were adjusted to prices, if they were rendered secure in their tenures, and if other things, like game-preserving and the retention of useless timber in their hedges, were to cease. In short, while the more respectable meetings, as they would be called, talk of Ministerial treachery, and Protection lost, and never allude to there being any fault at home, the farmers' hearts seem to be full of something that the landlords could and ought to do for them.

The Member for Shropshire seems to doubt all this. Then let me give him some proof. I have a little evidence on the point. Here is a Report from the Exeter Agricultural Association. The society met 'for the purpose of considering the propriety of memorializing the County Members on the present depressed condition of the agricultural interest.' The meeting is said to have been attended by a large number of tenant-farmers—though the reporter judiciously abstains from mentioning the number—while a few squires and clergymen are specified by name. Sir R. W. Newman, the chairman, began the business by reading the excuses of the County Members for non-attendance. William Porter, Esq., then opened the first fire, which was upon the County Members :—

He did think, when they had occasion to ask their representatives to give their strenuous support to the agricultural interest, it did look a little as if those representatives had not given that strenuous support which they ought, and which they had promised to give. [Cheers.] He recollected, at the last election, that many of them had come forward, and had stated certain measures which they were prepared and anxious to support; but it had been with them as it had been with many other Members, as soon as they had been elected they had ceased to recollect those measures—they had gone with their party, and had remembered only the men. [Cheers.]

Mr. Porter, after making several observations to this effect, concluded by moving the following Resolution :—

That this meeting, viewing with serious alarm the great depreciation in the value of agricultural produce which has taken place within the last few years, respectfully, but firmly, call upon the Members for the county to urge on the Ministers the necessity of supporting the agricultural interest, and by every means in their power to place agriculture in a better position.

This gentleman seemed to think that the fate of agriculture depends entirely on the County Members. Mr. J. Palk next addressed the meeting, and said :—

That, in the opinion of this meeting, land has to bear peculiar burdens (particularly the Poor, Highway, and County Rates);

and it would be a great relief to agriculture to make them a national charge.

To accomplish this truly patriotic scheme, the idea seemed to strike him that :—

The landlords and tenants must act together. Day by day they must strengthen the bonds which unite them. [Hear, hear.] It was folly to say that either could exist without the other; together they must rise, or together fall. It would never do for the tenants to be distrustful; the tenants must have full confidence in the landlords if they would hope to force upon the Legislature those measures which were absolutely necessary to the existence of agriculture.

This gentleman thought that if land-owners could be relieved of the liabilities attaching to their properties things would thereby be set straight. Mr. George Turner, who formed one of the deputation of the Central Protection Society to Sir Robert Peel, and bore testimony to the delusions under which the tenant-farmers brought the present Ministry into power, followed Mr. Palk, and he ended with this notable bit of logic :—

He had been an extensive practical farmer for a great number of years; and he declared to them that he had never paid so much upon his estate as he had done within the last three years, and he had never received so little income. If that was not a clear case for demanding some assistance from the Legislature, he did not know what was.

Then came one Mr. Chapple, who said :—

Every man who was farming land at 20*s*. an acre at the present price was losing money. [Hear, hear.] What, then, was to be done? It might be that the Members would say, 'Tell us what to do?' His answer to them would be—'Let them go to Sir Robert Peel, and tell him plainly that they will not support him to ruin us.' [Hear, hear.]

And he wound up with this peremptory Resolution :—

That the secretary be directed to forward a copy of these Resolutions to each of the County Members, with a request that he will use his most strenuous exertion to force on the attention of Her Majesty's Ministers the principles contained in them.

At such a meeting, what was the matter was easily told ; and if Members would only do their duty and speak properly to the Minister, British agriculture might be saved from ruin.

I will now read what passed among farmers when they were really saying what they thought, and when they were amongst real friends. The occasion was a dinner given in Herefordshire to a genuine friend of the farmer, Mr. Powell. The Chairman, in giving the health of this gentleman, said :—

This is not a meeting for any class of dependents to pay homage and respect which they do not feel, or to bend the knee to the rich aristocrat or grandee ; but to show our worthy guest that his public utility, as well as his private worth, is not only felt but acknowledged by us.

Mr. Powell said in reply :—

The farmers in general look upon the newly-formed Protection Societies with a cautious eye. You will rarely see the name of a tenant farmer attached to either of their lists ; they know their own position too well. The only Protection they want is to be put in a position to be able to protect themselves—[Cheers]—and this they could easily do if farms were let on leases and corn-rents.

These are new ideas for the British Agricultural Protection Societies, not a whisper of which is ever uttered at the genteel, respectable meetings where more legislative Protection is demanded.

And now let me read what occurred at a mixed sort of meeting at which a Marquis took the chair, but at which some farmers were present, one of whom had been very bold, and after making very free remarks had said :—

Would the landlords help them in reality? Would they pledge themselves that they will not take advantage of improvements when they are made? Would they guarantee leases? Would they take care that the crops were not devoured by game? If so, then the landlords might come to these societies with sincerity, shake hands with the tenants, and go to help the labourer. [Cheers.]

Here, the reporter says, the Marquis, who had long been fidgetty, became furious, declared that he would leave the Chair, tried to stop the farmer's remarks—which seem to have been too much to the point—and called upon the meeting to support the Chair. The majority of the meeting, however, seemed more disposed to support the farmer, who said :—

He bowed to the Chair; but he would add that, if landlords were sincere they would give security to their tenants. [A voice: 'No politics.' And great noise.] He was sure that all thinking people must admit that a hopeless despair was not the thing to stimulate exertion. [More noise.] He could not be that hypocrite to support agriculture on any other than sound and just principles. [Cheers.]

After this the Noble Chairman is said to have rapidly given one or two complimentary toasts, and then to have made his escape, when, of course, all the rest of the landlords likewise departed.

I have here another extract from the report of a farmers' meeting held at a place in Derbyshire, where one Mr. Binns discussed the condition of farmers. Mr. Binns said :—

> I am aware that in most of the farmers' clubs which have been established in different parts of the country, great anxiety has been evinced by certain parties to exclude the discussion of what they call (and I believe them) 'obnoxious subjects'—such as rents, leases, and game. But somehow or other, in almost every club of whose proceedings I have seen any account, these 'obnoxious subjects' have crept in. The farmers ought to use every effort to improve their condition, considering the diminished price of corn and cattle. If landlords would come forward when tenants were in difficulties, and say, 'we will meet your case by reducing the rent,' their struggles would meet with some alleviation. But such is not the case. Instead of meeting them with sympathy on a tenant's complaining, the answer in a majority of cases is, 'If you do not like to stay on the farm you may leave it; we have plenty waiting for it.' Let the farmers then in future depend more upon themselves. I know there are some landlords who act upon the principle, 'Live, and let live,' but unfortunately they are few, comparatively.

From the manner in which these sentiments were received, it is manifest that the topics they relate to are uppermost in the farmers' thoughts; and they are worthy of attention as assisting us to learn what the real grievance is amongst agriculturists properly so called. I will therefore refer to just one more meeting: a meeting of landlords and tenants on a friendly footing, convened especially, it appears, to promote the joint interests of both parties; but which, though held in the county of Sussex where such extraordinary unanimity is said to prevail, was a failure. The Hon. Member for Sussex presided; and a reporter says that including reporters and Mr. Darby, he could count only eleven persons. One farmer among them, however, spoke to this effect :—

No one can regret more than myself the absence of the influential men. Whether the landlords are ashamed to meet the tenants as a humble body, or whether they are afraid of hearing something that would not be palatable, I cannot say; but I can guess which works in their breast the most. The cause of their absence is, I suppose, that they consider the treatment they get on such occasions anything but what it ought to be; but from what I hear in the market that is not astonishing, for when they attend these meetings there is nothing but recommendation of great land-owners to set labourers to work, manure, drain your lands; but they omit one principal feature—they never tell tenants how they can afford to pay for it.

These meetings, which are a sample of those now occurring throughout the country, bear out my statement that the farmers are complaining of one thing, while the landlords are complaining of another.

And this point is a most important one to the opponents of the present system. This it is that has induced my Hon. Friend the Member for Stockport to move for an inquiry, in order to prove that agriculture is suffering from the system itself; and that freedom and not restriction in this trade (as in every other) is essential to its success, which success can only be shown by the people's having a plentiful supply of food. But at this the Secretary at War, who was appointed to meet the complaints of all sides, and who seems to speak with the authority of one whose judgment is superior to that of other people, demurs. He tells us that the remedy for all this is not to talk about it; that, if his own friends will be quiet, they will not suffer; and that, if we on this side will be silent also, we shall see that we have no reason to complain. Which is all very convenient, no doubt, to those who have to answer for the suffering, but not very conclusive to those who suffer. The story goes, that if everybody is quiet improvement will continue and that there will be no scarcity ; but unfortunately nobody believes it ; and though the country gentlemen may withdraw their confidence from the Government, the public will still urge their complaint.

Now, I beg to draw attention to this matter of agricultural improvement, which is to feed us all better than we have been fed. This is how it stands. The farmers say: 'We can do nothing without security for our capital, without rents being in some way adjusted to prices, without liberty to destroy game, without being more free in many respects than we have been.' The landlords say that they can do nothing unless they have more Protection, or unless the Protection that they used to have is restored to them ; that they cannot improve unless favour is shown to them. Well, the landlords appeal to the Government in this House about this Protection, and what does the House say? Why, it tells them that Protection never did them any good ; that they will not get back what they have lost, and that it is possible that more may yet be taken from them.

Then the farmers ask the landlords for what they consider is necessary to make the land more productive, and their business more profitable ; but the landlords answer : 'If you understood your business you would not ask for these things ; they cannot be conceded, and there are plenty ready to take the land if you are not satisfied with your present terms.'

And so it stands. According to the opinion of the only people who can give effect to them, certain conditions are necessary for the improvements by which more food could be produced: these conditions have not a chance of being conceded; but we are told that if we will hold our tongue there will be plenty of food, quite enough to meet the wants of an increasing population, owing to the vast improvement that will be made.

I ask whether there is the least reason to suppose that we should be satisfied with such a state of things? And whether it is not our right and our duty as guardians of the interests of the public and of the poor, to inquire particularly into all that affects property in land so far as to learn if there is a prospect, under present circumstances, of the community's being adequately supplied with food?

This inquiry has been made, and the result is that numberless impediments to the application of the capital and skill required for the due culture of the soil are shown to exist in this country. Land is shown to be desired and possessed for many other reasons than that of producing food for the people. Land is valuable for pleasure—such as preserving game; for acquiring political influence by means of the franchise given to tenants-at-will; for acquiring consequence in a county by the estimation in which such property is held; and especially for being made subservient to the object of founding families: all of which may be very desirable objects, but they are all notoriously injurious to agriculture—they are all impediments in the way of progress and improvement, and opposed to what is essential to turning the land to the utmost account. Unquestionably they may answer the purpose of some owners : tenants-at-will, for example, may pay better at contested elections than good crops of wheat. And in all these matters the proprietor has naturally, under ordinary circumstances, a perfect right to do what he likes : he has a right, and should be allowed, as far as legislative interference goes, to deal wisely with or waste his property just as he pleases ; but let him acknowledge the same right to the industrious over their only property—their labour.

In one of the instances that I have enumerated the action of the land-owner on the agricultural question is of very great importance. I mean that having regard to the mode of settling property in accordance with the custom of primogeniture. This mode of settling land involves the estate's being held by the proprietor for life only; and it is with a view to the eldest son's being secured in the inheritance of the fee till the resettlement of the property is again made, that the existing owner is generally limited to a life-interest in his estate. The importance of this to agriculture is that the owner being tenant for life, and having usually a large family, has little interest or inclination to lay out his income to improve the estate, feeling that in the wants of his younger children he has claims for any money that he possesses which might otherwise be employed for improvements.

In consequence of the discussion on these matters, a Noble Duke in the other House has proposed an inquiry; and I believe that a Bill has been introduced to enable the tenant for life to charge the estate with the money raised for the purpose of improvements. Still, a man must be an ardent improver who would consent to pay the interest out of his life-income for this purpose; though, possibly, if he felt that he was increasing the value of an estate to be equally divided among his children, he would then endeavour to augment the value of their inheritance.

The general result of the present system, as it is observed to exist throughout the country, is that the owner of the land is tenant for life and the occupier is tenant-at-will; and these are precisely the conditions under which it is most unfavourable to good agriculture that the land should be held. The consequence is that there is not that skilful, spirited employment of capital upon the soil, or that abundant and certain supply of food for the people of this country, that there might otherwise be. It is impossible to overrate the importance of this circumstance in the present state and progress of our population: but the whole thing will shortly be seen through and understood far better than it ever has been before; for I assert with confidence that the delusion with respect to the beneficial effect of a high price of food on their condition, under which the people have hitherto been made comparatively silent on the subject of the Corn Laws, has by the experience of the last two years been completely exploded. I consider that, after the official statement made the other night on this subject, it is placed beyond all dispute in future that the employment of the working classes is greatly and directly affected by the amount and cost of the food in the country; and that therefore it is impossible for working-men hereafter to be deceived by the preposterous fallacy that their condition is benefited by the dearness of food.

And now I call upon Hon. Gentlemen opposite, especially those connected with the Protection Society, either to acknowledge that they have been in error themselves in this matter, or to show the House and the country that they have not been parties to practising a cruel deception on the poor: one or the other they must do. This is a serious charge, considering the interest they have in the question; and I think that they should be anxious to vindicate themselves, if it be possible. To assert that it is an advantage to the people to make food dear by Act of Parliament, by which rents are raised, is certainly to mislead the humblest, the most defenceless, the poorest of their fellow-creatures; but whether or no it is wilfully done it is for Hon. Gentlemen to prove.

I speak of this seriously, because it has not been lightly and casually done. It has been done coolly and pertinaciously, and, I should suppose, at much cost. I have read the works that have been published by the Protection Society, issued with all the authority of men of rank, and wealth, and influence ; and I find that this fallacy of dear bread improving the condition of the people is the leading topic of all their speeches and pamphlets. And while it is endeavoured to show that the poor will benefit by food being dear, they seek to prove that the manufacturers have no desire to benefit the working people by making trade in the great necessary free. ['Hear, hear,' from the Member for Devonshire and others.] Am I to understand that there are still some persons in this House who maintain the doctrine? Then I deliberately call upon the Members for Devonshire and Lincolnshire to prove in what way dear food is of advantage to the working classes. I ask them to stand forward to-night (as they ought to have stood forward the other night) and reply to the statements of the Secretary of State which establish the fact that the employment of the people, and with it their whole well-being, depends upon and is promoted by the abundance and cheapness of provisions. I ask them this night to vindicate the proposition that they have helped to circulate and endeavoured to make the poor believe. They are bound, after acknowledging such views, to speak out this evening. I shall note carefully what falls from them ; and the House will draw its own conclusion if when called upon for it they shrink from the proof of what they have said. Till they have spoken I shall say nothing further on the subject. I will not even make other observations that I intended to make upon the conduct of persons in the highest station lending their names and authority to what I consider deceiving the poor and unthinking portion of the people, with the fullest experience that the Laws they are encouraging them to support are subjecting the labouring population to the severest privations.

Knowing well, however, that it is demonstrably true that whenever food as the first necessary is abundant there is an increased demand for labour, and that when it becomes deficient millions must become miserable, I consider that too much attention cannot be invited to the fact; for it will at least explain the variations that have already taken place in the condition of the people, and that may occur again.

Let that only be remembered which was alleged on the other side during the period of severe distress when each man was taxing his brains to conceive a cause other than the real one for the alarming destitution—to devise a reason that should account for it other than the actual, the obvious one, the one assigned and proclaimed unflinchingly and ceaselessly by the enemies of Monopoly.

If any one will turn to the debates, he will see that it was ascribed to machinery, to over-production, to over-population, to greedy capitalists, to joint-stock banks, to the want of emigration, and to the want of reciprocity with other nations. These were the things alleged in 1842, when we on this side kept reiterating that it was owing to a deficient supply of food during four successive years, and to obstructions placed by the Government on the trade with the countries from which we could draw our supplies.

Let any one deny if he can the fact that all these alleged causes of distress have increased, or have not diminished of late, though the real cause, scarcity of food, has, by God's blessing, been obviated; that there is much more machinery in use than ever; that there are more people by a million than there were; that production is much greater than it was; that joint-stock banks are as numerous as they were; that money never was more plentiful; that credit is generally good; and that there is not one State with which we had important trade at that time that has not since raised its tariff against us. How is all this to be explained? The Hon. Gentleman who seconded the Address this Session, remarked upon it and said that he should like to hear it accounted for in some way. The Ministers have had an opportunity of stating their views on the subject; and what did they say? They solemnly announced to the House the other night that they ascribe the improvement in the country to two circumstances: first, to the great fall in the price of food; secondly, to the reduction in the Protective Duties, and chiefly in those on the articles of necessary consumption. That is to say, the Government are asked to explain the prosperity of the country, and they proclaim that England's recent prosperity has been occasioned by an abundant supply of the necessaries of life, and a great reduction of the Protective Duties that had long existed.

The Prime Minister is jealous of any cause being referred to but that of his own legislation for this purpose. We might, if we pleased, say that the prosperity was owing to the seasons; but he emphatically declared that it happened together with this attack upon Protective Duties with the object of reducing the cost of living.

Here, then, is the authority for what we assert as to the causes of our present improvement. Here is my justification for calling for the repeal of the Laws that yet exist to obstruct the plentiful supply of food, which the Government asserts to be essential to contentment and prosperity.

Now, if Hon. Gentlemen opposite think that dear food is an advantage and makes the country prosperous, they have reason, I grant, for opposing me; but they have reason also for complaining of the Right Hon. Baronet. And they should settle this matter with him to-night; they should show him at once how he is wrong, and at least attempt to prove that they are right.

I, however, have reason to condemn the Government—with their views and experience—for not going further, and for suffering Laws that have the purpose and effect of the present Corn Laws to remain another day on the Statute Book.

But is it a debateable matter? Is it possible that we are debating about the advantage of cheap food? Have Hon. Gentlemen on the other side ever given it a thought, have they ever for a moment considered what depends upon it, how far all the economical arrangements of society proceed upon it? Why, the division of labour, the source of all our wealth, depends upon it. Men only devote themselves to other employments than producing food when they feel sure that food will be provided for them. They only produce other articles than food upon the faith that people will have the means of consuming what they produce, which faith they cease to have immediately people's resources are absorbed by something of higher importance to life than comfort or luxury.

Let food become scarce or require great sacrifice to obtain it, and instantly the means of consuming manufactures disappear, leaving the producers of manufactured goods without employment ; so that they must either produce food directly for themselves or become dependent as paupers upon the property of the country. And this is what actually occurs the moment the customers of those who produce other things than food are withdrawn or impoverished; and in the present circumstances of our country this is matter for grave consideration.

It is the tendency of every progressive country that fewer people should be employed in agriculture and more people in manufactures than in the earlier stages, so that the only vent now for our increasing population is in manufacturing employment. The time is come when every additional soul born in this country must look to manufacture, or employment other than agriculture, for the means of living. The market for our industries is in general consumption both at home and abroad : impair either, by increasing the cost of food or obstructing the trade, and you throw people out of employment ; you deprive the working classes of their customers with precisely the same results to them that would ensue to other men if you deprived them of the property on which they live. You may talk glibly here of producing this effect, because you suppose that the people will not starve since they have the parish to go to; but the parish is not an inexhaustible fund. And, moreover, have Hon. Gentlemen ever considered what is the effect now of one of those crises in manufacturing industry produced by injuring the market either at home or abroad? Have they ever considered what moral as well as physical ruin it brings; what loss of station, what temptations, what degradation, are occasioned by one of those extreme depressions?

Be assured that when the Legislature occasions a deficiency in the supply of food, it produces evils that it can never repair. A Government has complete power over the people when it undertakes to regulate the supply of food; it can give or take vitality from their business and their bodies as completely as we can from an animal in the receiver of the pump over which we have control. It may exhaust or restore at pleasure their means of living, by contracting or expanding the trade in food. The Right Hon. Gentleman was indeed right when he declared scarcity to be the greatest curse that could be inflicted upon us; what I question is, how far he had the right to ascribe that curse to Providence.

I remember hearing an eloquent man speaking on this matter during the scarcity, and he said that we should examine our own conduct first in the matter before we could consider ourselves qualified to blaspheme the Creator for what we styled His curse upon us.

And do you remember that, at the time when we were calling our distress for food a visitation of Providence, a pestilence was imminent in one of the Atlantic cities owing to the stores of provisions that became putrid from remaining in the warehouses for want of a market; and that had we not forbidden that food from entering our ports we should have been properly supplied and the city would have been spared a great disaster?

With such laws as those I am discussing, we ought indeed to pause before we ascribe our distress to anything but our own cupidity. Providence fills the earth with good things, and has endowed us with reason to enable us to obtain them. It is our own folly, then, and no want of God's beneficence, that causes us to suffer.

But these things are all appreciated by the Ministers. After the speech of the Right Hon. Baronet the other night, it is clear that they take the same view that I and my friends on this side do of the enormous advantages of having a regular, plentiful supply of food. They differ from their friends the Members for Lincolnshire and Devonshire, who consider that food should be restricted in its supply. The Government is fully prepared for what must recur if we are again visited with scarcity; they are officially acquainted with what was endured, and what was apprehended, in the most populous parts of the country on the last occasion; and they can hardly bring themselves to allude to what they know for fear of shocking the feelings of this House. Now, this being the case, I ask how can they reconcile themselves to suffer this moment to pass by without taking some steps for security against the recurrence of such evils ? It is the only point in this matter on which we of this side differ from the Ministers. They do not deny a single principle that we maintain : they say that food ought to be abundant ; that Protection is an evil ; that in every way the field for commercial enterprise ought to be opened ; that the means for manufacture ought to be facilitated to the utmost ; and that the raw materials and those that are essential for manufacture ought specially to be relieved. All this they agree to ; but they refuse to deal with the Laws that restrict the supply of food. For I contend that what alleviations have been made in these Laws have been avowedly not for the purpose of relieving the distress of the people, or to increase the quantity of food : they have been accompanied by arguments to show that this was not the purpose for which they were altered.

There have been two alterations in the Corn Laws : one in the English Corn Laws, the other in the Canada Law. The Right. Hon. Baronet opposite did not refer the distress of the people to the Corn Laws, and he appeared to have in view only such an alteration as should be consistent with the interest of those for whose benefit they exist, according to their own view of that interest ; and the Noble Lord the Secretary for the Colonies said distinctly that whoever imagined that it was his object to pass the Canada Act, either as a Free Trade measure or as a mode of diminishing the Protection of land-owners at home, would be grievously mistaken; and from all I have heard lately, I am not sure that he was in error.

What, then, is my position in demanding that we shall now proceed to legislate on the subject? The Right Hon. Baronet opposite admits an annual exigency to provide for the increase of the population. Each year, he says, 380,000 persons are added to those that existed in the preceding year, who must be fed. He tells us, also, that last year there were upwards of 1,500,000 paupers in England and Wales alone, which is nearly equal to one in nine of the population. And he says further that it is solely owing to the accident of good harvests and what he and his colleagues have done in reducing Protective Duties that there are not many more.

I now ask that some fresh means, some wider field, shall be given to our people to exchange the results of their industry and skill for food. If nothing is done now when the wisdom of this policy is admitted and its practicability is obvious, what will be the inference, wherever it is known, but that our people are impoverished by the selfishness of our legislation, and that, though we have the means of improving them in our hands, we refuse to act? This is the impression abroad wherever our circumstances are known. British wealth, British pauperism, and British Corn Laws—these are the topics that are dwelt upon whenever this country is discussed by reflecting men; and they are ever coupled with expressions of wonder and reproach. The belief prevails everywhere that the riches of our aristocracy and the poverty of millions of our people are connected with the Corn Laws; and it brings scandal on our name whenever it is uttered.

And does anything ever occur in these debates, I ask, to disabuse the minds of foreigners on this subject? What can be more calculated to confirm their impression than the Right Hon. Baronet's speech the other night, and the probable result of this discussion? I wish Hon. Gentlemen could hear and know what is said abroad about the British aristocracy owing to these Corn Laws. Foreigners see that no intelligent man of independence defends them, that all experience discredits them, and that they are maintained for no one earthly purpose but that of making richer those whose wealth is enormous already. And if these Laws remain unaltered after the admissions of Ministers upon all the material points connected with their mischief, their responsibility will be tremendous; and this they must expect to meet—they cannot hope to escape it.

They must, in the first place, remember that they cannot at once repair the mischief when it occurs by merely changing the Laws as it suits them; and that for whatever happens in the future from their not having altered the Laws now, they will be deemed fully responsible.

They should also remember that when a deficiency next occurs circumstances exist that will make the pressure much more severe than it has ever been before. The surplus available for our use is likely to be much less, on account of the greater consumption of wheat throughout Europe: within these few years, countries that used to export have become importing countries; and the population here and abroad has much increased.

At this moment Belgium is obliged to relax her Corn Law, and all the manufacturing districts are in a state of fever at the change not being sufficient to meet their wants. A petition to the Chambers has been sent me from Liège, representing the feeling that prevails upon the subject. I find that it echoes every sentiment and opinion that is expressed against the Corn Laws in this country; and it shows to what an extent they already feel the increasing wants of their population. There is hardly an evil that has been felt in this country, proceeding from the disturbance of every business occasioned by a deficient supply of food, that is not pointed out in that petition and apprehended for that country if the restriction on the import of food is continued.

In Holland, in 1834, they enacted a Corn Law in imitation of ours, for the benefit of agriculture; and a person who was many years in the Consul's office at Amsterdam told me that every evil that had been traced to our Sliding Scale had in every way been experienced under the Dutch Corn Law: it gave general dissatisfaction, it made food scarce, and prices in consequence were enormously high.

In parts of France they do not grow enough corn

for their own consumption; and I have been informed that the Canada Act, passed three years ago, has only added to the uncertainty felt with respect to our market in the corn-growing countries of Europe.

I should also mention another circumstance that will cause the pressure to be more severe when large importations are required: it is the Banking Act of last year. I am not going to discuss the general merits of that measure; I am not going to deny that in some respects it may make banking establishments more careful in the conduct of their business; but I do conceive that it will be the cause of greater sacrifices being made, and being made more suddenly, in order to export the only commodity that it is possible to export to countries with whom we have no regular trade for the purchase of the food that we require: namely, bullion. It will sooner and more suddenly cause the disturbance and distress in business that ends in a ruinous reduction of prices, by means of which manufactures would be exported for food.

Taking all these circumstances into consideration, I apprehend that when a revulsion does occur from scarcity it will be both more severe and more hazardous than before. The Government have yet time to avert it. What reason can they set against such ordinary prudence as availing themselves of it? Surely we are not to have that wretched plea of local taxation set up again this evening in opposition to the enormous advantage consequent on the free exchange of our industry for food! Such a plea is quite inexcusable from a Government with their eyes open to the evils of restricting the supply of food. In fact, it only shifts the responsibility of the Corn Laws from the landed proprietors to the Government. They can do what they please; they have a majority for relieving themselves and their supporters if they are oppressed. If there is any injustice at present in the distribution of these local taxes, let them be distributed more equally. I and others deny altogether that there is any injustice in the matter; and Gentlemen on the opposite side can hardly believe that there is: they do not prove it, and they shrink from any inquiry that would ascertain it.

When the Government announce that pauperism and crime are increased by dear food, what excuse is it for the continuance of Laws that make food so very dear that the cost entailed by these evils falls to a certain extent upon the property of those who have caused them? The fact is, that if the policy of making food scarce by law were abandoned, this charge upon property would be diminished.

The Right Hon. Gentleman the Secretary of State has declared that this is the effect of the failure of the Corn Laws. The remedy therefore is in the hands of the Government. The remedy for the evil of local charges is not to spread poverty and crime throughout the country in order to favour the property of the rich, to favour the idle or unproductive classes: the classes, moreover, who, if they swarmed in the country, would never add to its wealth—deriving their incomes from the sources they do. I do not impute this to them as a fault; they inherit their property, and do not acquire it for themselves; but they usually spend their fortunes unproductively: their expenditure is usually in consumption that has not reproduction in view. Nobody grudges it to them, nobody wishes to interfere with the disposition of property in this country; but, in the name of justice and common sense, do not sacrifice the industrious and the useful to the idle and unproductive.

This House does not act with the same carelessness in any other case that I know of. What is it that has engaged so much of its time and attention this year? Why, providing for cheap and rapid communication throughout the country. Observe, first, the object held in view—the ready transit of goods in order to enable the consumer to have his goods cheap; to enable the produce grown in one place to come into competition with that of another that hitherto has possessed a superior market; in fine, to enable persons to live, as well as to travel, cheaply. Note the jealousy with which Hon. Members regard Monopoly in these cases. Where cheapness and convenience is their object, they admit competition in the first place, for they examine the merits of rival lines. And then, when they give privilege, they take security that those who have received it shall perform what they have undertaken: Hon. Members restrict their charge and retain a power of regulating their business. They do not trust such men implicitly; Hon. Members expect that they would attempt to serve themselves and neglect the public if they did.

But how does the Legislature act with respect to

that great Company that undertakes to perform the most important duty to the people and the State that can be performed : namely, to supply the markets adequately with food? Why, it trusts them implicitly ; it expects that they will, of their own accord, increase the quantity at great outlay with the view to sell at the lowest price ; and then when the people complain that they do as all Monopolists ever have done, the Government puts forward a Secretary at War who tells them to be silent, to say nothing, and that all will be well : to leave the Monopolists alone and that there will be no cause to complain.

Is this consistent, is it rational, does it answer? I reply that the experiment of leaving them alone has already been made ; it was made from 1834 to 1838 when nobody disturbed them, they were fully trusted then, and we know the result.

In the month of March, 1838, I brought this Motion forward ; I was little encouraged either in or out of the House to do so ; I was told that I had better leave it alone ; that it would do no good ; and so much to this effect was said to me privately that I referred to it in my speech. I said : 'I make this observation somewhat in anticipation of that reproof usually offered to those who incur the odium of meddling with this matter: namely, that it is introduced at an unseasonable time; that there is no excitement on the subject; that the country is in a healthy state; and that it is mischievous to moot the subject at all—reasoning that, if I comprehend it, I cannot admit. I do not understand the morality or the wisdom that would postpone the consideration of a difficult question till we are precluded from entering upon it with calmness and caution.

'And with regard to the want of excitement that appears necessary to procure interest and attention for this subject, I cannot help surmising that the day is not far distant when there may be more excitement attaching to it than may be convenient to those who now complain of its absence. Nor can I admit the exceeding healthiness of the country that is urged by some as conclusive against the discussion of this matter. When I look around and observe the numbers that are now dependent on the public relief for existence; when I see a Commission now commencing its inquiry into the cause of the distress pervading 600,000 or 700,000 of our fellow-subjects; when I see that funds are being raised to assist our fellow-subjects to emigrate from their country; I cannot help thinking there is some great fault in our social and political arrangements.'

I made these observations, then, in order to guard against the confident tone with which it is usual, in the absence of pressing distress, to reject all warnings for the future.

I was followed by my friend, Sir Willliam Molesworth, a landed proprietor, though opposed to the Corn Laws; he fully admitted the apparent prosperity of that year and that even improvements had been carried out in agriculture. He said:—

Great improvements have taken place in agriculture in Ireland. Those improvements, together with abundant harvests, have produced, to a certain extent, nearly the same effect, in extending the field of production, as if the Corn Laws had been repealed; hurtful competition has in some degree abated; wages and profits have risen; and the people have been more contented and peaceable. But this effect is only of a temporary kind—population and capital will again grow up to the field of employment; hurtful competition will again take place; wages and profits will fall; and the bulk of the community will be again discontented and uneasy, unless the field of employment again increase in proportion to the addition to capital and population. Repeal the Corn Laws: new markets will be created. With our perpetually increasing and inexhaustible means of purchase, our importations of food from other countries might go on increasing.

This was said in 1838, and in about six months afterwards, early in 1839, we had the melancholy satisfaction of seeing all that we had foretold verified. What happened before the end of that year is familiar to the House: following close upon the fulfilment of our predictions came all the consequences that inevitably ensue from dependence upon the chance of one season and the result of the harvest at home.

I remember that I was at Hamburg at the time when the accounts of the bad harvest in this country spread abroad, and I was astonished at the confidence with which the distress that we should have to experience was spoken of there. They knew the exact amount of grain then in the Baltic ports, which was unusually small; and the price did, as they said it would, rise enormously as soon as they were informed of our harvest. There was but one feeling then: that this arose from not allowing the grower in Europe to look to England as a market. I know of nothing that has altered the prospect of affairs since then; and I am sorry to believe, that even the misery and suffering that have been seen to follow from our bad harvests, have apparently made no impression upon Hon. Gentlemen opposite. How long will they go on in this perilous course?

It cannot surely be contended that we are in a healthy state at this moment. There is a Bill before the House, forced upon it by the Reports officially made of the extreme destitution in parts of Scotland: a Bill to afford public relief upon a larger scale. A Report respecting Ireland has also been laid upon the Table, in which a most frightful picture is drawn of the state of a large portion of the Irish people. Surely there is distress enough to establish a case for further legislation in the direction pointed out by the Government as being conducive to the employment of the people and the diminution of crime and pauperism!

The Government are not in a situation to dispute either the distress or the remedy that I am pressing upon their attention. I am urging their own views; and will anybody pretend that to restrict the supply of food that comes to these shores as a customer for British industry can be a mode of benefiting those who want custom for labour and are without food? Who can deny that it is the natural right of the people of this or of any country to have the freest access to the means of subsistence that honest industry can offer to them. Sooner or later it must be conceded. Why delay it? Is it that I ask too much? How can this be said when two measures in different degrees of moderation have been received with as little favour as any Motion that I have ever made?

The Noble Lord proposed a fixed duty: he did so to meet the scruples of those who might object to this measure. How was he treated? The Member for Gateshead asked you to add a little to the stock here by bringing over the grain of our own colonies at the Antipodes. He was told that he ought to deal with the general question.

Well, here is the general question. How are Hon. Members going to deal with it? Their experience recommends them strongly to abolish the Corn Laws. Their only fear could be a reduction of price here; yet how has that operated? They expected that corn would be at 56*s.*; it has been at 45*s.* They say that every advantage has followed from this circumstance, even in the agricultural districts. They say that our consumption is 20,000,000 quarters, and they tell us that 10*s.* a quarter has been saved upon it. Well, that is 10,000,000*l.* sterling paid less out of the general means for one article, and has of course left so much more to be expended on the consumption of other articles the result of British industry. How would it have been otherwise than an additional blessing had the price been reduced sufficiently to cause another 10,000,000*l.* to be saved?

The whole financial policy of the Right Hon. Baronet is founded, if I understand it, on the ground of lowering the cost of living; he expects that we shall not feel additional taxation, if provisions essential to life are cheap. Considering what the taxes are in this country, how is it possible that the cost of living can be too low? The Revenue depends chiefly upon the expenditure that takes place after the first necessary of life is provided for.

A short time since the Right Hon. Baronet was horrified at being informed that a body of great men in the north had combined to raise the price of an essential to the poor man's comfort, by making the article scarce. He reproved them publicly in the House; he called upon them as good citizens to cease from the oppression of the poor by such unhallowed means. This he said with respect to coals. How is it that he does not apply this to corn? The poor can procure fire without coal more easily than they can get nourishment without corn.

I will add only one word more, which is as to the seasonableness of the time at which I make this proposition: the time is peculiarly reasonable for making it on account of the lowness of price. I was astonished the other night that the Home Secretary, so shrewd a reasoner in this matter, should have supposed that when the price is low in this country the landlord needs high Protection most! Why, it is the time when he wants it least; for the low price itself then makes the market so much worse for the foreigner, that the slightest addition to the difficulty of conveying the grain any distance is felt. It is, therefore, precisely at such a time that a duty of 4*s*. would operate: it might keep out all American grain just by that amount, if the price here were very low. But when the price is very high, the duty may be double that amount, and the community here may not be worse off; for the high price here, if the price is low abroad, may make it worth the foreigner's while to pay the duty. It is the difference of price here and abroad that determines the operation of a duty; when the price here is low, this country is more on a level with foreign countries, and then the distance would act like a Protective Duty.

Now, if the Corn Laws are repealed, the price may fall a little here, and rise a little abroad, and there will be but little grain come in; at present there is but little wanted, which is usually the case when the price is low: another reason why great importations are not to be expected at this time—there is less occasion for them, less food is wanted.

It is needless for me to detain the House any longer. I have urged, however inefficiently, all that has occurred to me as rendering this question peculiarly deserving of immediate attention; and enough, I think, to satisfy Hon. Members of the wisdom of not losing any more time without legislating on the subject. I have not resorted to declamation, and I shall not resort to it: the question has been too often mooted in this House to make any peculiar appeal to the interest favoured by the Corn Laws, which preponderates so greatly in the Legislature, either useful or appropriate. Everything calculated to touch their feelings of honour, honesty, justice, prudence, and humanity, has already been addressed to Hon. Members by abler men than I, and, if it is still unavailing, I am sure that I could add nothing that will have more effect. I will merely say, then, that if the House resists all concession now, I shall regret it more than

I have regretted such resistance on any other occasion, because never before has the time been so fitting for the change; and in the future Hon. Members will equally regret having neglected a moment so suited to the purpose. I beg to move: That this House resolve itself into a Committee, for the purpose of considering the following Resolutions:—

That the Corn Laws restrict the supply of food, and prevent the free exchange of the products of labour.

That they are, therefore, prejudicial to the welfare of the country, especially to that of the working classes, and have proved delusive to those for whose benefit the Laws were designed.

That it is expedient that all restrictions on corn should be now abolished.

XXIV.

BIRMINGHAM, November 15, 1845.

For a month after the debate on Mr. Villiers's Motion for immediate Repeal in 1845 the belief of an abundant harvest was general. Then a three weeks' rain made people apprehensive of famine, and in the manufacturing and commercial towns they scanned the clouds as narrowly and talked as incessantly of the chances of sun as the farmers did in the agricultural districts. Before the prorogation Lord J. Russell urged in vain upon the Government the necessity of providing for the contingency of a bad harvest. Till the end of September there was just enough sunshine to keep alive the hope of something of a harvest though a late one; but by the beginning of October the great failure of the wheat crop, both as regards quantity and quality, was an acknowledged fact; and by the middle of the month the almost total failure of the potato crop was beyond dispute. The 'Times' said that open ports would be adopted; but Cabinet after Cabinet was held and nothing came of them; there was a division in the Ministry, Sir R. Peel being unable to bring his colleagues to consent that Parliament should be summoned, or that the ports should be opened by an Order in Council. The 'Standard' announced on Nov. 7:—'We are, we trust, in a condition to congratulate the Leaguers upon the certainty that the ports will not be opened, inasmuch as the stock of provisions in Great Britain is amply sufficient.' On Nov. 15, a grand banquet was given to Mr. Villiers in the Town Hall of Birmingham by the advocates of Free Trade. Over 700 persons were present at it, including many of the most influential members of the Liberal party in the town and neighbourhood. The Mayor presided. Among the principal guests were Earl Ducie, Mr. Bright, Mr. Cobden, Colonel Thompson, and Mr. W. J. Fox. The chairman proposed the health of the guest of the evening, and Mr. Villiers made the following reply, which was reported in nearly all the newspapers of the kingdom that had any influence, and, together with some of the other speeches of the occasion, gave a tone to public opinion everywhere.

I AM deeply sensible of my inability duly to acknowledge the peculiar honour that you have paid me this evening.

When I consider the flattering circumstances under which I am your guest and the friendly manner in which your Chairman has expressed his sentiments towards me, I feel the greatest difficulty to convey to you my sense of your kindness.

I hardly feel myself entitled to be singled out for such special marks of distinction when I see around me so many who have exceeded me in the services they have rendered the great cause of Commercial Freedom.

In fact the only advantage that I can in any way claim over my colleagues is due to the possession of a seat in the House of Commons for some years previous to the commencement of their Parliamentary career.

But I believe they will support me in saying that when they did come into the House of Commons they found that I had not been idle: that I had been and still was toiling amongst difficulties more irksome than any that they have had to contend with.

Since I have been honoured with a seat in Parliament I have fearlessly endeavoured to do my duty, preferring always to serve the interests of the community to those of separate classes. And I can only say that if the humble advocacy that I have given to the cause that has this evening been connected with my name, can be considered a service, the gratifying manifestation of your opinions on the present occasion gives me the highest encouragement to persevere in it.

You know how the House of Commons is constituted, and the feeling that prevails amongst its members on the momentous question of the Corn Laws. You know also how unfortunately they identify their own interests with the maintenance of the Corn Laws; and that those who oppose them act under the greatest disadvantage. But I can answer for the distinguished men present on this occasion, as well as for myself, that nothing has cheered us more under all our difficulties in the part that it has been our lot to take against the Corn Laws, nothing has sustained us more in our course, than the confidence we felt that sooner or later the intelligent and independent portion of the community must appreciate the importance and the truth of our principles.

I derive, therefore, from this assemblage a satisfaction more than personal. I accept it as a sign of the progress of the cause, and as a gratifying verification of what we have expected. And here allow me to express the hope that coinciding with us in our views upon this question you will not underrate the importance of openly declaring your opinions. The Legislature no doubt must ultimately decide the question; and we who sit in the House of Commons have of late seen the most conclusive signs that those who will have to decide it feel that they are in error, and cannot much longer maintain their selfish position. They think that they have an interest in the Corn Laws; but evidence has been pressed upon them by their own Ministers and by circumstances they cannot dispute, which leaves them no doubt that it will be impossible to maintain much longer class interests which are at variance with the interests of the community.

But there is one thing that they do not appear to know: at present they seem to be ignorant of the sentiments of persons throughout the country of the intelligence and respectability of those whom I have now the honour of addressing. They want some sign of the real opinion held by the independent portion of the public. They choose to assume that if you abstain from agitation, you concur with them; and they pretend that the public either support them in their opinion or are indifferent to the operation of the Corn Laws.

I do not believe that the aristocracy of this country are better than other men; in fact I think that they are much the same as other men: they are very much the same as those in other classes of society who, if they help themselves to something to which they are not entitled, are loath to give it up. Like other great bodies in this country they will not move unless the steam is up: it is not a gentle pressure but a high pressure that they require. Sir James Graham was never nearer the truth than when he said (and it is one of those things that he has not unsaid) that the aristocracy of this country when backed by public opinion are omnipotent; but that without it, or if they run counter to it, they are virtually powerless. The truth of this has been specially shown in reference to the Laws that restrict the supply of food. What the aristocracy now require and the want of which I believe stands at present between us and the repeal of the Corn Laws, is some definite, intelligible, and unmistakable expression of opinion throughout the country. They want to be assured that the public generally are as much impressed with the evils and mischiefs of the Corn Laws as we are. Satisfy them of this, and I firmly believe that another Session will not pass over without the concession of total Repeal.

If this is the case, need I say how important it is that the opinion of this town should be known? how important it is that this great capital of the manufacturing industry of the country should speak out firmly on this and on every future occasion? What Birmingham did when its opinions were strong, its spirit aroused, and its determination taken, is yet fresh in the recollection of many in both Houses of the Legislature. We all know that what was deemed all but rebellion a few years since is now admitted to have been a salutary and beneficial course. And I am satisfied that Birmingham cannot manifest its sentiments on this occasion without exercising a powerful influence on the Legislature.

It is for this reason peculiarly gratifying to all sitting here, as well as to myself, to witness this unequivocal testimony of the state of feeling in this town. We look upon it and accept it not as an expression of personal regard, but as the public expression of determined adherence to a great principle and a righteous policy, the immediate adoption of which you identify with the permanent well-being of the people at large.

Commercial freedom is an object in every way worthy of your exertions. The Chairman well characterized it as connected with all the best interests of commerce. Commercial freedom is only an extension of that liberty, in its truest sense, for which you have fought before, and instalments of which the people of this country have frequently succeeded in obtaining.

Commercial freedom is as much a right of the English people as any liberty for which they have struggled, and which they have obtained. And such are the circumstances of our country that if its commerce should continue to be restricted as it has been heretofore, it might as well be without many of the liberties which it now possesses, and of which it so justly boasts.

The people of this country have acquired the power of saying what they please, and thinking as they please, and praying where they please: they have secured to themselves civil and religious liberty, and the liberty of the press. And the result has been that with which every extension of our popular liberties has been attended: the country has become greater and the people have become better. Nay more, the people of this country, in consequence of what they have gained, have become more intelligent, more enterprising, more powerful, and more peaceful than any other nation; and it is on this account that they are the more aggrieved by the galling restraints still imposed on their commerce.

What is it to a man to be possessed of greater intelligence or skill than his neighbours, if he is prevented from employing it to the best advantage;

if he is barred from gaining the necessaries and comforts of life by means of it? What are intelligence and skill to a man if his wages are to be at the mercy of Monopolists? What is it to millions of men to be surrounded by abundance, wealth, and luxury, if they are doomed themselves to depend on the chance of fair weather for the bare food of life, failing which they are reduced to utter destitution? And is not this the condition of multitudes of our fellow-countrymen in these two islands? Is it not the great question now slowly agitating the country whether the calamity of insufficient food is not about to befall the labouring population? Does any man believe that this state of things is necessary, or a visitation of Providence, or that it is an evil that human prudence could not have foreseen and provided against? It is the natural result of legislating against food. It is the inevitable consequence of the Laws that we are denouncing: a consequence that has been foreseen, and that the Legislature and Government have been warned against over and over again.

By the Corn Laws the superior kinds of food are rendered inaccessible to the people, who are thus driven to use inferior kinds; and if the scarcity that we now apprehend should occur, the people will be reduced to destitution. Such has been the constant result of making food difficult to be procured by the mass of the people. No man, then, who has been a party to the legislation that occasions such evils has a right to talk of the visitations of Providence in connection with this matter. We will not on so great a question accept as an authority in favour of calling these evils visitations of Providence those who proposed, and those who still maintain the enactment which I assert, and which you all believe, is the true cause of the mischief. It is to the Corn Laws that the very great distress now existing in this country is attributed by persons of the highest intelligence and widest experience who have either written or spoken on the matter. And it is the frequent observation of enlightened foreigners who visit us that they witness extremes in the social condition of this country that are to be met with nowhere else. With greater wealth and abundance in our possession than any other country in the world can boast of, they see side by side of it a mass of poverty and suffering that is not equalled or even approximated elsewhere. And this they almost invariably trace to the Laws that we are now met to oppose, which purposely make food scarce.

The other day Lord John Russell, when addressing the citizens of Edinburgh, passed an eloquent panegyric on the Constitution of this country; and to much that was said on that occasion of the particular advantages that the English people enjoy every reasonable man in the kingdom is ready to assent. But no Englishman now dares to boast of his institutions in any part of Europe, without being exposed to the reproach that in his country Laws are still maintained the pernicious consequences of which fall wholly and with terrible effect on the poor. 'With all your boasted freedom,' they say, 'with your long catalogue of sacred rights, vindicated, fought for, and obtained, see what injustice is daily perpetrated in your land under the forms of liberty!' Other people complain loudly of the despotism that crushes them to the earth, but where do you find such practical injustice wrought as results to this country from the Laws that within the last thirty years have been passed to make the wealthiest aristocracy in the world wealthier still by means that expose millions of the people to want?

We may be taunted, as we have been taunted before, with keeping the argument all on one side and not hearing what the other side have to allege. Never were we more willing, never were we better prepared than now, to listen to all that the friends of Monopoly think proper to advance. The substitution of the Sliding Scale—their latest invention for making food scarce—is due they assert to their solicitude not only to make food plentiful and cheap, but to make us, in respect of it, independent of the foreigner. The present is a seasonable moment for examining the virtues of this device. By the Sliding Scale food, we are told, will be rendered abundant, and by this abundance we shall become independent of the foreigner. I repeat it, there is now a fair opportunity for ascertaining how far it has succeeded in accomplishing one of these ends, and how far the accomplishment of the other has proved an advantage to the country.

And here let me say that there are other Sliding Scales besides our own in the world, for in this matter other people have unfortunately for themselves imitated our example, and the present time is suitable for examining all of them.

Sliding Scales were attempted in Holland and Belgium. And how did they fulfil the expectations of the people of those two countries? The very first moment that a deficiency of food was threatened the authorities without loss of time assembled together and consigned the Scales to that place from which it was the honest hope of all they might never return.

In both countries, as in our own, the people have had the ill-fortune to have the producers of food preponderating in the Legislature; and they have not unnaturally hit upon the same device for making food abundant. It has not, however, with them been allowed to stand in the way when there arose an apprehension of scarcity. With the fear of scarcity the Sliding Scales vanished and a complete system of Free Trade took their place.

I know of no better instance of the mischiefs of the Protective System, and of the advantage of the principles we contend for, than that which Holland furnishes in this respect. Upwards of two centuries ago Free Trade prevailed in Holland. Then not one grain of corn was raised in the country; and yet Holland was alluded to by contemporary writers as the granary of Europe. Amongst others, Sir Walter Raleigh observed that Holland was able to supply the wants of the other countries of Europe when they were visited by a deficiency. It enjoyed a perfect Free Trade in corn, and the consequence was that it could always command a surplus wherewith to supply the wants of its neighbours. Raleigh says: 'Ever since it resorted to the system of freedom of commerce, it has always had an abundance of food not only for its own people but, on an average, about 700,000 quarters besides, available for the communities around it that are ill provided.'

Does anybody believe that Holland ever had occasion to substitute the system of the Sliding Scale for that of Free Trade while it enjoyed that blessing? What is the condition of Holland now? The Dutch substituted the miserable system of the Sliding Scale for that of Free Trade, and the instant that they find themselves likely to be pinched for food, they are obliged once more to resort to the old system which they so unfortunately abandoned.

And what confidence have we lately shown in the system of Protection? What do we read now in some of the public journals? Why, that Ministers of the Crown have been meeting four hours a day for the last week, for the purpose of seeing how they could decently get rid of their Sliding Scale. The only scruple that they at present appear to have upon the subject is that they were the authors and promoters of the scheme which they are now desirous of throwing overboard.

And what in reference to their late doings is the universal opinion of the country? Why, that if there has been one act of folly greater than that of establishing the Sliding Scale, it has been that of not seizing the favourable moment offered for abolishing it. I am not exaggerating in the slightest degree when I say that this is the prevailing opinion throughout the country. The Ministers had a great and a glorious opportunity of getting rid of this mischievous scale, but they did not profit by it.

The Sliding Scale, as I said, promised to make us independent of foreigners. Is such independence likely to be a signal advantage to us at this moment? What everybody is just now regretting is that foreigners have not enough for us to depend upon should we be in want, and that we cannot in our present exigency reckon upon a foreign supply. Those who devised the notable scheme seemed to forget that this state of things was likely to follow: that if we made ourselves independent of foreigners, they would become independent of us.

In looking at the organs of Monopoly, I find that they face this difficulty by saying that Sir Robert Peel is not afraid, that he is ready to meet whatever emergency may arise, because he is ready to give a bounty to foreigners to induce them to send us food. It is extremely good of him; but I should like to know who is to pay the bounty? I do not suppose that Sir Robert is going to pay it. I take it that the people of this country would have to pay it, and that the remedy proposed implies nothing less than that we are not only to pay more than we should do in this country for our food, but that when we want more we are to be especially taxed to enable us to buy up the food of other people.

I really believe that there is no merit whatever in the Sliding Scale but this, that it cannot now deceive anybody.

To confirm my assertion I recommend the people of this country to indulge for a while in retrospect. What was the state of public feeling during the months of August and September last? Were not the state of the weather and our prospects for the coming year in connection with it, the all-engrossing topics of conversation? Were not these all-important subjects then anxiously revolved in everybody's mind? All were concerned to know whether we were to have rain or sunshine; whether food was to be dear or cheap. And what meant all this solicitude about the weather? Why, everybody was uneasy about the state of the weather because they see that the food of millions is made to depend on the most variable thing in the world—the English climate, and that abundance or scarcity, dearness or cheapness, is made to turn upon the clouds of August and September. What is the meaning of this? Why are people anxious about the price of food? Because they have certain ideas fixed in their minds at present connected with the dearness or cheapness of food. There has been so much experience of late of the consequences of abundance or scarcity of food in the condition of the people that there is no one in this country, I believe, who is not prepared to say with confidence what must inevitably be the result of the one and the other. You cannot divest the people of this country of the idea that when food is cheap and plentiful, credit will be good, trade brisk, manufactures prosperous, wages high, and the country generally in a state of prosperity. And that when it is scarce and dear, money will be scarce, credit impaired, manufactures depressed, wages low, all local burdens increased, and that capital, which in prosperous times is available for railways and other great public works, must necessarily be withdrawn to pay for the increased charge of food. These are the ideas that now obtain with all thinking men. It is only natural then that there should be anxiety as to whether the harvest is good or not.

But the real question is, whether all this apprehension and anxiety is necessary? Ought we to be dependent solely on our own harvest? Or having ascertained that it is desirable that food should be cheap, ought we not take the best, most certain, and readiest means to secure that object? And have the means to make food cheap been taken by the Legislature? It cannot be too widely known that there is not a single article in great demand in this country, subject to the regular principles of commerce, that is at any time deficient in supply. There are many articles of which we obtain our supplies from foreigners; but which, unlike food, being free from all legislative interference, are nevertheless regularly and abundantly supplied.

There is no exception to the rule that these articles are at all times supplied not only with regularity and in sufficient quantities, but with a tendency to fall in price. It is a fact that the Monopolists should be eternally called upon to explain, that with Free

Trade we have always a sufficient supply and low prices, whereas when we play such pranks as making a Sliding Scale with regard to any article we are immediately exposed to all the evils of an uncertain and often a deficient supply and high prices.

Such is the result of our experience of the Corn Laws. And I want to know in this, the thirty-first year of their operation, whether there is one single thing of any other kind to be alleged in their favour? We expect to know something of the character of a man when he is twenty-one years old; surely it is time if anything can be said in favour of these Laws that we should be made acquainted with it now, in their thirty-first year! What we really know is, that they occasion great anxiety for about two months in every year; that they throw the country into a state of confusion about every four years; and that they have always occasioned a great loss to the country generally, and severe privations to the poor in particular.

I do not know anything in which our friends exerted themselves to so much advantage in their attacks upon these absurd Laws as in showing the influence of more or less food upon the moral and physical condition of the people. They have worked out this point in a manner that ought to satisfy everybody. That the working-man suffers privations when bread is scarce and dear, and that he gets the comforts and advantages he desires when it is plentiful and cheap, is now proved to demonstration.

And this exposition has also not been without its

effect on our opponents, the Monopolists. When I first entered Parliament, I remember being told that the Corn Laws must be maintained as a national object; that they were necessary to the maintenance of the national credit; that the National Debt could not be paid without them; and that they raised wages. Now, however, we no longer have the plea of national credit brought forward in support of the Corn Laws; we are told: 'All we want is time. Give us time and Protection, and you shall have plenty of corn, and food shall be as cheap as you wish.' But I have an objection to waiting. I mistrust the man who proclaims himself the advocate of cheapness and plenty and yet keeps a Corn Law in his house. I distrust people who combine to keep up a Monopoly in order, as they say, to make things cheap. That is not the way business is done in this world. The manufacturers endeavour, it is true, to make things cheap, but they do so under the pressure of competition. But when a man says, 'Leave me a Monopoly in order that I may make the article in which I have the Monopoly cheap,' I distrust him. I distrust Protective Societies for Agriculture, for I never see that they do anything with the purpose of cheapening food. They assemble often, unquestionably, and they talk much; they tell each other how cheap corn can be grown by improved methods of cultivation; what new inventions have been made in agriculture; and the great advantages that would result from their adoption. But in my view all they prove is that if they would only put their shoulders to the wheel and not trust to

Protection they would be able to meet any competition that could be brought against them.

But after all the learning and all the talent brought out by the Protective Societies we see nothing done by them. If we could perceive that they did anything at their meetings besides reading long lectures to instruct the farmer, I should say they were really in earnest. If they drew up a report on agriculture and said: 'We have made the farmers on our estates our political tools ; we have, by our legislation, placed them under great disadvantages ; we make them pay high rents by holding out expectations that we know can never be realized ; we make them improve the property for our benefit ; and we compel them to preserve a species of vermin which it is our sport to hunt and kill. The result of such treatment and interference is that the farms are badly cultivated, and the people badly supplied with food ; instead of which we recommend that all landlords in future should secure their tenants in their farms. We shall be the first to do it ourselves. And, further, we recommend that vermin shall be destroyed by the tenants.' No doubt in this case the learning of Liebig and Smith of Deanston would soon be turned to account, and be useful in developing the resources of agriculture. But while the Protection people confine themselves to lecturing and do nothing, they have no claim on our confidence ; nor have they any reason to call on us to wait the result of their improvements.

There is another reason why we should pause

before we trust these upholders of Monopoly. Though they say, 'Give us a little time and we shall be able to give you all you want,' unfortunately whenever food has been cheap and abundant they were the only people that were annoyed at it and discontented. Last year, had you been in the House of Commons, you would have heard what I now tell you confirmed; you would have seen a certain gentleman[1] with a large bundle of papers in his hand, speaking with much energy and firmness, hurling threats against the Treasury Bench; and if any stranger had entered at the time and been told that the speaker was a member of the Society for the Protection of British Industry, he would have supposed him to be some great philanthropic statesman propounding a scheme for raising the condition of the people; but how astonished he would have been when he found the bundle of papers consisted of prices current of almost every article of agricultural produce, animal and vegetable, and heard him quote the one after the other to show, by way of complaint, how much bacon was less per pound and flour was less per stone than he and his friends had been led to expect they would be when they assisted in bringing the present Government into power.

The prices of 1841 were brought forward and compared with the then prevailing prices; charges of breach of faith were made against the Minister; and threats of withdrawal of confidence heard. The discussion on the occasion was what was termed

[1] Mr. Miles.

in the House practical; and it absorbed the interest and engaged the attention of the whole party who want time to produce cheaply. The Hon. Member got the ear of the House, and it went forth that that was a bad night for the Government. And this was an instance of a gentleman high in the confidence of the party representing the agricultural interest and trusted by them, occupying the time of the House of Commons two hours and a half in complaining of the great fall that had occurred in the cost of the necessaries of life. An exhibition calculated most certainly to astonish those who look upon our Contitution as characterized by intelligence and benevolence, and who consider the British Legislature as remarkable for its Christian character.

The man who brought this complaint forward is however a most respectable man. He sits in Parliament as a country gentleman, and besides doing his part in passing laws for 28,000,000 of people, he attends Quarter Sessions and officiates as a Magistrate. For my part I rather like the simplicity with which he stated his views on the subject. There was no concealment or hypocrisy in the matter; and on this account his speech was, in my opinion, a valuable one. Indeed it is impossible to overrate its importance. I was glad the other day to see that the speech had even been spoken of by one of the Hon. Gentleman's own party as a remarkable one. One gentleman was indignant at the indiscretion of his Hon. Friend[1] who said a short time ago that when he heard the speech he

[1] Mr. E. Scott.

saw that the game of Protection was up. He spoke the truth, however: the game of Protection was up from the moment that speech was made. Listen to these Protectionist gentlemen, or read any of their published opinions, and you would not, as a rule, for a moment suppose that their object in supporting the Corn Laws is to make the necessaries of life scarce and dear. It is well therefore that the indiscretion of one of the party let the cat out of the bag.

A nobleman, of whom I do not wish to speak with disrespect, referring to his experience of the last Session, said that the Corn Laws were doomed. He meant that they were found out. The Noble Lord will shortly be seen to have been a true prophet.

Another Conservative, a captain in the Navy, said: 'I have learned two things this year. I have heard that the population of the country is increasing at the rate of 1,000 a day, and I see that the object of Protection is to make the necessaries of life scarce and dear. Why, it is worse,' he continued, 'than the Chinese, for they do all they can to provide for an increasing population and make food plentiful and cheap.' And he went down to his own county and boldly told them there that it would never do to go on as they were with the population increasing at an enormous rate, and a system in operation that failed to provide them with adequate subsistence.

This statement had a good effect upon the House. Shortly afterwards Lord John Russell thought it necessary to bring the condition of the working classes before the House. 'The working classes do not,' said his Lordship, 'keep pace with the increasing wealth of the country. The wealth increases rapidly, but the condition of the working classes has not improved in like proportion.' Lord John Russell made a most able speech on that occasion, and referred to circumstances that have occurred during the last fifty years by which the condition of the people has been affected. He referred also to matters for which Parliament is responsible, and which it might remedy; but he came to no other conclusion than that the sole cause that prevents the people from bettering their condition is those Laws that make the necessaries of life scarce. He further asked the House to take the question into immediate consideration; and it was curious to see the manner in which the proposition was received by the Government.

The price of food was then low, and the Government had to meet two things: they wanted to take the credit to themselves for the prosperity then existing, and at the same time to keep well with their own friends. But that was a difficult task because their friends wished food to be dear, and the Government had admitted that the existing prosperity depended on its being cheap. Sir James Graham, who succeeded the Noble Lord, did not oppose the Motion; but he moved the previous question. He admitted that the game of Protection was up. He made a clean sweep of all the rubbish that had been put forth in favour of Protection; and a more clear and comprehensive argument against Protection to maintain price than his no one ever heard. He stated the effect of the price of the necessaries of life on the condition of the working classes, and proved that when food had been abundant and cheap the moral and physical condition of the people had improved. No speech delivered by a Free Trader could have been more conclusive as to the advantage of the cheapness of the necessaries of life than that of Sir James Graham, the Secretary of the Home Department. And no one of the Government supporters, no one of the Protection party, said a single word in reply. The single-minded gentleman to whom I have referred said not a word. He was content with having complained of cheapness and plenty ; he did not deny the results on the social condition of the country.

I myself had a Motion on the paper on the very subject ; but my friends advised me not to bring it on after the speech of Sir James Graham. I had evidence from every part of the country showing that the people are more prosperous, happy, and moral when food is cheap than when it is dear. Ten days after I brought forward my Motion for the Repeal of the Corn Laws that exist only to make the necessaries of life dear and scarce ; and no answer was offered but that the people were then well off ; that there was plenty of employment ; that trade was brisk in every department. And it was asked why, as the Laws had failed of their purpose, disturb the existing state of things? The Minister admitted that the Laws do not meet the objects for which they were framed ; but he said : 'Why interfere with them at such a time of general prosperity?'

Many voted in the minority who had not voted before, determined to trifle with the country no longer. The Howards, the Cavendishes, the Fortescues, and Russells refused to be any longer parties to what was clearly exhibited in the course of the Session to be either a fraud practised on those who were said to be protected by the Corn Laws, or an enormous injury to the community at large. I believe that if there were a public meeting in any part of the country, no high-minded men would now be found to support Laws so shabby in their purpose, and so dangerous and mischievous in their results; and I do not see how those people who are the real or pretended 'friends of humanity,' can continue to countenance Laws that have been demonstrated beyond all question, by late exposures, to be a giant cause of misery.

I, too, like to test these Laws on the ground of humanity. Yes! It is on the ground of their inflicting positive physical evil on those least able to bear it that I want to consider them. I do not underrate their commercial, political, or financial bearings. I have considered them all, and nothing is more complete than the arguments against the Corn Laws on these heads. The mischief and folly of Laws that interrupt the commerce of a country by preventing food from being made a medium of exchange cannot be equalled. And I do not believe there is any town in which the rights of capital and the interests of individual enterprise are more egregiously injured by commercial restrictions than they are here.

You are large exporters to countries where the produce of the soil is the only means of exchange, and you have your commerce limited and the business of this great town interrupted by a mischievous and a violent interference with the rights of capital, of which the feudal or dark ages afford no more flagrant instance.

Again, I know nothing more important for you to consider than the bearing of the Corn Laws on the financial condition of the country. You see great works set on foot in times when capital is abundant, and men find from the prosperity of trade its application in this direction profitable; but let there be anything like a scarcity of food and a large abstraction of the national means to pay for it, and instantly we see public works are stopped and that confusion ensues of which we have been too often the witnesses before.

The Corn Laws are equally bad from a political point of view. They prevent that knitting together of nations in the bonds of mutual interest which tends to avert that great curse—war. And what is the further result of these restrictions as regards other nations? We are looked upon as a nuisance throughout Europe. We are looked upon as foes everywhere when we might be revered as friends by all.

But at this moment I am calling your attention to the practical bearing of the Corn Laws as a food question. There is now a deficiency of food. One chief article of home produce is supposed to be lost, and there is great difficulty in obtaining a supply from any other country. The price of the necessaries of life is rising everywhere. It has now reached that point at which it was when, after long privation, starving men broke into the shops of tradesmen and plundered them to get food. The price has now reached that point at which it was when the scenes of Paisley and Stockport were enacted: scenes to which Sir Robert Peel said he could not refer without emotion, and which were due to that scarcity, of which Sir James Graham said that it was invariably accompanied by the prevalence of crime, poverty, mortality, and political discontent, throughout the country. The price has now reached that point at which it was when the Revenue declined; when the imposition of the Income Tax was found necessary; and when the public works, commenced under more favourable auspices, were checked. There is a prospect of the recurrence of such a state of things. There is no confidence to be placed in the apparent prosperity of the country.

In 1838 everything appeared as healthy and sound as possible. It was in that year that I implored the House to take the Corn Laws into their consideration, warning them that the course of prosperity might be stopped by the failure of a harvest. In March they rejected my Motion by an overwhelming majority, and in the September following the whole country was alarmed by a deficient harvest. We have now many of the signs of that year; the same results may again follow. I ask, then, when was there any political question submitted to an intelligent community more ripe for decision? When were the people more strongly called on to urge the Government to provide against prospective want in this country?

The Government have not decided on anything; they wait for you to suggest what their decision shall be. There never, in my opinion, was a time when it was more necessary for the people of England to speak out. I am convinced that it would be a libel on the character that you have honourably acquired, to suppose that under such circumstances you would be found lagging behind the rest of the community, and that you would by your silence give evidence of want of public spirit. In a cause of justice and humanity you will never be found wanting: and I am sure that you would not descend to notice the humble efforts of an individual like myself if you did not intend to rise up yourselves and accomplish the work. Gladden the hearts, then, cheer the courage of millions by calling on the Government to strike down at once and abolish for ever this selfish and mischievous obstacle to the supply of food for the people. And if they should resist your appeal, and Parliament should sanction such refusal, require the Ministers to put the electors on their trial, and see whether they are the proper depositaries of power, and faithful guardians of the interests of those unenfranchised millions who earn their bread in the sweat of their brow.

XXV.

COVENT GARDEN THEATRE, December 17, 1845.

The refusal of the Government to assemble Parliament or to open the ports with the prospect of famine staring them in the face, threw the whole country into a state of excitement, and was met by prompt action on the part of the League. They had once asked the country for a fund of 50,000*l.* and got it; they asked later for another 100,000*l.* and were successful; they now asked for a quarter of a million. On the two previous occasions the great towns responded with their thousands, and individuals with their hundreds; now firm after firm, and manufacturer after manufacturer sent in their 1,000*l.* each; and the prompt subscription of the Quarter-of-a-million Fund made many converts. Amidst all the excitement Lord J. Russell on November 22 addressed a letter to the electors of London dated from Edinburgh. In it he declared it to be no longer worth while to contend for a fixed duty, and he urged upon all to unite together to put an end to a system that had proved to be 'the blight of commerce, the bane of agriculture, the source of bitter division among classes, the cause of penury, fever, mortality, and crime among the people;' and, as the Government appeared to be waiting for some excuse to give up the present Corn Law, 'by petition, by address, by remonstrance,' to afford them the excuse they sought.. On December 4, the 'Times' announced that it was the intention of the Government to repeal the Corn Laws and to call Parliament together in January for that purpose. Another morning paper called this an 'atrocious fabrication by the "Times";' but the 'Times' had true information, and on December 11, Sir R. Peel's resignation disclosed the Duke of Wellington's withdrawal of his reluctant consent to Repeal, supported by the Duke of Buccleuch and Lord Stanley. Lord J. Russell was immediately summoned from Scotland by the Queen. On December 17, Mr. Villiers presided at the great Covent Garden meeting.

THE sole purpose for which I have to ask your attention is to explain to you briefly why I occupy the chair this evening. It was only a few minutes before I entered this theatre that I was informed by some of my friends around me that the gentleman who so frequently and efficiently presides as Chairman of these meetings had become suddenly and seriously indisposed; and I was asked if I would on the emergency supply the place of my friend Mr. Wilson. When the request was made to me to preside at this meeting, I had an impression that it was no easy duty to discharge and at first I declined to undertake it; but finally I yielded for the one object that for the last six or seven years I have continually had in view in my connection with the Anti-Corn-Law League: namely, to cordially co-operate with it whenever my services could be rendered available.

I well remember the difficulty there was to advance the question of Repeal before the establishment of the Anti-Corn-Law League; and I have always been of opinion, and I continue to be so still, that if some such powerful organization as the League had not existed, there would even now be little prospect of success. And, therefore, as I have long and earnestly desired to see the repeal of the Corn Laws, I have ever thought it my duty to place my best services at its disposal whenever they might be required.

Notwithstanding the errors that are said to have been committed during the course of past years by some of this body—errors that have been most candidly admitted by many of its leading members, I am of opinion that if our opponents should come to their senses and concede the abolition of the Corn Laws before the day arrives when the people are maddened by the privations and distress that these Laws necessarily produce, this great triumph of justice will be mainly the result of the active endeavours continuously sustained by the Anti-Corn-Law League.

One of the reasons for which I sincerely regret the absence of our friend Mr. Wilson on this occasion is that it was his intention to have detailed to you the extraordinary exertions that have been made recently by our enlightened friends and by those who have represented the branches of the League in the provinces; and to have afforded you satisfactory and clear proofs of the extent to which conviction of the necessity of Repeal is gaining ground; for wherever they go the important services of the representatives of the League are fully appreciated. It probably would have been one part of the address that Mr. Wilson would have thought right to make to you, to congratulate you most cordially, as I do now, upon the accession of strength that we have lately received through the adoption by some of the most eminent statesmen in this country of the principles that have been advocated in this theatre. We know now that these men, the only statesmen to whom the Crown could have recourse to form an Administration for the government of the country, have come to the conclusion that they will no longer be parties to withholding one of the most obvious rights that the people of this, or of any other country, can claim or enjoy: the simple one of feeding themselves.

We have the only men who can, without exciting ridicule and contempt, be called to the councils of the Crown, at last allowing themselves to be announced to the country and the world as opposed to the policy that we have so long been condemning.

Of Lord John Russell's opinions there can at

present be no question. He has in a clear and intelligent way made them manifest to the whole world. We have all read his recent address to the electors of the City; and therefore, about his views and, I trust also, his intentions, there cannot be a doubt.

It was with no surprise that I read that address, because I remembered that in the last Session he for the first time voted for the Motion that I submitted to the House for the total repeal of the Corn Laws.

In the speeches he made on several occasions during the Session, he exhibited himself perfectly alive to all the injury and mischief that the Corn Laws have produced on the working classes of society ; and he distinctly predicted that a time would arrive when we should be precluded from deciding this question with calmness and quietude. He predicted the time when some great emergency would arise, when a scarcity of food would be manifest; and that then we should be suddenly called upon at once and totally to repeal the Corn Laws.

All men believe either that the emergency has actually occurred to the extent stated but a short time since, or else that the people are about to suffer very considerable privations. Lord John Russell, therefore, has come forward in right season, and at a most opportune moment, to declare that he will be no party to placing any obstruction either to the supply of food to the people, or to the interchange of the products of their industry for the products of the industry of other nations.

It has been asserted that Sir Robert Peel also has brought his great mind to the conclusion that the people ought to feed themselves; and not only has the statement not been contradicted, but it has been confirmed by his resignation. In what way these changes of opinion have been brought about seems to me to be a matter of indifference to us. It may have been by the bad potatoes or the good arguments. But whatever the cause the fact is that the changes have taken place, and it is the business of those who assemble here and of the people at large to turn the circumstance to the best account.

Now this apparently is a great difficulty. But if these public men are true to you, and if you are true to yourselves, there cannot really be much difficulty as to the course that should be pursued.

If Lord John Russell is thoroughly convinced that the Corn Laws ought to be abolished, and has been summoned to the councils of Her Majesty, and has been given a commission to form a Government—let him declare that he will undertake that commission, and that he will form that Government upon the principle of abolishing the Corn Laws. If Sir Robert Peel is properly represented, and if he has not had the folly to resign his office without just cause, if he is now honestly convinced that the Corn Laws ought to be abolished—let him come forward and frankly support Lord John Russell.

If we are satisfied that these two men and the two parties they lead are really earnest in the purpose of getting rid of this giant grievance, it becomes the duty, as it is the interest, of the Anti-Corn-Law League, to direct all its energy, activity, and intelligence to the support of Lord John Russell and Sir Robert Peel. I believe that if we can find in the total abolition of the Corn Laws a common ground for these three parties to stand upon, the month of February will not pass over without our relieving the Statute Book of one of the foulest blots that ever disgraced it.

But if I might be allowed to offer one word of warning, it would be, that if the people of this country depend upon anything, if they rely upon any person or persons with more confidence and reliance than they do upon themselves, they run the greatest risk of being disappointed. We have now got the two great political parties in such a position, that if only we do justice to ourselves and to the cause, I believe that nothing can prevent our success. The time, the moment has come (and it will be but a short one) when all men are required to make every effort and every sacrifice in order to convey to their rulers the unmistakable and distinct determination of this country no longer to submit to the iniquitous Tax upon Food.

I beg to apologize to you for having thus intruded my own views on your notice. I was not announced to do so this evening, and I will not stand another instant in the way of your enjoyment of that eloquence for which you were specially invited to attend this evening. I beg leave to call upon Richard Cobden.

XXVI.

COVENT GARDEN THEATRE, January 17, 1846.

Lord J. Russell, with the full assurance of every aid and support that in his private capacity Sir R. Peel could give him to effect a settlement of the question of the Corn Laws, tried to form an Administration but failed to do so because Lord Grey refused a place in a Cabinet of which Lord Palmerston would be the Secretary for Foreign Affairs. Consequently Sir R. Peel on December 20 resumed office, and reconstituted his Cabinet on the same lines as the previous one, all his old colleagues taking office with him again excepting Lord Wharncliffe, who died it was said from the tension of the crisis, and Lord Stanley, who retired and was succeeded by Mr. Gladstone.

We have come to that stage in the progress of our cause at which every one is anxious to know what prospect there is of our immediate success, and what is going to be done next.

The last time that we met in this theatre our spirits were much elated at the state of affairs owing to the position of political parties. Several events of the highest importance have occurred since then. These have been estimated in various ways by politicians of different parties. But when we assemble in this theatre we profess to have nothing to do with party politics; and therefore we have now simply to consider these events as they bear upon our cause.

I venture to express an opinion that there is nothing in recent events at all calculated to discourage the hopes that we entertained on the occasion of our last meeting. The moral of all that has taken place since that time seems to be that the cause of Free Trade is in the ascendant, and that our struggle is rapidly approaching a successful issue.

At the time of our last meeting, Lord John Russell had received the commission of the Crown to form a Government, after having placed on record his perfect accordance with ourselves. We have had the satisfaction to learn since then that the colleagues whom he proposed to call to his assistance were entirely agreed in opinion with himself, and consequently with us. And we have further reason to believe that if he had succeeded in forming a Government, he would have received the cordial support of Sir Robert Peel and such friends as he could influence.

We have also the satisfaction of knowing that he did not fail to complete his arrangements for forming a Government from any cause whatever connected with any difference of opinion upon our question. And though it would have given the personal friends of Lord John Russell great satisfaction to have seen him filling the post to which he was called—a post that I believe he would have filled worthily, and one that, notwithstanding what has been suggested by our friend 'Punch,' he, I think, would have had strength to maintain—the force that will now be presented in favour of Free Trade in the House of Commons is, in my judgment, greater than it would have been under any other circumstances.

Sir Robert Peel has returned to power; his dissentient colleagues have apparently returned to reason, and nothing has transpired to make us believe that any of them have reverted to their former opinions in favour of the Corn Laws; and though in these days it is certainly hazardous to reckon on the course of any public man, yet I cannot believe that Sir Robert Peel has resumed office for the purpose of convulsing the country with disappointment, and drawing upon himself universal mistrust.

If his will is not wanting, he is now in a position to advance Free Trade far more successfully than he could before. Recalled to power as a matter of necessity, he is at once relieved from all former party considerations. He has at the present moment not only all the patronage of Government at command, but he has also the goodwill of the Opposition who now for the first time are united, and determined to extend to him earnest, cordial, and zealous support if his measure is honest and complete, and equally determined, if he should falter or fail, to resort to any and every means by which they could procure a measure of justice to the people.

Under these circumstances I feel sanguine of success. I cannot think that the year will pass without some satisfactory settlement of this question. I have almost faith in our rulers that they will not disregard the voice of common sense now so unequivocally expressed in the country. The question must be settled without delay: whatever the Government may wish to do the time for trifling with it is past. There has always been a reality in our cause that time and circumstances were sure to aid; and of late everything has combined to show the true character of the enactment we oppose until at last it stands before the country stamped with the odium of being a law restricting the food, the work, and the trade of the people. Ministers it seems will not now undertake the administration of the country if they are to be held responsible for the continuance of the Corn Laws.

It was only the other day that we learned from a letter which Mr. Gladstone wrote to his constituents that the party who are now pledging themselves in every quarter of the country not to surrender one atom of the Corn Laws, have been tested as to whether they will undertake the administration of the Government conditional on the continuance of the Corn Laws. From that letter it seems that they have shrunk from such a task. They wish the Laws to be supported, in order that they may enjoy all the advantages of them when they can be maintained quietly, and to escape all the risk the instant there is any danger in continuing them.

If we look at their speeches, we shall see that it has been from no modesty or diffidence on their part that they have refused to form a Government—if the offer to do so was made to them; for in perusing their addresses to each other on the subject, they seem in the first place to claim superior integrity, a majority in both Houses of the Legislature, and seven-ninths of the population on their side. Now it is difficult to conceive—if they believe what they say, if they have this amount of public spirit, if they are convinced that the Corn Laws are absolutely necessary—why they would not undertake to form a Government. However, they shrank from this duty, it seems, and they content themselves now with exhausting the language of vehement abuse against all those who are opposed to them and in authority over them.

To this point it is well to draw the special attention of the country. We have arrived at that period in the history of Monopoly when no man will undertake and the strongest Ministry refuse to retain the administration of the government of England if it is to entail the responsibility of simultaneously supporting the Corn Laws. This is the issue of that enactment after thirty years' experience: thirty years' experience of a measure to impede the supply of food to twenty-eight millions of people. And yet we are told that we are not safe; that we are not yet out of danger; that the party who are determining to uphold every part, every iota of these Laws are still so formidable that they may yet defeat any Minister who undertakes to form an Administration for the purpose of abolishing them.

I myself cannot conceive that there can be much danger when I consider who the party consists of; how they are managing the defence of their system; and the movement now taking place in various directions throughout the country against them. We are told that they are about to follow closely in the steps of the League; that they are going to raise a large sum of money for the purpose of meeting it in everything it may attempt; that if the League should raise a quarter of a million, they will raise half a million. And we are also informed that in the opinion of Mr. Newdegate, the Member for Warwickshire, should it come to a display of physical force, they will bring against the people who are for Free Trade —for unrestricted commerce in this country, a force of which at the present moment we have not the least idea. Something of this kind was I think stated two years ago, when these Protection Societies first appeared; and though it is very seldom safe to prophesy, I remember that, knowing what their cause was and who their advocates were, I did venture to predict in this place that they would speedily disagree and soon after disappear.

It would seem that I was not very much out in my calculation; for I observe that Mr. Miles, at a meeting on Monday, said that he was glad to see his friends again because he had been asked in the summer what had become of the Central Protection Society. I heard the question asked: a member of the Society answered it, and said that they were doing nothing. He was then asked what the local Societies were about, and he replied that they were under the direction of the Central Society.

As to their disagreement, we have already had specimens of that. Even the Dukes cannot agree: if the Duke of Norfolk speaks, the Duke of Richmond is ready to sink into the earth; and this I take to be very much the feeling of the whole peerage at some of the Duke of Richmond's proceedings. If one had to judge between the two, the Duke of Norfolk's nostrum would probably be entitled to greater indulgence as being more innocent than the Duke of Richmond's. The Duke of Norfolk at this crisis only prescribes to the labourers to burn their own insides;[1] the Duke of Richmond recommends them to burn the 'Times' newspaper; and his logic amounts to this: when they differ in opinion with other persons, they should resort to fire for the suppression of their opponents' views. A lesson not very likely to be forgotten, I think, by the labourers privileged to receive his Grace's instructions; and a hint of which, perhaps, they had heard something before.

I have done what, probably, few persons besides have done—I have looked through the speeches of these friends of Protection; and it seems to me that if a moiety of their half-million is to be devoted to the circulation of their speeches, the League ought to claim that as a contribution to their fund. I can conceive nothing more advantageous to our cause than the circulation, gratis, of these speeches. I find that one-half, at least, contains a complete admission of our case and of the charges we bring against the Protectionists.

Our charges against the Protection Party are that they maintain Laws by which food is made difficult of access to the poor; that they diminish its quantity; in fine, that they make dear and scarce a necessary that otherwise would be cheap and abundant. These speeches prove exactly what we have been labouring

[1] An allusion to the Duke of Norfolk's famous 'curry-powder charm.'

to show. They say: 'If the Corn Laws are repealed, see how low the price of food would fall; and if the trade were free, see in what abundance that food would enter the country.'

Nice calculations, moreover, are made by them to show what much more wholesome and nutritious food might be introduced than can be now obtained, if the Corn Laws were repealed; but they pretend to an accuracy, for which there is not the slightest ground, as to the great fall in prices the repeal of the Corn Laws would necessarily entail.

Mr. Miles, at the meeting of the day before yesterday, quoted a statement which he considered to be authentic, to show what a prosperous trade between this country and America would follow Repeal. One really can hardly believe that people exist who are using such statements not as the rest of mankind would—as the very strongest reason for the adoption of the measure by which plenty might be brought about—but as an argument conclusive against any such measure, and of force only in support of the Laws positively and actively opposed to it.

What a noble thing for the gentry of this country to be banded together for the great and lofty purpose of preventing abundance—preventing a sufficiency of wholesome food from coming into the country for the sustenance of the people! What a glorious attitude to assume in face of the Sovereign, who has just expressed her grief at the distress of her people and given a ready assurance of her immediate assent to any measure of relief, in answer to an address setting forth that one great article of the subsistence of her people has failed this year! What an exalted position not only to be standing between the benevolence and good will of the Sovereign and the sufferings of the people, but between the abundance that God has provided on the earth for all His creatures, and the necessities of that portion of them dwelling on this island!

Yes! there are gentlemen of England now pledging each other, marshalling themselves together, subscribing their half-million of money, and vowing that they will succeed. All for what? Not to prevent the invasion of an enemy; not to avert misfortune coming upon the kingdom; but simply and solely to arrest the progress of the attempt to bring health and comfort to the people, by bringing food, of which there is now a deficiency, into the country! What a proud position for the aristocracy of a nation whose glory and power have been talked of and vaunted throughout the world! Declaring themselves mere dealers in fish, flesh, and bread! invoking each other in the name of their order to stand firm to the prices they fixed in 1841; and cheered on to perseverance in their strange duty by the lines of the poet who celebrated their constancy! How little idea that poet had when he was immortalizing their constancy of old, to what base use his verse would be applied. By the wildest stretch of his imaginative power he could never have supposed that the British aristocracy would in 1846 prove their constancy to nothing but a Sliding Scale and scarcity! Constancy in making food difficult of attainment to the poor, till at last the labourer proclaims to the country that for forty successive years he has never once tasted meat; that he knows it by sight, but is ignorant of its taste for he has no money to buy it with!

This declaration has been made by one of those unfortunate peasants at Goatacre, and it has not been disputed. And his condition is at this moment the condition of numbers in all parts of the land where the great lords and gentry are arraying themselves for the purpose of preventing the importation of food into the country, that would enable these labourers to *taste* what they have only *seen* these forty years past. Let them only be constant in this cause, and perhaps they may live to see another set of peasants arise, who will talk of bread as these talk of meat: they will know a loaf by *sight*, but the price will place it beyond their reach for the *taste*.

I have a right to say that this is the effect of the course they pursue, because they never condescend to allude to any of the great considerations that we have so often brought under their notice: the effect of a scarcity of food in producing poverty among the people, the means it affords for tyranny, the ills affecting human life among the labouring classes that ensue from it—all these are unheeded by them. They have never disputed that the population of this country is increasing annually at an enormous rate. They never pretend that any provision is made to meet the wants of that population; nor do they pretend that any provision is made to prevent those periods of deficiency that have sent thousands and tens of thousands to the streets, to the unions, to the gaols, and to the grave, simply through poverty.

There is not one word mentioned at the Protection meetings that would not equally apply if the famine that most men expected only three months since had occurred, and that most men yet fear may occur in the middle of this year. On the simple claim to uphold the principle of Protection, Monopolists, without looking to the consequences, contend that they are entitled to make food dear. And if we were now in the midst of a famine, there is not the slightest reason why they should not hold exactly the same language that they do under our present circumstances.

Wherever the potato has failed from disease in other countries (and the disease was known in other places before it arrived here), the failure of the crop has always been greater in the second year than it was in the first, and still greater in the third year than it was in the second. Is it, then, anything but wisdom to provide against a recurrence of this misfortune? And yet to what do these gentlemen pledge themselves all over the country? That not one iota of their Protection shall be abated; that there shall not be any diminution of the obstructions now imposed to the introduction of food. 'No,' they say, 'sufficient for the day is the evil thereof. We have had these famines before, and when they do occur we accept them as visitations of Heaven; we offer up prayers in the churches that they may cease, and we request the archbishops to urge on their Christian flocks to be liberal in their charity to provide for the people.' These things have been, and, as far as the humanity or prudence of Monopolists is concerned, they will be again; and if any Minister ventures to provide against the responsibility of such occurrences he is charged with cowardice and treachery.

As far as I can collect from their addresses, they are now charging the present Minister with cowardice for not having boldly faced famine. He ought not to have changed his opinion on the subject of this Anti-Food Law because of the apprehension of famine. He ought to have met such apprehension like a man: he ought not to have made any provision for it. There is only one inference to be drawn from their speeches: the charge of cowardice and treachery. Treachery, treason to whom? Not treason to the State, not treason to the poor; not treachery to the great sources of our power in this country. No, but treason and treachery to the proprietors of the soil.

In an apology that was made for the great landowners yesterday in the 'Morning Chronicle' (I question whether it was by a very friendly hand), the writer is extremely anxious that we should be most careful in our allusions to them; that we should deal tenderly with them: because, he said, from the cradle to the grave these persons are placed under circumstances so unfavourable to the development of their minds, to the knowledge of men and to the management of their own affairs, that they may be well excused if they commit grave blunders in the management of the affairs of the country. A great consolation to those who live under their rule, and have to suffer the effects of their misgovernment! But if this is really their condition, I think that we could teach them to be a little more modest in their mode of dealing with other men.

They charge the present Minister with treachery; they say that they gave him his present position; they seem to imply that he wears their livery still, and that he has no business to engage in another service. Now this claim of theirs to name the Ministry of the country seems to me something very like an insult to the whole nation. How have they acquired such power? They will say through the county representatives: they say that they have the counties in their hands. How have they got them in their hands? Lord Stanley has enlightened us on this point. He says that a few families meet previously to the return of a Member, and then decide which of their relatives or retainers shall represent the county. I do not think that it is very wonderful under these circumstances that we see in that quarter so much anger at what has been recommended by the League: namely, that the friends of Free Trade should seek to acquire portions of landed property in the counties in order to increase their power in the representation of the country. The land-owners call this 'unconstitutional' and 'uncalled-for innovation.'

It appears to me that if one ground can be urged stronger than another, for every friend of Free Trade, for every advocate of liberty, for every hater of tyranny and oppression, to come forward and invest his property in this legitimate manner, it is the violent assumption on the part of the landed proprietors of their right to name, in the first place, the Members for the counties, and next the Ministers of the State.

I remember that soon after the meeting of Parliament after the general election, this arrogant pretension was advanced with respect to the present Minister by some of these magnates, who said that they had made him and they would unmake him, if he did not do their bidding; that they had given him his place; and that they had bound him by a bargain to attend exclusively to their interests. Well, I must say, for the credit of the people who are yet disposed to expect some good from the administration of the Prime Minister, believing that he understands the interests of the country and that he has shown some inclination to support them—I must say that he did at the time repudiate with proper spirit any such obligation to the aristocracy, or any such inclination to do their will. And I will here quote his words to show that he then entered into an obligation not to serve any section of the community, but to do his duty by the nation at large. When some independent Member called upon him to say whether a statement made in some place to the effect that he, the Prime Minister, had bound himself in this manner to them to do the bidding of a selfish minority were founded on fact, he replied:—

It is my intention to act upon a sense of public duty; to

propose those measures alone that my conviction of what is requisite for the public makes me think desirable. It is right that there should be an understanding as to this. What can be my inducement to take office and to make the sacrifices the acceptance of it enjoins? I want to serve my country; I want to acquire an honourable fame. Should I go through the labour that is daily imposed upon me if I could not claim for myself the liberty of promoting those measures that I believe to be conducive to the public weal? I will claim that liberty and propose those measures; and I assure this House, and the country, that no consideration of political support will induce me to fill such an office as that which I fill by a servile tenure, and nothing would compel me to be the instrument of carrying other men's opinions into effect. It is not valuable from patronage or distinction; it is only worthy of my holding for an hour on account of the opportunity it gives me of serving my country; and the moment I feel convinced that the power of doing that is denied me, I tell every man in the country that he has conferred no obligation on me; but free as the wind, I reserve to myself the power of retiring from the discharge of those duties that could no longer be filled with satisfaction to myself or advantage to my country.

[A gentleman in the boxes here called for 'Three cheers for Peel!' Several voices replied: 'Wait till the next meeting.'] I think that precaution is very proper. I have referred to those sentiments, which I myself heard uttered by Sir Robert Peel, to show that the landed aristocracy have no claim on him; that he is not bound to them, but is bound to do his duty by the community at large. He has pledged himself to do so. I believe that now he is in a position, and that he has the power to do so; and I only refer to it to justify the expectation of many liberal-minded men that he means to, and will perform his duty to the public.

One has had experience enough of public men in general to have little faith in any of them in particular;

but when interest and duty are obviously combined one is led to expect that a man will not shrink from doing that which he has promised and which he is interested in doing. The Protectionist gentlemen, who during the last four years have been making such a noise in the country, have been ready to support the Minister in spite of his recent declarations, and notwithstanding that he has pursued a course that according to their present assertions is completely opposed to their views. They have acted as supporters of the Government, and I have no doubt that, as such, they have not refused the patronage that a Government is able to bestow on its friends; consequently they come rather late with the charge that they are taken by surprise—which charge they intend to make the ground of opposing any measure that may be proposed to meet the wants of the country.

These gentlemen are, in my opinion, out of court in their present position. There are only two grounds on which they could have justly claimed the continuance of their Monopoly with any grace: they ought either to have extended Protection to every other interest, or else they ought not to have allowed it to be withdrawn from any. They ought to have been able to point to the results of their Protection as justifying their being made an exception to the rest. Whereas they have, in fact, been actively carrying out the policy of Free Trade and applying the principle of it to every interest but their own. One after another all these interests have been attacked: Protection has, indeed, been removed altogether from many; the weakest and most defenceless have been attacked without the least scruple, and the landlords have not objected to the policy. They have been constantly told that their turn must come next; they have been reminded that the same hand that attacked the other interests would assail them; and they ought to have been prepared for it. Other persons have alleged word for word what they now state in defence of their own interests: the cause of the poor in their employ, and the investment of their capital on the faith that they would not be disturbed. There are whole towns, great districts, and individual properties that have been most injuriously affected by the new railroads sanctioned by Act of Parliament; and the parties so injured by them claimed from Parliament the same Protection against loss that landed proprietors are now claiming. They prayed and petitioned against the improvements that were about to be made; but the landed proprietors and Protectionists always disregarded their claims with the utmost philosophy and coolness, and in all such cases invariably sanctioned the principle of competition.

The thousands of the working classes of this country who are constantly thrown out of employment by the introduction of machinery, or some improvement superseding their labour, have also come to Parliament and prayed for some Protection against the use of machinery to keep them in employment. In return they have been met with the soundest views of political economy, and told how erroneous their claims were; and nothing that they ever prayed for was granted. Again and again they have been sent away with no other comfort than the axiom that particular interests must yield to public good.

People, then, may well ask why these proprietors of the soil whose possessions nobody interferes with, whom everybody is willing to leave in the fullest enjoyment of their ease and wealth, who by no sacrifice of their own have acquired their fortunes, are to be protected and not exposed to the principle of competition when that principle is proved to be of advantage to the whole community?

Are the landed proprietors able to point to any result of this Protective System that can justify an exemption in their favour? Will they take us to the rural districts to justify the continuance of their System? Will they point to the county of Wilts to convince us of the comfort and the happiness that it brings to the labourers they employ?

We have had allusions this evening to the meeting that was held at a village in Wiltshire: will they take us there by *moonlight* to see the flourishing condition of the peasantry? But what the unfortunate people in that village proclaimed, is no novelty to any person who has studied their case. I venture to say that for twenty-three years out of the thirty during which Protection to the landed proprietors has existed, you will find public documents recording precisely the same condition of the labouring classes in the agricultural districts as that which was proclaimed by the peasants at Goatacre.

There was an Inquiry in the House of Commons

in 1824 into the wages of the labourers; and in the pages of the Report of that Committee will be found word for word what was asserted on this occasion by the peasants: that they could not be in a worse condition; that come what might, let there be any change, it would be for their improvement. Witnesses in 1824 stated that it was simply owing to the smallness of the remuneration they received that they were hurried into the commission of crimes; and that they were as degraded and demoralized as any people to be found on the face of the earth. Why, it is conformable with every inquiry that has been made into the agricultural districts, that these wretched people are almost at the bottom of the scale of society.

A few years ago the Commissioners of the Crown drew up a scale, marking the condition of the different classes in this country; and the agricultural labourers were literally placed at the bottom, lower even than the felon or the pauper. There is, in fact, no condition more depressed than that of the agricultural labourer. I ask then whether, with this accumulated evidence which is notorious, it is not testing the temper of the country rather too highly to say that the Protective Laws and Protection to agriculture exist for the benefit of the unfortunate agricultural population?

It was I think about twelve years since that a Member for Bedford, a Conservative in politics, made personal inquiry of these labourers themselves, then confined in great numbers in the gaols of the agricultural counties. They had been charged with many offences, at a time when there were great riots and much incendiarism ; and this gentleman, who from his politics was not disposed to lay too much stress upon such things, declared that he had collected from these miserable people in gaol that they had been tempted and led into the offences of which they were paying the penalty simply through the low rate of wages they received from their employers. How is it possible to bring such people as evidence in favour of the Protective System ? Those poor fellows at the village meeting in Wiltshire, at once refuted the two leading fallacies upon which the Protectionists have been trading for years past. Monopolists say: 'If food is dear, wages are high ; if you have a Free Trade in food, land will go out of cultivation.' But what do the labourers themselves say ? 'From forty years' experience, we tell you that whenever the price of food rises, the wages of labourers do not rise in proportion. As for the land going out of cultivation, we would undertake to prevent that. There is no fear for the land ; that won't go to waste. Give it up to us, and we will cultivate it.'

Now if the land-owners cannot point to these unhappy people as any proof in favour of their System, how can they answer for the manner in which they have fulfilled the condition of their great Monopoly ? Have they adequately supplied the people with food ? Is it not notorious that every four or five years we have deficiencies deranging the whole business of the country ? We are constantly exposed to periodical famines ; and what do the Protectionists say when confronted with them ? They cannot deny the fact; they only say that the country *could* produce enough to support the whole people. Our answer then is: 'Why do you not produce what is sufficient ?' They bring scientific men down to their agricultural meetings to tell the farmer what he could, should, would, or might do if he adopted this or that improvement. And the invariable answer to all these admirable lectures by the only people who have the means or the intelligence to make the improvements is : 'All that you say is very true; but we do not hold the land under circumstances that would enable us to make these improvements. We want greater security of tenure before we can invest our capital in your land.'

What said Lord Stanley[1] only a year since, speaking at an agricultural meeting ? He said: 'Great improvements are required in the agriculture of this country ; but no man has a right to expect that his tenant will improve his land unless he gives him the security of a lease ; and the value of that lease will vary with the duration of its term.'

Now I ask whether there is the slightest prospect of leases being more generally given than they have been hitherto ? Look at the meeting of the Protection Society held last Monday : what is it they say ? 'We must increase our influence in the counties in order to meet the efforts of the League.' Do you believe then that they would in reality increase that influence by giving their tenants leases and rendering

[1] The late Lord Derby.

them independent? The Tenantry-at-will System has been very much increased of late, simply for the purpose of acquiring influence in these counties. They want now more and more influence; and therefore there is less and less prospect of agricultural improvement. This is the reason why they will never give us a Committee of Inquiry in the House of Commons. Mr. Cobden has asked them for it again and again, in order to learn what good these Corn Laws do to the farmer, but they have never heeded him. They will not grant a Committee of Inquiry, because they know that the farmers would come forward on any such occasion and give evidence that would be very prejudicial to their cause. The farmers, as well as the labourers, have their Goatacre meetings, where they talk of things in a manner widely different from the way in which they are discussed at their Parliamentary Protection Meetings. They have their grievances; and they are not alarmed at the consequences of Free Trade in the way that the landlords and their dependents are.

I happened recently to communicate with one of the most respectable land agents in this country, a man who acts for twelve or fifteen different landowners in the country, all of them peers of the realm. I asked him the other day whether he shared in the fears respecting the results of Free Trade professed by the landed interest? He told me that so far from it, no one among the whole agricultural party could be found a more staunch and earnest advocate for Free Trade than he was, or more perfectly convinced of the gross delusion of the statement that Free Trade would be injurious to agriculturists. I asked him in what way he thought Free Trade would benefit the agriculturist? He replied that the first benefits to ensue from it would be a better cultivation of the land, a greater employment of labour, and a clearer perception of the abuses connected with the ownership of land. I next asked him whether the farmers placed much confidence in the statements made against Free Trade, and whether he believed they would sustain much loss by the repeal of the Corn Laws? He said that he had recently been letting some farms belonging to a nobleman, and that he had asked every one of the tenants whether they would wish to have a clause inserted in the lease providing that if the Corn Laws were repealed they should have their leases cancelled. He proposed that each party, landlord and tenant, should six months after the Corn Laws were repealed—if they were—have the option of cancelling the lease. All these tenants took time to consider the proposition; but every one of them came back after reflection, and refused to have the clause inserted. There was so much doubt among themselves, they said, as to whether the repeal of the Corn Laws would be beneficial, or prejudicial, as some people said, that they would not run the risk of the landlord cancelling the lease.

Nevertheless, it is still maintained by these Protectionist gentlemen that Free Trade would bring utter ruin to the tenant farmer. And we, therefore, repeat that there is not the least ground for such a statement.

I have just quoted the opinion of a well-known land agent, a man of unquestionable respectability, who would willingly come to the Bar of the House of Commons and give evidence to the same effect before the assembled Parliament if he were invited to do so ; and no one can deny the authority that such experience and character as his would give to his word. But now I will call your attention to what was said with respect to the evil or advantage likely to result from the adoption of this system of Free Trade in the presence of 20,000 people about three weeks ago by the President of an agricultural society, who is also High Sheriff of the county of York, and much esteemed by all his class and the whole county in which he dwells. I will read a passage from his speech with respect to the effects of the adoption of Free Trade anticipated by our agriculturist. He said :—

What the effects of these Corn Laws have been upon trade and manufactures, I leave to others who have felt them, I fear too bitterly; but as to the influence which these laws have had on agriculture, I, as a farmer, as a country squire, and as the president of an Agricultural Society, may be supposed to be able to form some opinion ; and I do not think it fair to take as a criterion such a district as that I live in—a district bordering upon a manufacturing one ; and one, too, in which any blow struck at trade is always felt immediately and acutely. But I have lived for two years in a purely agricultural county in the south of England ; and I have observed the results of Protection there ; I have seen there the Protected labourer, I have seen what is his condition. I have seen Protected land, I know what is its condition. I declare to you that I never saw labourers or land in a more wretched or destitute plight than they are in Devonshire, part of Gloucestershire, the Isle of Wight, much of Dorsetshire, and some of Somersetshire.

This, I think, is a very important testimony in favour of the justice of the cause that we are advocating with so much earnestness. And as it is no light thing to be charged with reckless proceedings in favour of the views we entertain without any regard to the interests and well-being of any large section of our fellow-subjects, we are bound in our own defence to show what would be the real effect upon the interests that are supposed to be peculiarly concerned in the change we call for. And when we find persons who possess the greatest means of information, whose interests are deeply involved in the change, and who tender us their opinions as to the likely result, I think we do right in considering them. And I know nothing that is calculated to give us more confidence than the opinions expressed by such persons, unless it be the speeches delivered at some of the Protection meetings; for the Protectionists cannot agree among themselves upon their own question.

There was a great meeting in Hertfordshire the other day, at which Lord Salisbury[1] was present, and at which he made a violent speech in favour of Protection. He said that he would not bate a tittle of Protection; that they had not near enough of it, and that nothing would induce him to surrender any portion of that which was now possessed. At that

[1] The late Lord Salisbury.

same meeting Lord Essex was also present, and he said that he could not go that length; that there were a great number of protected things—things I presume that he does not grow himself—that ought to be allowed to come into this country duty free. He alluded to all the inferior grains that are now protected, and declared that it would be an enormous advantage if we were to let them in without paying duty.

For thirty years people have been upholding the System of Protection, and it has taken them all that time to find out this, which they say would be a great boon to agriculture! They allege that if all the inferior grains were to come into this country free, it would be an enormous advantage to those who have to feed their cattle. Thus Lord Essex, who does not oppose the duty on wheat, says that duties on inferior grains are a positive evil to the agriculturists; and that you could not confer a greater boon upon agriculture than to withdraw all Protection from the food for cattle.

Then, with respect to the peculiar burdens, I defy any person to read the speeches of the Protectionists and find two of them agreed upon the matter. They have been called upon again and again to bring in their bill on that account and let us see the amount of it, in order that we may judge whether we can settle it with them; but they have never done so; they never will allow any inquiry to be made into the matter, because they believe that the examination would go farther than they wish, and extend to exemptions as well as burdens—and they have a strong suspicion that the exemptions preponderate.

Looking at all these inconsistencies, and marking the experience that we have had of the mischief of the Corn Laws; looking at the weakness of the defence of the Protective System afforded by the Monopolists, and the success that has attended Free Trade as far as it has gone, how can a Minister, who is convinced of the dangers and mischiefs of the Corn Laws, give any weight to the authority of such opponents? The men who take the lead at Protection Meetings are eternally predicting woe of all that is conceded to general interests. They are always supposing that what is given to the public is taken from them; that the last abuse that has been abandoned is the thing most essential to the greatness of the country; and they have been proved to be wrong in almost every prediction they have uttered. And, though there may be among them some of Liberal politics, yet even these have not been less wrong in their views on this subject. Upon the passing of every measure of commercial reform during the last four years they predicted some dire calamity to the country. And what is now the ground that they assume against any further change? It is that the country is in a state of unparalleled prosperity; and that therefore it would be very unwise and dangerous in them to make any further reform.

Look at all these opinions uttered during the last four years, and then look at all the changes in the Custom Duties that have been effected: each of these was to ruin the country—ruin and misfortune were their inevitable result! And now again they come forward and cry out: 'Don't touch corn, don't touch our Protected Counties! They are more prosperous than they have ever been. Leave well alone. It is impossible to do better.'

I cannot conceive that this party will influence any Minister, from any disinterestedness manifested by them in the vindication of their System. But it is of no use disguising from you the truth, that they can, as the Legislature is at present constituted, obtain a numerical advantage over any measure that may be proposed if they assume it to be adverse to their interests; and therefore I should wish you to be prepared for such an event. I believe that a great struggle will take place; and that the more full and satisfactory, the more thorough the measure is, the greater will be the effort made to defeat it. I beg you, then, to be forewarned; and I earnestly hope that, both in justice to your own interests and for the good of this country, you will leave nothing undone to prevent yourselves being defeated by as selfish and unpatriotic a party as ever arrayed itself against a people.

XXVII.

HOUSE OF COMMONS, February 26, 1846.

On January 19, 1846, the Queen opened Parliament in person, and herself read the Speech from the Throne, which lamented the failure of the potato crop in Ireland, and indicated a Free Trade policy to cope with the deficiency of food that would consequently have to be met. In moving the Address, Lord F. Egerton stated that his opinions on the Corn Laws had undergone a considerable change, and Mr. Beckett Denison seconding it said that he had been 'driven' by experience to alter his. Sir R. Peel then rose to make his explanation. On the question of the Corn Laws his policy was completely changed; and 'very deliberately adopting the speeches of Mr. Villiers as his model,'[1] he proceeded with great ability to show that all the grounds on which Protection to native industry was advocated had been proved to be wholly untenable. On Jan. 27 he moved, that the House should resolve itself into a Committee of the whol House on the Customs and Corn Importation Act, and introduced his measure to a crowded House. With regard to Corn he proposed to substitute for the existing Sliding Scale, a maximum duty of 10*s.* when wheat was at 48*s.* a quarter, falling 1*s.* with every shilling of rise in price, till the price reached 53*s.*, when the minimum duty of 4*s.* a quarter should be attained, the immediate effect of which would be to reduce the duty at the then price of wheat from 16*s.* to 4*s.*; this modified scale should last for three years, and cease, by a positive enactment, on Feb. 1, 1849, when the ports should be entirely thrown open. The debate on the measure was postponed till Feb. 9, and extended from then over twelve nights, when a vote in favour of the Government was carried by a majority of 97 in a House of 577. Mr. Villiers spoke on Feb. 26, and his speech closed the eleventh night's debate. The debate when the House went into Committee lasted four nights more, and on the third reading the Bill was carried on May 16, at four in the morning, by a majority of 98 in a House of 556. During this prolonged discussion every worn-out argument against Repeal was renewed, and every exploded fallacy in support of Protection was revived, to block the course of a measure imperfect only because, though going a long way towards it, it fell a little short of full justice to the people; whilst at the same time no species of vituperation and personal invective was spared those who introduced it and those who supported it. But it was all in vain; rain and dire famine had both come to the help of a just cause; and

[1] Prentice, *History of the Anti-Corn-Law League.*

on June 26, 1846, the Ministerial measure was passed, and the repeal of the Corn Laws was virtually enacted, for which Mr. Villiers had ceaselessly striven since March 15, 1838.

I HAVE some scruple in rising after the Hon. Gentleman who has just sat down, from observing the order in which Members who have risen to address the House have been selected. I believe that the Hon. Gentleman and myself are at present agreed, for he comes recently from the hustings where, stating both his own views and those of the farmers of Dorsetshire, he declared in favour of the immediate repeal of the Corn Laws. ['No, no!'] Then the Hon. Gentleman has been entirely misreported; for there is not one newspaper that reported his address that did not in the report express sentiments to the effect that if there was to be a change in the Corn Laws, he, the Hon. Member, for one would be in favour of immediate Repeal. The Hon. Gentleman, it appears, now denies that he ever said in the county of Dorset that he was for immediate Repeal.

[Mr. Seymer expressed a wish not to be misunderstood on the point. What he said was that he should oppose to the utmost the measures of Her Majesty's Ministers; but that if he failed in that opposition, he thought, on the whole, that if Repeal was to be carried out, instead of being deferred three years it would be better that it should take place at once.]

I am glad to see that the accuracy of the press is so well supported by the Hon. Gentleman. I am happy to hear his confirmation of the report to which I alluded. ['No!'] Why do you say no, when the

Hon. Gentleman has just said yes? He has said that if the Corn Laws were to be repealed, it would be far better to have them immediately repealed than postponed for three years. I claim him, therefore, as a supporter of the Amendment to this Measure which it is my intention to propose, and if the Hon. Gentleman is really representing the sentiments of the farmers, I believe that he will vote for my Motion.

The Hon. Member has told us that the tenant-farmers are an independent body of men ; but the proof he has given us of it is that most of them go to their landlords to ask how they ought to vote. He stated that a great number of persons whose support he received held lands from landlords of Liberal principles, and that fortunately for him they got leave to vote as they liked.

He has, however, I admit given one proof that the farmers are independent. He says they are generally loyal and well-affected. Now, this is a somewhat more cheering proof that they are not wholly under the influence of their landlords. I believe it to be the case. I believe they are very quiet, good sort of people, and in general too steady to be really influenced by the disloyal and inflammatory language that they may hear from those above them. The complaints of the farmers are not against the State ; they do not quarrel with the Government ; their grievances are nearer home. Those who know them are aware that they have domestic grievances that are never redressed ; the landlords instead of remedying them have been going about and telling the tenants that the Government of the country is endeavouring to injure them: that it is composed of men void of honour, truth, and honesty. The farmers, however, are much too sensible to be led away by interested language of this kind; and in their hearts they are, as the Hon. Gentleman says, for the immediate repeal of the Corn Laws and for the total abolition of a system by which they have been so cruelly deceived.

I think that the Hon. Gentleman's speech went to show us how very much the farmers are under the influence of the landlords with respect to their votes, and that therefore their opinions are not necessarily those of their landlords. I will just refer to a speech that was made before his. It is the most extraordinary address that we have heard lately, and occupied nearly an hour and a half in its delivery. I refer to the speech of the Hon. Member for Rutlandshire,[1] the last newly-elected Protectionist Member in this House. The Hon. Member gets up, and like the chorus in the Greek plays, recapitulates all that has passed: how we come to be where we are, who has done this and who has done the other, arriving in the end at only the same conclusions as those of his party who preceded him in the debate: that if the Corn Laws are abolished England's sun will set for ever. He professes to tell us the result of his election: he says that it indicates the opinion of the public on the question. The fact is it simply indicates what the Hon. Member for Dorsetshire stated—the influence that the landlords in Rutlandshire, as well as in

[1] Mr. G. Finch.

other counties, have over their tenants ; and that they have returned the Hon. Gentleman, as many another has been returned, solely to represent their own views and opinions.

There was, however, just one novelty in the Hon. Gentleman's speech : namely, that it is important to put an end to the trade with America and France because these are countries with which we might possibly go to war. But the wisdom of that argument is so obvious that it hardly needs to be pointed out.

There is, in fact, little or nothing that I can say respecting the question before the House that has not been better said upon this occasion by Her Majesty's Government ; and I believe that no service would be more highly appreciated by the public than that of facilitating in every way the progress of the Ministerial Measure.

Hon. Gentlemen in one corner of the House certainly do not seem to favour such consideration. They have marked out for themselves a course of obstruction, which perhaps they can justify, but if they can, they will be more clever than other people. And I cannot help contrasting the patience with which the House now bears with them, with the treatment that persons who brought forward this question at former times have met with. I have still tingling in my ears those hideous noises, those horrid yells that were raised to stifle all expression of opinion when a minority in this House, the promoters of this discussion in the past, stood up and pleaded for the sufferings of their constituents and asked for an inquiry into the connection of the Corn Laws with all the misery and privation that they witnessed—nay, even a partial inquiry into the terrible distress which they ascribed to the influence of these Laws.

I think that a striking contrast is also presented between what took place on the passing of the Corn Laws in 1815 and what is now occurring with regard to their abolition. The people were exclaiming in the streets against the enactment of those Laws; soldiers surrounded this House; and Members complained that they had not time to present to the House the petitions foretelling all the misery and distress that their operation would entail upon the people. Notwithstanding which the Corn Laws were hurried through with the greatest speed that the forms of this House allow of in the passing of any Bill into law.

But now Hon. Gentlemen opposite are pleading for themselves, for the great and powerful; and therefore the debate is protracted beyond what has ever been known in the discussion of any other question—prolonged more than any other debate within the memory of any Member of this House. For three weeks have we sat here listening to the same statements over and over again. After all the experience that has been gained of the mischief of these Laws; after they have been discredited by every enlightened authority; after all the argument being on one side, and that side supported by every statesman of note; after all this, here we are having the same things repeated over and over again for the space of three weeks. Such is the difference between the way in which the interests of the rich and the rights of the poor are considered in this House.

However, as the time is to be wasted I do not think that I should really be doing justice to the principles I have advocated in this House, I do not think that I should be doing justice to those whom I represent here and those with whom I have co-operated so long throughout the country, if I did not express my joy and satisfaction at the concession that has been made to wisdom and justice in the propositions and avowals of Her Majesty's Ministers.

As the subject has been so much forced upon the consideration of the House during this debate I cannot help forming an opinion as to whether the concession has been made from self-interest and at the sacrifice of honour on the part of Her Majesty's Ministers ; and I declare most solemnly that it seems to me that the concession that has been made is the result of the responsibility that, as Ministers and statesmen, the Government have felt of the danger to the country of a continuance of the Corn Laws.

And I must explicitly state for those who have depended chiefly on fact and argument to persuade their opponents, that it is most gratifying to observe that the abandonment of the Protective System has been conceded by the leaders on both sides under circumstances that place them entirely above the suspicion of any interested views. For I do not believe that when the Noble Lord the Member for London declared in this House at the beginning of last Session, that he considered the system of Protection, as it is called, to be the bane of the interest that was thought to be secured by it—I do not believe that when he proposed, in the course of last summer, that the House should resolve that those duties were injurious to those said to be benefited by them, and when he moreover addressed his letter to his constituents telling them that he was ready to give full effect to his conviction—I do not believe that when he did this he did it from any other than an honest sense of what was due to the community. But I am not so sure that in doing so he was not considered by many to have marred the interests of his party.

With respect to the Right Hon. Baronet at the head of the Government there has been so much discussion about his conduct that it is impossible not to have also formed an opinion upon his position in this matter; and I must avow that I cannot see in what respect he has deserved the reproaches that have been showered upon him by his party. As far as I have collected what has been said in the House, the Right Hon. Baronet does not propose this measure himself without reluctance. He has made the proposition being satisfied himself that it ought to be made; but he did not make it until after he had submitted to others the propriety of their making it to the House. It is no fault of his, as far as I can discover, that he is Minister at this moment, or that he is the proposer of the measure now under consideration.

I think, therefore, that on this ground and certainly on every other the public have no reason to complain that the Right Hon. Baronet should have been the Minister to submit such a measure to the country. And if I collect their opinion on the matter rightly they are pleased that the Right Hon. Baronet has freed himself from the trammels with which every Ministry has hitherto been surrounded on this question, and that he has at last cleared himself of a class domination to which all past Governments have been too long subject, and become truly the Minister of the country.

Up to the present time it has been the boast of the landed proprietors that they have chosen the Minister of the country. And they have always threatened him that if he withdrew his support of the Corn Laws he should cease to hold power. The Right Hon. Baronet, actuated by a due sense of his position, has at last disregarded this dictation, has come forward and proposed a measure in the interest of the whole community, and now throws himself upon that community unreservedly for support. I believe that the public in general rejoice to see him relieved from the shackles of his former party; and I further believe that they will not only carry him through this measure, but through every other in which he will honestly consult the public interest.

I know that this measure is not a complete one; I am aware that in one respect it falls short of what the country wished. I have been asked by the Hon. Member for Newcastle-under-Lyme whether I shall indeed venture to recommend the adoption of it. Why within a few hours after the measure was proposed I put on record my congratulations to my constituents at their being likely to receive so large an instalment of what they had so long been struggling for. If I had not taken that step then I should certainly have been disposed to take it after the opening speech of the Member for Bristol, who proposed the Amendment now before the House, and who said that if this measure were passed, he and his party should regard the System of Protection as abolished for ever. And if I had not taken it even then, I should unquestionably have felt justified in doing so after witnessing the opposition that the Right Hon. Baronet has received from the other side of the House.

The violence of that opposition will be accepted by the country as an apology for many of the deficiencies and much of the incompleteness of the measure. The Right Hon. Baronet will be looked upon as an honest negotiator, and as having obtained the utmost that he could obtain for the people. The public will see from the conduct of Hon. Members opposite what difficulties the Right Hon. Baronet has had to contend with, and what a fierce spirit has been opposed to him on account of his measure.

Gentlemen opposite, however, are not aware, perhaps, of what service they are rendering to the Right Hon. Baronet, and the popularity they are gaining the measure by their conduct in the course they are pursuing. For my part, I believe that the very violence and passion that have been exhibited upon that side of the House against the present Bill have of themselves endeared it to the public; and that every Member who has deserted the Minister—thus exhibiting the sacrifice that he has been obliged to make in order to propose a measure of national advantage—has helped to place him on a pinnacle of public favour that he could not otherwise have attained.

The Hon. Member for Newcastle-under-Lyme asked me whether I should dare to show my face among my constituents after supporting this measure? I would ask the Hon. Member and any of those who countenance him, whether two years hence they will venture into any public meeting and show their faces after supporting an Amendment that I must designate the most daring defiance of public opinion and the general interest that I have ever known. It makes no distinction between the different issues involved in the scheme, acknowledging the expediency of many of them; it says simply and peremptorily to the whole measure: 'We will have none of it, we absolutely abjure the principle of it.'

Many parts of the Right Hon. Baronet's scheme are admitted to be beneficial to agriculture. There are numerous persons, for example, without the means of subsistence who might expect to obtain it if some of the clauses of the Bill were carried: they might hope to exchange food for their industry which they cannot do now; but simply because that article is dealt with from which many here derive their income the whole measure is to be rejected. [Cries of 'No, no!' from the Conservative benches.]

You say, 'No, no!' but are there not many of you who have said that some parts of the scheme are most desirable and expedient and would greatly benefit agriculture? You say, 'No, no;' but I ask if Noble Lords have not at some of their Protection Meetings affirmed that several of the clauses of this measure would be most advantageous to agriculture? [Cries of 'No, no!'] No, no? Why I can point to counties where Protectionists have come forward and said so. [Cries of 'Name, name.'] There was Lord Essex, in Hertfordshire: he said that Indian corn would be a great boon to agriculture. ['Oh, oh!'] Why, he is a Protectionist, and would not let foreign wheat come in! But, nevertheless, he would import foreign food to feed cattle. You, however, will not even allow those who are graziers, and who want to feed their cattle, to have their food from abroad. You may shake your heads, but I say that it is so. My Hon. Friend the Member for Newark, who has just been returned a rank Protectionist, shakes his head; what does he mean? Does he mean that he would let in Indian corn not fearing that it would supersede the use of the nobler grain? He would let it in! Then why vote for this Amendment?

The Bill is opposed *in toto*. The Irish people might starve. ['No, no!'] Oh! the ports may be opened? How long is it since that was agreed to? Since it was discovered that there is but little corn to come in? There was nothing said last autumn about opening the ports. Then Hon. Members protested that there was no scarcity, that there was nothing but the basest cowardice on the part of the Government. 'Afraid,' they said, 'afraid of the people's starving! Was there ever such pusillanimity! Was there ever such turpitude!' I heard this expression myself again the other night.

This is what they said then; but now they have discovered that grain is actually going out of this country from the warehouses to neighbouring States, and that there is such a scarcity on the Continent that there is no more grain to come in, and so they say, and the Hon. Member for Somersetshire says, 'God forbid that we should prevent anything coming in to save the people, if they are starving!' Anything may come in so long as it is sure that prices will not fall. With little prospect of advantage the ports may be open now. ['No, no!'] Well, if that be not so, I do not understand what is meant by 'No, no!' when I assert that obstacles are opposed to all the objects comprehended in this measure.

We have heard in the course of this debate that it is for the purpose of discussing the great principle, the great System of Protection—the policy that has long prevailed in this country, that the debate has been so long continued. Now this is the eleventh day that we have been discussing what is called the System of Protection, and I want to know whether we have yet a clear idea of what that System is, according to the views of Hon. Gentlemen opposite? Or what it is they mean by the principle of Protection? What it implies? In fine, whether anything, so designated, that can be dignified by the name of a policy resting on general principles and involving the general good has been raised in question during this discussion?

It has been asked on this side whether the System of Protection can be universally applied. 'Oh, certainly not,' is the answer. We are told that we cannot regulate the price of labour, whatever we may do with the price of food. It has been admitted that this cannot be done. Can the cases where Protection ought to be applied be defined? Whether or not it is possible to define them, they have not been stated. 'Is Protection,' we ask, 'opposed to the principle of competition?' 'God forbid!' say the Protectionists, 'so far from it, indeed, that Lord Stanley, our leader, defines Protection to be, competition subject to regulation.' But they cannot tell us the principle on which it should be regulated. They say they do not mean to oppose all the advantages proposed in the measure now before the House; but they want to maintain the principle of Protection.

I thought that the Hon. Gentleman the Member for Shrewsbury[1] would have told us something about the principle; that he would have shown us how its application could be made national or general; but instead of enlightening us himself he only complained of others not enlightening him; and lamented that his friends around him had not told him what the principle is.

Now, I ask the House whether candidly this great System which was said to be in question, has not dwindled down into a complaint that the fanciful obstruction to the trade in food for the purpose of making it dear and scarce called the Sliding Scale,

[1] Mr. Disraeli.

is in danger of being removed? Every Member who has spoken upon the subject has hardly been on his legs five minutes after he had risen to vindicate Protection before he commenced to attack the horrors of Free Trade in food, and to depict the advantages of the Sliding Scale, which, it seems, is dignified by the term of Protection to agriculture.

But here, again, have we got any information on the influence of this mode of protecting agriculture? Have we had the slightest intimation as to how the science of agriculture is advanced by this means? How capital can be wisely applied to the cultivation of the soil? Have we heard anything but the wildest assertions as to what prices would be if there were a Free Trade in corn? Not one single syllable has been uttered to show how this impediment to trade tends to advance agriculture. Not one single agricultural authority has been quoted in the whole of this debate to show that the Sliding Scale, or what is termed the System of Protection to agriculture, promotes improvement in that business. Not one single man engaged in agriculture, not an individual who would be an authority in any parish or hundred in this country, has been quoted in this debate to support the assertion that Protection is essential to the proper cultivation of the soil.

Many have been quoted on the other side who have said that agriculture depends upon nothing of the kind, and that there is no advantage in an Act of Parliament to secure high prices. A gentleman deeply interested in the business of farming, whom I could quote, has been in the Gallery of the

House following the debate. He is about the largest occupier of land in the country, and he was examined for three days before the Agricultural Committee of the House when it last sat, having been summoned as a great authority on agricultural matters. Well, he has been during the last few nights in the Gallery of this House; but he has been wishing that he was in the House itself that he might answer the silly things that he has heard from advocates of Protection for agriculture about the necessity of Protection. He occupies 3,800 acres; he holds land in six counties; he is a receiver of rents in eight counties; and he states that he is for the total, and immediate, and unconditional repeal of the Corn Laws as the best thing for the farmer.

When we see men such as he in favour of a repeal of the Corn Laws, it certainly is not wonderful that inquiry was resisted. Hon. Members opposite would never allow a Committee to be granted; they would not hear any one at the Bar of this House on the subject, doubtless because they apprehended such evidence being given as that to which I have just referred. They would never face an inquiry because they have no witnesses to call on their side. ['Oh, oh!'] Oh? why they never name such persons in support of their case. They are surely on their trial before the country now; why not then cite intelligent agriculturists in support of their views of Protection? I repeat what I said before: if the House goes into a Committee of Inquiry, I will call farmers from every county in England; I will call land agents; I will call every class of men who are competent to give evidence from their own experience; and they will all give evidence contrary to the views of Hon. Members opposite. ['Oh, oh!']

Hon. Members say 'Oh!' but there is a club of land agents in this city, and I have reason to believe that a majority of its members are of opinion that a total and immediate repeal of the Corn Laws will do no harm whatever to the landed interest.

One would have thought that the Hon. Member for Essex and the Hon. Member for Suffolk who have both spoken—who seem to plume themselves on being identified with the soil, who would indeed be angry if that were questioned—would have given us some information. I listened with great interest to them because I know how ready they are upon this subject. The Hon. Member for Essex,[1] after cutting some very questionable jokes, in the first part of his speech, ended by reading a chapter from Dr. Arnold about men with one idea.

Then there is the Hon. Member for Suffolk. He was returned specially as the farmers' friend—the man who knew more about the farmer than anybody else. I do not know how many besides did the same, but I listened to what the Hon. Gentleman said, and all that I could gather was, that he was reading the Solicitor-General's speech made some time ago at Cambridge. Essex and Suffolk are two of the chief agricultural counties, and that is all that we can collect from the two Members for those counties.

[1] Sir J. Tyrrell.

Those Hon. Gentlemen will go any length to turn out the Government and to oppose the Right Hon. Baronet's Measure, and yet we cannot obtain a single notion from them as to the way in which the Sliding Scale benefits agriculture.

A very intelligent man in the county of Norfolk—I dare say he is a constituent of the Hon. Member for Norfolk, whom I see in his place—has written a pamphlet in which he says that if the landlords will do what they will not do, and if you will make the tenants do what they are not able to do, that we shall have plenty of corn without Free Trade. He declares that the farmers of the present day must take for their text, for their rule of proceeding, that low prices are quite compatible with good agriculture ; that they must never look to high prices but must produce a great quantity ; and that they must depend for success on low prices and plentiful crops. That doctrine is, I think, totally opposed to that of the Hon. Member for Norfolk, who by the Corn Laws practically tells the farmer: 'Never mind the cultivation, never mind how you manage your farm, because we will get you an Act of Parliament, and we will secure you high prices, which is all you want.'

Then I ask whether on this occasion the House has heard any great results from this system of Protecting as regards agriculture?

The Hon. Member for Norfolk tells us of none. Are we to look to the farmers or labourers as offering examples of its success? During this discussion we have heard scarcely a word about the condition of the farmers; but if we look at the speeches out of this House, we find from them that the farmer who has prospered during the last thirty years is so rare a bird, so strange an animal, that if he were to be seen, he ought to be stuffed and sent to the British Museum. It has actually been said at the agricultural meetings, that the farmer who has thriven under this system is worthy of being preserved in a museum.

Then, as to the labourers, have we had any evidence of their prosperity?

We have been told that the Goatacre meeting was got up by the Anti-Corn Law League. This, however, is not the fact. The League had nothing whatever to do with that meeting. I know that it was simply one of a series of meetings that have been held for some years past by the labourers of Wiltshire, who have always declared the same thing: that they could not be worse off than they are, and that any change among them must be for the better.

But only look at the Reports of every Commission that has been appointed to inquire into the condition of the agricultural labourer, and you will see from 1824 down to 1843—the date of the last Report—just precisely the same account of the agricultural labourers: that their condition is as bad physically as it is possible to be; that they live under circumstances the result of physical suffering, the most unfavourable to their morals and their happiness; and that this is more particularly the case in the most distinctly agricultural counties.

I wonder that the Hon. Member for Suffolk did

not allude to the agricultural labourers of his county, because they are specially mentioned in the Report of the year 1824 and have been constantly referred to since.

In Suffolk there are more of what are called gentlemen farmers and of clergy than in any other county; and yet the people there are described as being as demoralized and as much subject to privation as in any other county in England.

The Hon. Member for Shrewsbury asks if the people have not thriven under this system of Protection? I say decidedly they have not; and to those who say otherwise, I would ask if they have thriven why have we not had an account of their prosperity during the eleven days that this debate has endured? And why do we not learn how it could possibly benefit the poor? In fine, why have we up to this moment been left with no better definition of the results of the system than that which was obtained from Lord Stanley in another place?

Lord Stanley was asked what he meant by this system, and he was obliged to avow it to be a system that raises the rent of land and the price of food; but not the wages of labour. But, as Protectionists, Hon. Members opposite are all proud to acknowledge Lord Stanley as their leader. The principles, therefore, that he has avowed are those for which they have been fighting for eleven days past, and in support of which they are going to a Division: a system that raises the price of food, raises the rent of land, but does nothing to benefit the labourer! A system that accounts for a prosperous farmer being such a rare bird that he ought to be placed in a museum! A system that is the key to the condition of the agricultural labourer—now the bye-word of demoralization and distress!

We are legislating for the public at large, and we are bound to know what the effect of this system is upon the community. The Right Hon. Baronet the Secretary of State for the Home Department tells us that he has ascertained its effect; and he has, in my opinion, most accurately stated it. Hon. Members have heard the result of his official observation; and they have avoided dealing with that point altogether. I am wrong; yes, they have met it in one way; they have railed at the Ministers for treachery; they have charged the Right Hon. Baronet with letting the cat out of the bag. But they have not answered his statement. Up to this moment they remain exposed to the charge of promoting a system that produces terrible distress. The Right Hon. Baronet who has been in office during two periods, one when food was dear through the operation of their Laws, the other when it was cheap through the blessing of Providence, has clearly stated the effects of this system.

He has told the House, as the result of his experience, that at one period in consequence of high prices the poor were in want; that they were wretched; that they were tempted into crime; that the rate of mortality amongst them had increased; and that all these miseries had fallen upon them from the success of Protection. And when, by the bounty of God, the system failed and Protectionists came to this House to complain that the prices were low, and to urge that high prices were necessary to their interest; when they denounced the Minister because they did not get a sufficient price for their produce; he told them that, though the price of food was low, that of labour was high; that crime had diminished; that death, disease, and all the miseries that before befell the people were less; and that, therefore, he had come to the conclusion that the success of the Protective System is calculated to promote the misery of the people, and its failure to ensure to them prosperity and happiness.

Up to the present moment the Right Hon. Baronet has received no answer on this point. No one rose in reply to question these results when he stated them last summer. No! when he said that under a high price of provisions wages did not increase, but that much misery followed, somebody should have risen and said, that low-priced provisions do not promote the comforts of the people, which I have often heard said in this House before. But Hon. Members did not say that; because they knew that it would no longer be believed.

When the Right Hon. Baronet made this speech last May, it was the subject of general remark that the Corn Laws were doomed.

Even in the agricultural districts it was seen that the effect of high prices of food was to produce misery; and that when the prices of food fell the greatest advantage was felt by the agricultural labourers.

Well, now, I say that the charge involved in the

statement of the Right Hon. Baronet is a very serious one and ought to be met before the close of this debate, otherwise the indication of the good fortune of Hon. Members opposite is that of the misery of others. In order to know whether Hon. Members are well off under the Corn Laws and whether they should contend for their maintenance, we must look not only to current prices, but also to the calendars, the statistics of pauperism and crime and the rate of mortality, which equally indicate the high or low price of food.

After eleven days' debate nothing has been done to refute the statement of the Right Hon. Baronet. And the Noble Lord the Member for London remains unanswered too. In his letter to the City of London, he asserts that the intention of the Corn Laws is to make food dear, and that the effect of such dearness is, in his opinion, precisely what the Home Secretary has told the House it is. Protectionists cannot escape from this purpose of the Corn Laws, because there is no meaning in them if they are not to make food dear.

It is very well for the Hon. Gentleman the Member for North Devon to say: 'God forbid that the price of corn should be high; I do not wish scarcity; I know that it is a great misfortune;' and all that sort of thing. It is all very well to say so; but how is he going to vote? How has he voted on previous occasions? I ask this because there has been talking about the Corn Laws for twenty-five years; and there has never been any other purpose in view but to maintain price. I refer him to the period between

1822 and the present year; and to the fact that prices have never been low during that time but that the country gentlemen have come here to complain of agricultural depression, whilst, on the other hand, prices have never been high but that the people have come here to complain of distress.

In 1822 the price of food was lower than it ever was before. The Hon. Member for North Devon must remember all that took place then: it was made the subject of positive grievance by the county Members that prices were so low. But the low prices were not the result of importation. We have heard to-night that cheapness produced by importation and cheapness the result of abundant harvests are two very different things. Unremunerating prices are what Hon. Members opposite have always complained of. They never distinguish between low prices and the causes that produce low prices. I forget who it was—but I believe it was the Hon. Member for the West Riding of Yorkshire,[1] who attempted to-night to draw a distinction between the cheapness produced by foreign importation and an abundant harvest. Gentlemen opposite will do well to look to the years 1822, 1835, and 1845. There are three distinct periods when the prices have been low, not from importation, but from the care of God, of which they have come down here to complain. ['No!'] It is of no use denying the fact, there are the records to prove it.

Lord Castlereagh came down and proposed a scheme for making food dear. He suggested a vote

[1] Mr. B. Denison.

of money, in order to buy up the 'surplus food,' as it was called, to secure a remunerating price to the landed interest; and there was a vote of money proposed in the House to relieve the landed interest from the support of the poor.

In 1835 and 1836 there were also, as I said, low prices that proceeded from good harvests and nothing else; and yet the Marquis of Chandos came here and proposed a repeal of the Malt Tax and that the House should go into Committee upon the grievous state of agriculture. And I believe there were Committees appointed in both Houses of Parliament to consider the unparalleled distress of the agricultural party, although not from importation, but simply from an abundant harvest.

Again, what was the meaning of that two hours' speech which we heard last year from the Hon. Member for Somerset, flourishing the prices current in his hand, and complaining that the Government had not secured them a better price for flour, beef, bacon, veal, pork, &c.? He did not complain of low prices occasioned by importation, because there was less imported during that year than for some time before; but he stated that there was distress owing to prices falling, on account of a more abundant harvest than usual.

I say, therefore, that what Hon. Members complain of is low prices, and that the object of the Corn Laws is high prices. And I urge once more that after the statement of the Right Hon. the Secretary for the Home Department, who declares that he cannot resist the evidence that high prices produce distress, because wages are not increased in a corresponding ratio, they must say on what ground they claim for the continuance of a system that is intended to raise prices.

But it is also contended that the Corn Laws are not only a protection to agriculture, but that they also protect domestic industry. What is meant by 'domestic industry'? It must, I suppose, mean something in which the working classes are concerned. But is there any evidence that the working classes agree with this view of the case; that they believe themselves interested in a system that produces all the misery that the Right Hon. Baronet says takes place whenever this scheme fulfils its purpose? Has any Gentleman opposite quoted the opinions of the working classes in support of the position that the Corn Laws are beneficial to domestic industry? Has any Hon. Member produced a shred of evidence that the working classes approve the idea that they benefit by the high price of food? There is not a single town in all England where the working men concur with Hon. Members opposite, and have not more or less declared themselves against their doctrine. I believe that the address to their fellow-workmen throughout the country published by the working men at Sheffield and agreed to in an open-air meeting was assented to by all of them. They say:—

These Laws have deranged our monetary system, making numbers of our manufacturers bankrupts, checking the natural current of trade, and reducing thousands of families to misery and starvation; nor do they produce any real good to the great mass of our agricultural population; for those who till the earth, and make it lovely and fruitful by their labour, are only allowed the slave's share of the blessings they produce.

Again, at Liverpool in 1843, some working men undertook to inquire into the condition of their own class belonging to that town; and the conclusion arrived at from the inquiry into the state of 5,000 families dwelling there, which was verified at the time by respectable merchants of the place, was as follows:—

That the labouring classes are in a state of great distress. That their condition has been getting worse for the last four years. That we find that disease and crime bear a relation to the price of food. That high prices of provisions compel the people to live on coarser food, thus injuring their health, and abridging their comforts. That manufacturers and dealers are fast sinking, from an inability in the bulk of the population to purchase from them those articles necessary to their existence. That we find that high wages and full employment are coincident with low prices of provisions, and that high prices of provisions are coincident with low wages and want of employment. One thousand and fifty-two families are supported by pawning, charity, or prostitution. One thousand and seventeen families are supported by savings, credit, relations, and casual employment. Other families are now on the parish; out of 5,000 families, 3,600 come from the agricultural districts, not being able to find employment in their own districts.

This is the way that the Corn Laws support domestic industry.

Surely it is a mockery and an insult to tell the poor that you oppose this measure in order to promote their industry!

There are things that have been said against the measure that would certainly be better unnoticed were it not that the authority of the Member for Sunderland, who has urged them, may influence and mislead some people. The Hon. Gentleman has a singular position at present; and owing to the great success of his undertakings whatever falls from him is taken as Gospel.

Well, the Hon. Member for Sunderland is very much alarmed at this measure; and he has used all his authority to frighten the House and the country upon three grounds. In the first place he is afraid that the price at which wheat can be brought into this country from abroad will be too low for agriculture here; he is afraid also of the effect on the Exchanges; and he is afraid of the injury that may be done to our Home Trade. He told us the other night that he had brought foreign corn into this country at 25*s*. a quarter. He said that in 1837 he was a party to a transaction himself in which wheat, after paying the charges of freight and duty, was lodged here at 25*s*. It is impossible to doubt the truth of what any gentleman says he did himself, and quite impossible to doubt anything that the Member for Sunderland says; but when the Hon. Gentleman states a fact of that kind, he wants the country at large to draw a general conclusion from it. He wants people to suppose that when food can be purchased and consumed at 25*s*. a quarter, and can be imported at that price from abroad, the farmers of this country cannot compete with the foreign grower. That is the purpose for which the assertion was made, or it was of no use at all. I think that the Hon. Member ought to have specified where he imported his grain from; for during the last week his statement has been quoted in different papers, as if it regarded the general import price of foreign wheat.

The Hon. Member will, I presume, admit that we shall have to import a considerable quantity of grain from Poland and Russia, and that Dantzic will necessarily be one of the ports from which we must receive grain. We shall have to get a million, or two millions, or as some people say, four millions; and we must depend on that port to a great extent. I happen to have here an authority which I defy any one to question: namely, the prices of grain at Dantzic during the whole of the year 1837, in which year the Hon. Gentleman imported his wheat at 25*s.* a quarter, and the price of freights from Dantzic to Liverpool or London.

[Mr. Hudson was here understood to say that the wheat which he had purchased came from Odessa.]

But as I understood the Hon. Member's statement, wheat could be bought for general consumption at 25*s.* a quarter; his statement is of little use if it has only reference to damaged wheat at Odessa, because I say that we must depend upon Dantzic for a large portion of our wheat. The Hon. Gentleman says that he brought grain here—good grain, capable of being consumed as human food, and brought it into the market at 25*s.* a quarter. I say that the finest quality, capable of being consumed as human food, never was sold at Dantzic during that year under 29*s.* a quarter. [An Hon. Member: Odessa.] But the Hon. Member is telling the House the Free Trade price of wheat, and Hon. Gentlemen all began triumphing on that account, because they believe that it will be inferred that wheat which ought, as they say, to be at 56s. here will be only 25s. in future. Now the prices of wheat at Dantzic for the highest and lowest qualities during the year 1837 were as follows :—

	Highest quality per quarter	Lowest quality per quarter
	s. d.	s. d.
April	31 0	23 5
May	32 0	24 0
June	33 0	25 5
July	30 0	20 0
August	32 3	20 0
September	32 0	24 0
October	29 6	23 5
November	30 0	25 5
December	29 0	28 0

During the same period the prices of freights from Dantzic to London and Liverpool were never less than 4*s.* 9*d.* and sometimes 6*s.*, and the other charges were 3*s.* And yet the Hon. Gentleman assures the House that if the trade were open, foreign grain would be imported here at 25*s.* a quarter; this he infers from what took place in the year 1837 after our ports had been closed for four years.

There is another peculiarity attached to that year: namely, that a very large amount of Baltic wheat went from Dantzic to America; which shows that the Hon. Member was still more fortunate in having been able to land one cargo here from somewhere for 25*s.* a quarter.

But the Hon. Gentleman is one of the school that maintains that there is no objection to an importation of foreign corn if it be not paid for in gold. I will therefore just tell him what was the case when we were importing grain between the years 1840 and 1844.

In 1839, there is no doubt that the bullion fell from upwards of 9,000,000*l*. to 2,000,000*l*. in the course of six months, and this fall was owing to large importation; but our importations for the three following years were as large, only they were regular also; and the Hon. Member will see that the bullion returned to this country, and that the regular importation of wheat was paid for by manufactures.

In 1840, the import of wheat was 2,600,000 quarters; but the bullion in the Bank had increased to 3,500,000*l*. from 2,000,000*l*.

In 1841, the import of wheat was 2,300,000 quarters; but the bullion in the Bank that year was 4,900,000*l*.

In 1842, we imported 4,206,000 quarters; and at that time the bullion in the Bank of England had increased to 19,000,000*l*. Our exports also had increased in a corresponding ratio; and these exports to the great grain countries took place when our exports to every other country failed.

And now, without reading all the particulars, I will just state what was the result of the exports before we began to import grain from the grain-growing countries down to last year.

In 1837, the export of manufactures was 12,800,000*l*.; in 1842, after we had enjoyed four years' import of grain, the export of our manufactures was 16,800,000*l*. It is necessary to bear in mind that this increase of trade with foreign countries took place when our exports to every country were falling off, showing that after the first year of a great and sudden demand for articles we had not before imported, there arose a regular trade.

The Hon. Member for Sunderland has referred to what has likewise been alluded to by other Members in this debate: the value of the Home Trade. It is a very common argument with agricultural gentlemen, that the Home Trade is far better for us than the Foreign Trade, and that we ought to be careful how we deal with it. That is precisely our case; it is because the Home Trade is so good that we ought to be careful not to injure it; and nothing injures it so much as high prices of corn. The Hon. Member is well acquainted with the Midland Counties, and therefore for his information on this point I select the evidence of the Mayor of Leicester—a large manufacturer, given before the Import Duty Committee of this House:—

In speaking of the consumption of Leicester you say that the market has been falling off for two years. Are the Committee to understand that this has been from the increasing poverty of the industrious classes of the country?—I do imagine that to be the case.

Have the artisans been obliged to give more labour, and to do more work for the same wages in consequence of the pressure which has existed in Leicester?—Certainly, wages have been lower in consequence of it, and I never saw anything like the distress that there has been among the artisans employed in the town of Leicester.

To what do you ascribe the decreased demand for their goods?—To the high prices of provisions, which have diminished the means of the labourer to purchase, because if his food takes a large proportion of his wages, it leaves him less to lay out in clothing, furniture, and other articles.

Have you any experience with respect to the demand for your goods, when provisions have been low?—Yes; it is the invariable rule in our trade that when provisions are low, we have a good demand; it is a rule observed by the manufacturers, and established as a maxim in the trade. If the harvest is good, we may have a better home demand; but if we have a bad harvest, I do not know what will become of the population, for it will make corn high, and leave the workmen destitute of employment, and the distress will be very great. Ours is a home manufacture depending upon the home market; and upon the well-being of the workmen generally the prosperity of the manufacturers of Leicester entirely depends.

Are you quite certain that the falling off in the demand for Leicester manufactures amongst the purely agricultural population has been as great as amongst the manufacturing population? —The falling off has been as great. The hosiers who travel there tell me that the wages of the agricultural labourers are so low that it leaves them nothing to lay out in manufactures. They have first to obtain the necessaries of life, and it leaves them nothing to lay out in stockings.

Then although the price of food has increased their wages have not increased in proportion?—Certainly not in the agricultural districts; in the manufacturing districts wages are lower than they were two years ago when food was lower.

Would you attach any importance to the protecting duties being removed, which you are said to have yourself?—The bulk of our manufacturers would be glad to see them removed. We passed a resolution to that effect at a large meeting held in the spring of last year. We had a large town meeting, and resolutions were passed declaring our willingness to abandon all protective duties on manufactures, if all prohibitory and all protecting duties on agricultural produce were also removed.

Was that resolution the result of the opinion of the general aggregate of the manufacturers in Leicester and the neighbourhood?—It was.

Facts of this kind were elicited on the Import Duty Committee from nearly every manufacturer of articles of general consumption; and we urge them in opposition to what is stated in defence of artificial prices as necessary for the Home Trade.

I would now ask the attention of the House to what is said on the other side in reply to these great economical considerations which the Government have had brought before them, and to propositions to the same effect which from time to time have for years past been submitted by Hon. Gentlemen on this side.

It has been stated, and stated truly, by the Right Hon. Baronet, that the population of this country is rapidly increasing, and that the Census shows that there is no chance of finding employment for them except in Commerce and Manufactures.

I wish to call the special attention of the House to the answers that the Hon. Member for Northamptonshire and the Hon. Member for Bristol make to this statement. But first of all I would remind the House that Commissioners of the Crown recently reporting the results of their inquiry have declared that produce equal in amount to that of the county of Surrey is annually required to feed the increased population of this country; and places as large as Birmingham and Manchester to find room for their shelter. The Hon. Member for Bristol says, that manufactures have been carried a great deal too far; and that we ought rather to consider the propriety of restricting our manufacturing districts. The Hon. Member for Northamptonshire, who is a leader of the Protectionists, and who undertakes to speak for that party, and to tell them the views that they ought to propound, in opposition to this side of the House—he, the Hon. Member for Northamptonshire, says that we may talk as we please about the increase of our population, and our want of food to meet that increase; but that the true policy for this country is not to import food from abroad; that we ought to confine ourselves to native produce, and to a system under which we produce three quarters of corn where we might procure five.

Now let the country distinctly understand the political economy of this party. They say that the manufacturing districts of the country are increasing too fast and that their limits ought to be confined; and that concurrently with this restriction we ought to produce less food at home instead of more, and that we ought to import less food from abroad notwithstanding the increase of population.

This is the argument used by Hon. Gentlemen opposite, and deliberately stated in their organs—the 'Quarterly Review,' 'Standard,' and 'Herald.' In these organs it is unblushingly affirmed that if the manufacturing districts were razed to the ground, if half the metropolis were razed to the ground, the country would be greater, happier, and more prosperous.

And quite consistently with such views this measure is opposed—it being alleged that we want no more manufacturing towns; and that we ought not to produce more food at home or import more from abroad however rapidly the population may increase. These are the principles of the Protectionists.

We, on the other hand, say that we want to provide food for an increasing population. We find by the Census returns that there is less scope for employment in the agricultural districts now than there was in 1831; and in answer to this, it is argued that we ought to have fewer manufactories, and less production of food.

Throw out this measure, say the Protectionists, and we will form a Government that upon our principles will provide for the exigencies of the country and the needs of the people. But, let me ask, have they for a moment considered how they are to maintain the Corn Laws after they have defeated the present Government? The Corn Laws must be supported now by force or by opinion. ['Oh!'] Is there any other way? It has already been tried to support them by force. Force was employed when the Laws were introduced; and four years after they were carried they were maintained by force. In 1815 the people of this town were put down by force for openly resisting the Corn Laws; and in Manchester in 1819, four years after their enactment, the people were cut down for calling for their repeal. And again, in 1830 they were threatened when they were suffering dreadfully from their effects; and it was in contemplation once more to stifle their voice by force; but by 1830 the time was past for suppressing opinion by the sword.

It was however said in high quarters that there was another way of putting down the people if they ventured to manifest their feelings too strongly against the Corn Laws. Former Governments had the power to put the people down by means of rotten boroughs. In 1830 the time came for the rotten boroughs themselves to be put down. But the people finding their condition unimproved, their interests neglected, and their demands rejected, became disappointed with the results of the Reform Bill ; a great popular organization was formed in order to obtain a further extension of the suffrage ; and when a scarcity from bad harvests, which since the Corn Laws had passed had been periodical, occurred in 1839 they were indisposed to join the middle classes in demanding the repeal of the Corn Laws alone.

This feeling was turned to account by the Protection societies. Everything that could be done to delude the minds of the people upon the question of the Corn Laws and the advocates of Repeal was done by those societies and their emissaries out of Parliament, and by their partisans in Parliament. Indeed, it was the deception they practised upon the people to reconcile them to the Corn Laws that really gave rise to the Anti-Corn-Law League. It was their proceeding that really caused the members of the Anti-Corn-Law League to exert themselves as they have done ; that lead them to do so much in circulating—not any new principles, or vague theories, but the deliberate opinions of the most enlightened men that the country ever produced, in order to influence public opinion against all restrictions on commerce and in favour of the total abolition of the Corn Laws.

With what result their efforts of late years have been attended is now well known ; and it is obvious to every rational mind that the Corn Laws cannot any longer be maintained either by force or by delusion.

Protectionists now quarrel with a Minister who is applying himself to the settlement of this question. I would ask: have they devised any means themselves —have they contemplated whether it is possible for them to maintain the Corn Laws under circumstances from which the Minister has shrunk: under the regular recurrence of periods of scarcity? If a season of scarcity should occur again; and the people under the pressure of that scarcity should call, as they have always called on former occasions, for political reforms; or if it should so happen that the people rose up against these Laws, what state would such a Government as the Protectionists could form be placed in under such circumstances after having refused to alter the Corn Laws?

I ask the House only to imagine such a Government as we have seen described as possible: a Government with a Noble Duke at its head, and consisting of some Hon. Gentlemen whom I see opposite. In what position would such a Government find itself in a period of scarcity and tumult with the responsibility placed upon it of restoring order and contentment? Is it possible to imagine a Government placed in a more pitiable—I will not say despicable —situation? What would be done? Would it not be exactly what has been done before? Would not Hon. Gentlemen have to come to the Right Hon. Baronet the Member for Tamworth and pray him to resume the reins of power and to do precisely what they are now quarrelling with him for attempting?

The Hon. Member for Rutlandshire blamed the

Right Hon. Baronet at the head of the Government for not having stuck to his guns. 'Stuck to his guns!' What Minister, let me ask, would have stuck to his guns under similar circumstances? Would the Hon. Member stick to his guns if starvation were spreading throughout the country, and he was unable to persuade the people that the starvation they suffered was not the fault of Hon. Gentlemen opposite, nor the result of their legislation? Would they who blame the Right Hon. Baronet stick to their guns under such circumstances, and after it is made clear to the whole world that sticking to their guns only means sticking to their own interests? The fact is, the Protection they require is Protection from themselves; and the Right Hon. Baronet is providing this for them, though they cannot see it.

Other countries have been referred to by the opposite side and their example cited as a warning. The Hon. Member for Dorsetshire, at the commencement of the Session, said that he was not so much afraid of agitation with respect to this question, or of high prices; but that he was afraid of such men as Necker or Turgot getting into the Government. There is some analogy, I admit, between the condition of this country as regards the Corn Law question, and the state of France when Turgot became Minister.

The Hon. Member for Dorsetshire, who expressed his fear of a second Turgot in our Government, is, I am sure, acquainted with the character of that Minister and the views he entertained with respect to his country at that time. He was a very sagacious man. I venture to say, notwithstanding the pretensions of the economists of the present day, that there is no man possessing more comprehensive views upon political economy now than he possessed then. Turgot was called to power in 1774, and no man entertaining more honest and intelligent opinions than he did could have obtained it. He undertook the government of the country after writing a very remarkable letter to the King, in which he pointed out to him the difficulties he should have to contend with in his administration of public affairs. He stated in that letter that he despaired of doing good; that he knew that he should be calumniated; that a confederacy would be formed against him because he should represent to the King that a certain class ought not to live upon the substance of the nation; and, after dilating upon his difficulties, and expressing his confidence in the good faith and justice of the King, he said that he accepted office, desiring to die with the character of having acted honestly and having done as much good as possible for his country.

Now, what was the first act of his Ministry, and the one, probably, that excites the fears of the Hon. Member opposite? He repealed the Corn Laws in France. He said that there were two things that ought to be cared for by every country desirous of escaping bankruptcy and revolution—and this be it remembered he said fifteen years before the Revolution took place in France. The two things were, the maintenance of the Revenue, and provision against scarcity of food. And for this purpose he insisted above all other things that trade in corn should be free.

Consistently with these views, the first act of Turgot in 1775 was to set free the internal Corn Trade of France, and to place on record his views of the expediency of setting free her external Corn Trade. What was the case then in France? It is really worth the while of Hon. Gentlemen opposite to observe it. When Turgot succeeded to power he found that each province was by its Corn Law made dependent upon itself for its supply. Each province was protected from the abundance of its neighbour, and hence they were constantly exposed to all the evils of scarcity, leading to riot, misery, and confusion. He removed the barriers to the trade in corn between the provinces; and then he proceeded to place the finances of the country upon a sounder basis. And now—after he had thus boldly and wisely struck at the two great sources of danger and evil—mark the cause of his fall; because, if care be not taken, the same fall may await those in this country who would act with similar courage and wisdom.

It is, if I remember rightly, in Condorcet's 'Life of Turgot' that the combination that was formed against the Minister is described; and it appears to have included all those who lived on the Revenue without rendering any service in return; all those who profited by abuses of all kinds in the State: farmers of the Public Income, foolish people of Society—women of fashion, and frivolous young nobles. That is the sort of persons who were opposed to

Turgot's policy, and who intrigued against him, and against every Minister from 1775 to 1789 who foresaw the consequences of the system that he was anxious to reform. Turgot complained, and strove to defeat them. And this is the Minister whom the Hon. Member for Dorsetshire fears may be imitated by a Minister of this country.

Mr. Carlyle, in one of his recent works, has referred to the sentiments of the privileged classes in France in the year 1787, and has represented some of them as saying, that they could not live upon the rents of their estates alone, that they could not parade themselves at Court, that they could not maintain their station, unless they had something more than the natural profits of their own possessions; and that they could only sustain their order and their usual expenditure by privileges and exemptions to which the rest of the community were not entitled. And so they would not support any Minister who refused to support them in these extravagant pretensions and views; and every Minister who disputed them was driven from power from the time of Turgot till 1788.

In that year, however, the harvest was bad throughout France; and in 1789 the people were threatened with famine; then came riot, disturbance, and speedily in their train a comprehensive change such as was referred to by the Member for Shrewsbury the other night, which struck deep into the roots of Society and effected vast changes in the relations of different classes.

As Hon. Gentlemen opposite have referred to this period, let them study it and take warning by it; for I declare that with the deep-rooted conviction that the people have of the character and purpose of the Corn Laws, I know nothing that would enable the Government to support its authority in this country if placed again under the circumstances of scarcity of food and a failure of revenue; and I ask them to consider, when they reflect upon what they have experienced of late years of the effect of scarcity, whether the Right Hon. Baronet in proposing his measure, is not fulfilling the conditions of true Conservatism; and, whether they can, professing that character themselves, and in the absence of any security against a recurrence of scarcity, be justified in the course they are taking. For, be it remembered, they have not themselves proposed a single measure of security against a time of scarcity. They heard the Right Hon. Baronet opposite say what he apprehended from it; that he dreads the very recollection of the last period of scarcity, and danger, and sedition; that he is, therefore, desirous to prevent the recurrence of such periods. But they have offered no security, they have taken no precaution against its recurrence; and mind, after all the discussions that have taken place, and the enlightenment of the people on this subject, it would be impossible to deceive them again: henceforth they will hold the Legislature strictly responsible for what occurs.

Hon. Members must recollect that the system they wish to maintain is to prevent the growth of food in other countries for the supply of the wants of our own population; and from this circumstance they cannot in any case be held relieved from responsibility for at least two or three years to come.

There is something like famine already existing in Ireland; and we are not sure that there may not be a bad harvest next year. What do Hon. Members mean to do if there should be a bad harvest, and if owing to the discouragement they have given to other countries to produce for our markets, there should be little to be obtained from abroad? If the people are without food, and call on them for supplies, what will they do? Hon. Members have undertaken to feed them, and the people are not fed. What answer will they give in 1846, and 1847, and 1848, if distress should ensue?

Surely there is sense in taking this into consideration. In a period of scarcity it would not be merely a question of Corn Laws. People are then in a peculiar state of mind. Men's minds are in no ordinary state when suffering from want. Her Majesty's Ministers are fully alive to this fact, and they openly avow that they contemplate with horror and alarm the recurrence of such an event; and hence they are taking steps to prevent it. They know that when men are made desperate by distress, and driven to madness by suffering, and by the privations of those who are dear to them, they will accept only too readily any causes that are assigned for their misfortunes, they will only too easily grasp at any remedy that promises them relief. It is most certainly for the interest of the aristocracy of this country that the public should not be placed under such circumstances, as most surely it is for their interest to prevent the public mind from reflecting upon the manner in which they have been governed for the past half-century.

My Noble Friend the Member for London has referred to the immortal services that the aristocracy have rendered to this country. I do not deny that such services have been rendered by them. I am glad to hear that such has been the case; and from not being so well versed in the ancient annals of the country as my Noble Friend, I cannot dispute it; but I think that if there should recur another period of anger and distress, the people might be forgetful of such services, and that they would be disposed to reflect chiefly upon that period of some forty or fifty years past of which they themselves have direct cognizance.

I therefore conjure the landed aristocracy at this very moment, in the full possession of the present opportunity, to consult their own true interests, and to sacrifice selfish prejudice to the cause of justice, by a hearty concurrence in the measure proposed by the Government, and by the abolition *in toto* of Laws that, as long as a vestige of them remains, will be evidence against their wisdom and their honour. Lose the occasion, and I venture to predict that they will suffer the fate of every one who has ever sought to trample on, or who for a while succeeded in tyrannizing over, this race and nation to which it is their great good fortune to belong, and over which it ought to have been their pride to rule with justice and intelligence.

XXVIII.

HOUSE OF COMMONS, January 31, 1850.

Protectionists did not show themselves ready to accept a Free Trade Policy as an established fact after the passing of the great measure of 1846; they constantly manifested a desire to raise anew the question of a Protective tariff, especially with regard to corn, for the purpose of securing a Parliamentary guarantee of price for agricultural produce. The land-owners were receiving higher prices for their land than they had ever enjoyed before, though the agriculturists were still complaining of distress. In Jan. 1850 Mr. Villiers, at the urgent request of Lord J. Russell, agreed to move the Address in the House of Commons in answer to the Speech from the Throne, in order to mark the entire agreement between the Whig Government and the Free Traders in considering the policy of the Act of 1846 as irrevocable. The most convincing proof of the improvement already effected in the condition of the people at large was furnished by the reports from all parts of the kingdom of the rapid extension of commerce and the vast increase of the manufacturing industries; the Revenue Returns were better than they had been for years; and Mr. Villiers had the pleasing task of pointing to the prevailing prosperity as the first-fruits of the legislation having for its main object to secure the permanent enjoyment of the blessings of cheapness and plenty, that he had done so much to promote.

I RISE to move that a humble Address be presented to Her Majesty in reply to the gracious Speech that has just been read to this House.

In doing so, I assure the House that I am fully impressed with my own incompetence for the task; and I am convinced that no one who has preceded me in discharging it has ever felt more in need of the forbearance of Hon. Members.

Indeed, but for the circumstance that there appears upon all sides a disposition to refer the present condition of the country to those recent changes in our commercial policy that have been the subject of such frequent discussion in this House, and in which I have borne my share, I should have deemed myself the least appropriate person to have been selected for this purpose.

However, I do entirely concur in the view that to my certain knowledge Her Majesty's Ministers take of the condition of the people ; and having perfect confidence that my Noble Friend at the head of the Government will not compromise—that he will not in any way surrender, but that he will maintain in their integrity, the measures that he conceives to be closely connected with the happiness and well-being of the people, I have no scruple in other respects to ask the House to respond to the Speech that has just been read.

And now I cannot do better than advert in the first place to those topics in Her Majesty's Speech that cannot fail to unite the feelings of the House.

The deep affliction that Her Majesty has experienced from the death of her illustrious relative, the late Queen Dowager, has been communicated to this House ; and I think I should be only correctly representing the opinion of the country if I were to say with regard to her late Majesty, that her blameless life, her unostentatious character, and her numerous charities, as well as the exemplary manner in which she fulfilled the duties of her exalted station, have secured for her memory a feeling of deep respect throughout the nation ; and the House, I am sure, will not hesitate to join in the expression of cordial condolence and sympathy with Her Majesty in the bereavement she has endured.

It is stated in Her Majesty's Speech, and the statement is one that this House always receives with the greatest satisfaction, that 'Her Majesty happily continues in peace and amity with Foreign Powers.' It is further announced that Her Majesty has, in conjunction with France and by means of a friendly mediation, prevented hostilities from 'occurring between the Governments of Austria and Russia on the one hand, and the Sublime Porte on the other.' The causes of this apprehended rupture are indicated in the Royal Speech: certain persons, subjects of Russia and Austria, sought, it seems, refuge and protection in the territories of the Sultan, whereupon a claim, based on Treaties of ancient date, was made by the Emperors of Russia and of Austria, that those persons should be surrendered in order that they might be punished according to the offence with which they were charged. A doubt having arisen on the part of the Sultan as to the correctness of the construction of the Treaties upon which this claim was made, the Sultan referred to the Governments of England and France to aid him in the solution of his difficulty. I believe that it is now generally known that the Governments of France and England adopted the construction put upon the Treaties by the Sultan, that construction being unfavourable to the surrender of the persons in question; and that the construction having been allowed to be just, the final arrangements with regard to the persons who sought refuge in the dominions of the Sultan were in accordance with the propositions that had emanated from the Sublime Porte.

The result, therefore, of Her Majesty's mediation, in conjunction with France, has been to prevent hostilities between the Imperial Governments of Russia and Austria and of the Sultan—involving, perhaps, the peace of Europe; and that friendly relations have been, or are about to be resumed between the three Powers.

I believe that there never was a time when the interference of this country in the affairs of other countries with which we are not directly concerned was regarded with more dislike than at present; but I think that this is in some degree due to a want of discrimination between the differences of character under different circumstances of such intervention: a discrimination most necessary to be observed; for there is a great difference between an interference that has for its purpose to dictate to a people the form of Government under which they shall live, or to contribute force to a Government to resist its people, which it would otherwise be unable to do, and that kind of intervention that assumes the form of friendly mediation, having in view the cause of peace and humanity and the prevention of hostilities the issue of which might be dangerous to ourselves. I conceive that in this latter case interference is not only justifiable but politic; and I think that it is one of the best consequences of the position we now hold in the opinion of the world, that when we do intervene in the cause of peace and humanity we can do so with effect.

I refer to the position that we now hold in the opinion of the world because it is with satisfaction that I see this country at present looked upon with a trust and respect that has seldom if ever been exceeded which I am disposed to explain by the true character of the people being better understood by the world than it ever was before. I believe that other countries are perfectly satisfied that the people of this country have no object more at heart than to maintain peace with the whole world; that they have neither a wish to aggrandize themselves nor to take political advantage at the expense of any other country; and that as regards power they are perfectly satisfied with the vast results of their own peaceful pursuits. And though, doubtless, we must always sympathize with those nations who, following in our footsteps, are struggling to obtain their liberties, yet I believe that there is no way in which we can aid those people so well, or influence other Governments so much, as by pointing to our own example which shows that the greatest amount of liberty enjoyed by any nation upon the earth is consistent with peace, with order, and with the acquisition of vast wealth: a proof to the people of what is to be gained by firmness and moderation, and to Governments of what is to be averted by timely concession.

Her Majesty has announced in her Speech that she has been in communication with different Powers for the purpose of making arrangements consequent upon the changes that we effected last year in the Laws for regulating our navigation. It has been also announced that Her Majesty is negotiating at this moment with other States who have intimated their willingness to reciprocate the advantages that by those changes have been extended to them; and that the United States and Sweden have already interchanged every advantage that we offered to them by the recent abolition of our Navigation Laws.

It is rather early, perhaps, to express any opinion of what will be the general result of the alterations in this part of our commercial system; but, so far as one can see, there is at present every prospect of all similar restrictions to the intercourse of nations being swept away, originating as they did at a time far less enlightened than the present, and continued far too long for the convenience of the world as it is.

It is gratifying to observe that all the apprehensions that were expressed by those who resisted the reform here appear to have been unfounded. Seldom has there been the exhibition of so much sentiment and feeling mixed up with private and pecuniary interest as was evinced upon the question of the abolition of our Navigation Laws; but I think that it has also rarely happened that the mischiefs and evils of an old system and the advantages of a change have been so quickly and so clearly brought into view.

There is every prospect that the predictions made by the advocates of the Navigation Laws, and their alarms also, will prove unfounded ; and there is every promise that what was prophesied and expected as to the advantages of the change will be realized. The interest that was most affected by the change has not for some years been in such a state of activity as it is at this moment. General activity is apparent in the dockyards throughout the country ; and whether on the Tyne or the Thames, or the Wear or the Clyde, the same account is given that the business of ship-building never presented a more cheering prospect.

I should also mention that some of the persons engaged in the Ship-building Trade who were foremost in predicting evil consequences from the change, are now amongst the most busy ; thus showing little faith in the statements they themselves made, and justifying us in the discredit we cast upon them.

It is further disclosed that we have advantages for building ships that are hardly possessed by any other country; and that so far from the shipping interest being likely to suffer by the alteration, we can not only build ships at home cheaper than they can be built in other countries, but, which is still more satisfactory, that other countries can build their ships cheaper here than they can in their own yards.

It appears moreover that whatever advantage we supposed to be possessed over us by other countries resulted from the system that prevailed in this country ; and that in consequence of the reform we have effected in that system with respect to the structure of our vessels, and with regard to the moral character of masters and mates, and their knowledge of their business, we are now qualified to maintain competition with the navies of any country in the world.

I do not intend to weary the House with many details on this matter, but I cannot help reading a letter dealing with it, written by a man whose character and position give authority to his words, that I have received from Liverpool :—

As regards shipping there is a much better feeling since it was ascertained that the Navigation Laws were irretrievably doomed; builders are well employed, new contracts are making freely, both at home and in the colonies, and first-class British-built ships are readily taken up as they arrive. In fact, the supply of twelve-year ships falls short of the demand, and advanced rates have been paid in some cases for homeward freight. There are now building on the stocks 2,850 tons, against 2,220 tons in 1849. Some British ships have been taken up in the Mediterranean and elsewhere, and loaded for the States, and a few foreigners to load for England—the first-fruits of reciprocity. I enclose some of the shipping circulars, particularly pointing attention to that of Thom, Currie & Co., from the importance of that firm.

A passage in one of these circulars is to the following effect :—

As soon as it was decided that the old laws were doomed increased energy evinced itself, and in the assurance that the position of the ship-owner would not be further compromised, buyers and builders resolved at once to be up and doing.

I have also got a return from the port of Sunderland, and I find that of the vessels building in the port of Sunderland on December 31, 1847, the amount of tonnage was 22,140 tons, and on December 31, 1849—the Navigation Laws having been doomed six months previously—it was 29,210 tons. Of ships sold, there were sixteen in December 1847, and twenty-four in December 1849. The number built in December 1848, when there seemed some doubt as to the Navigation Laws being abolished, was 142 of 37,878 tons, and in December 1849, 155 of 44,333 tons.

I might go further into detail on the subject of the Navigation Laws to show that I am right in congratulating the House on the change that has been made; but knowing that there are some members more perfectly informed on this subject, who are likely to afford the House further evidence, I will not longer detain its attention on this topic. I cannot, however, help repeating, after six months' experience of the change, that everything foretold by the opponents of the change has hitherto been falsified, and that everything promised by its advocates is likely to come true.

The Speech from the Throne has informed the House of the satisfaction that Her Majesty derived from her recent visit to Ireland. That Her Majesty's reception in that country should have been marked by every indication of attachment and loyalty, occasioned, I believe, no surprise to those who are best acquainted with the feelings of the Irish people. Often complaining of this country, and sometimes with reason, the people of Ireland have seldom been wanting in respect for the Crown. They cheerfully acknowledge the legitimate right of Her Majesty to the dominion of their country; but of Her Majesty personally they knew only that from the time of her accession she had manifested a marked interest in their welfare, ever desiring that all reason for complaint should be removed, and anxious that justice and favour should be equally dispensed in each portion of her kingdom. It was, moreover, supposed that Her Majesty had long wished to visit Ireland; and with these prepossessions concerning the Sovereign, it was not surprising that among a people of their generous nature, her arrival among them should have been welcomed with delight. Having been present in the capital myself when Her Majesty was there, I am bound to say that I never saw so vast a concourse of people congregated together who demeaned themselves with so much order and propriety. People from all quarters of the country and of all opinions assembled in Dublin on the occasion, and, without yielding to any extravagance of feeling or losing their self-respect, they seemed to have come together for the common object of manifesting regard for the person and character of Her Majesty.

According to information that I have received, nothing has occurred amongst the Irish people generally since Her Majesty's departure from Ireland to shake those feelings of attachment and loyalty that were evinced in her presence.

We are reminded by Her Majesty's Speech that great distress still prevails there, and that vestiges yet exist of the awful calamity with which the country was lately visited. Indeed it is impossible for those who know the extent of distress that the famine occasioned to suppose that at so early a period all traces of its effects should have disappeared; but it is gratifying to know that in many respects the material condition of the poor of Ireland is improving, and that, owing to the abundance of the necessaries of life, the amount of suffering is less. This is indicated not only by the less frequent resort to public relief, but likewise by signs of greater contentment, and the diminution of crime and outrage.

It is matter for satisfaction, considering the apprehensions that were expressed with reference to the amount and mode of the relief afforded in Ireland, that the fears of those who were opposed to it have not been realized. It was imagined that if relief were once given out of the workhouse to the Irish people they would become generally demoralized, and that a habit of reliance on public charity, incapable of being afterwards checked, would be engendered. Nothing of the sort has occurred: as soon as the necessaries of life became more reasonable in price and the means of employment abundant, out-door relief greatly diminished. At the commencement of 1849, we find that the in-door relief included 206,254 persons; in 1850 it is reduced to 204,407. The amount of the out-door relief on January 1, 1849, was 479,576*l.*; on January 1, 1850, it was reduced to 104,650*l.* The decrease of in-door relief, therefore, is 1,760*l.*, and of out-door relief no less than 364,926*l.*

As far as we can ascertain the prospects of the operation of the Poor Law, it appears that the administration of the system becomes more simplified, and the means of preventing imposture more certain. Most striking evidence of this is afforded by the increased workhouse accommodation provided in the country during the last year, showing that what is considered in this country a sufficient test of imposture is likely to be applied there generally with effect. The workhouse accommodation on January 6, 1849, was for 251,717 ; on January 5, 1850, for 290,720.

I stated that there was a diminution of crime in Ireland, consequent on the improved condition of the people. I find from a Return of the number of outrages reported by the constabulary in 1847 and 1849, that the number of cases of cattle and sheep stealing that occurred in 1847 was 10,044 ; in 1849, 8,157 : of other outrages, the number in 1847 was 10,142 ; in 1849, 6,749 : the total of offences being for 1847, 20,986 ; for 1849, 14,906. The total number of animals stolen in 1847 was 15,291 ; and in 1849, 13,631.

I now come to an announcement in Her Majesty's Speech that I am sure will be most gratifying to the House : I allude to the reference there made to the condition, in this country, of manufacturing and commercial interests and of the people generally. Her Majesty is happy to congratulate the House that the state of the manufactures and commerce of the country has greatly improved, and that the condition of the people is very much better in consequence of the easier access to the necessaries and comforts of life.

This is a most important fact : important at any time to those who are aware of the vast consequences that are involved in the prosperity of our manufactures and commerce, and the condition of the people, affecting as they do our whole social, political, and financial system.

But though an official announcement of this fact has been waited and watched for with very great interest in this country, I believe that there never was a time when attention was more directed to the subject out of the country than at present. Everybody is anxious to learn the existing condition of England. The whole commercial world consider that we have lately made a great and momentous experiment on our industrial and commercial interests, and they are watching the result. This announcement contained in the Speech, therefore, has a peculiar importance just now.

The fact is, the nations of the earth are beginning, notwithstanding the sneers sometimes cast upon the subject, to direct their attention to Political Economy. There never was a period when they were more desirous of acquiring wealth, or when the people were more impatient of its unequal distribution, than they are now; and the problem that is at present waiting solution is, in what way nations can accumulate the greatest possible amount of wealth consistently with the fairest distribution of it.

I do not dispute that there are two systems totally opposed to one another, each of which has professed to accomplish this object. The one consists in regulating and restricting the trade of the country by the State, and maintaining particular industries and interests that are unable to maintain themselves: this is called the Protective System. The other is to leave to the unfettered intelligence and energy, almost to the instinct, of a free and civilized people, the discovery of the means by which they can obtain the highest possible reward for their capital, skill, and industry : this is called the Free Trade System. Now what excites the special curiosity and interest of the world in us is that, considered, as we are, to be the head of all the commercial nations of the earth, we have been seen, after years of experience of the Protective System, to abandon it for that of Free Trade.

This interest has been much enhanced by the very confident predictions that were made here and elsewhere as to the disastrous effects that must follow from the change. The great issue upon the Protective and Free Trade Systems was taken on the free importation of food ; and upon this point some of the most positive prophecies and warnings are on record. I have no doubt that many persons have been shaken in their faith in what they thought to be a sound principle by the confidence with which persons of authority and station in this country have spoken as to the result of the experiment. And the real importance of the announcement made in Her Majesty's Speech is, that it enables us to know with certainty the truth with respect to the change.

No doubt it may be said that a trial of only one year is hardly a fair test of any experiment of the kind ; and that as yet there has not been sufficient time to judge of its results ; but if the predictions of evil had been in any measure justified, I think that the time has arrived when we should have had some intimation of the evils likely to ensue.

Now, of the objections urged by those who opposed Free Trade in corn, the House is, I am sure, very familiar with the following: first, that Free Trade in corn would greatly impair the Home Trade; secondly, that the condition of the working classes would be greatly deteriorated; thirdly, that our Currency must be exported to pay for it; and fourthly, that the Revenue would decline.

It was said on the other side that, inasmuch as food is the basis upon which all human industry proceeds, according to its supply, whether scanty, or adequate, or abundant, so will the means of the community be available for the production, distribution, or consumption of all other articles; that an objection founded upon the evils of having more food instead of less, is fallacious; that as trade consists only in the exchange and distribution of articles required for human use, or as such articles are demanded in proportion as the first necessary of life is procured with more or less facility, trade will invariably be better when food is plentiful and cheap; and, lastly, that since with our system of taxation, revenue depends more upon expenditure than on income, the Revenue will be greater, and not less, as general consumption increases. Abundance of food, therefore, we said, must always be a cause of prosperity in such a country as this. These were the arguments put forward for and against the system of Free Trade.

Now, I want the country and the world at large to judge between us; and I hope the House will decide at present by examining the results. What are they? We have heard something about them from private sources; but this is the first occasion on which any official announcement as to the state of the country has been made.

We are told that commerce and manufactures are thriving, and that the condition of the people is greatly improved from having fuller command of the necessaries of life. The evils denounced as about to overtake us were to be in proportion to the quantity of commodities, especially of food, that was to be imported. It was certainly beyond my expectation that we should so soon have an opportunity of putting this matter to the test. For what am I now in a position to state to the House? No less than that within the last sixteen months we have imported more food than we imported during the sixteen preceding years. Surely if any of the threatened consequences of Free Trade in food necessarily follow its adoption, there would have been some indication of them at present; for neither party imagined that the imports of grain would so soon have increased to so large an extent. Nothing approaching it, indeed, has, I believe, ever occurred in the history of this country: we have been importing at the rate of a million quarters a month.

My honest conviction at this moment is, that not a single thing that was feared by the opponents of Free Trade has come to pass, nor is there the slightest prospect that such will be the case. On the other hand, the advantages expected by the Free Traders are already experienced: the Home Trade has improved; the condition of the working classes has been ameliorated; not a sovereign has left the country, for there is as much gold as the Hon. Member for Warwickshire could wish; while, as we shall be informed by my Right Hon. Friend the Chancellor of the Exchequer, the Revenue is improving. I am in possession of letters, circulars, and documents coming from every part of the kingdom, in which the writers not only admit that they are well off (a very rare thing with the people of this country) and that their condition is improved, but in which they also ascribe their good fortune chiefly to the cheapness and abundance of the necessaries of life.

I really had doubts whether the improvement would be so soon evinced in the Home Trade; but only this day I received a letter from the north of England, describing the state of the manufacturing interests in a place chiefly concerned in supplying the interior of the country: Bradford and its vicinity. This letter, dated Bradford, January 28, 1850, and treating specially of the circumstances of the working classes in that town and neighbourhood, and of the rate of wages and the general condition of trade, says that:—

A constant, steady, and great improvement has taken place during the last twelve or eighteen months. The exports to the United States have increased—the demand for the Continent has revived with the more general return of tranquillity, and with regard to the Home Trade, while a very large increase has taken place in the demand for our goods in the manufacturing districts, the experience of our firm would not lead us to the conclusion that there has been in 1849, as compared with 1848, any diminution in the demand for Bradford goods in the agricultural districts, but quite the contrary. . . . . Repeated advances in wages have been given, and I feel justified in stating that owing to the high rate of wages and the low price of clothing and food, the working classes as a body were never so well off as at present.

Another letter from Leicester—where there was a good deal of agitation on the subject of Free Trade, and apprehension that the country would be ruined in consequence—written by a person whose authority and position in that town place his statements beyond question for accuracy, informs me that:—

The demand for the last year has been fully equal to the manufacturing capability of the district—all the workmen have been fully employed, and two advances in wages have been established and maintained in the staple trade, of the permanence of which there is every indication. . . . . I assure you nothing has ever been so satisfactory to me as the realization of the results to the working classes of Corn-Law Repeal.

And, finally, another correspondent in Leicester—the Chairman of the Leicester Board of Guardians, affirms that the trade of the place has never before been so prosperous. He tells me that the population of the Borough, which is a Poor Law Union within itself, is now about 60,000. The Poor Rates in 1848 were 37,000*l.*; in 1849, 32,000*l.* 'I have resided in Leicester twenty years,' he says, 'and I never knew it in so prosperous a condition as regards its general trade. The wages of the working men of the staple trade, for many years notoriously low, are advanced, and there is a prospect of further advances ; and the cheapness of provisions, especially of bread, is regarded as an inestimable benefit.'

I quote these letters merely as specimens of the evidence that may be collected in every part of the country showing that the Home Trade, about which so much solicitude is expressed in this House, does not suffer.

The comparative number of bankruptcies alone is some indication of the state of trade. In 1848 there were 1,763 bankruptcies ; in 1849 only 1,146, showing a decrease of 617.

With respect to the condition of the working classes, the indications are of the most satisfactory description ; and as the working classes have a great many friends in this House, I am sure that it will be a source of high gratification to them to hear it.

Whether we look to the agricultural class on the one hand or to the manufacturing class on the other, the improvement is equally apparent : it will be found that the people can command a larger share of the comforts of life ; that they have higher wages, and that uniformly they are far better off than during the past year. I see that the Hon. Member for Warwickshire expresses some doubt ; then, let the truth of my statements be ascertained. An important indication in the matter would be the amount of public relief given. My Right Hon. Friends the Chancellor of the Exchequer and the Chief Commissioner of the Poor Laws will be able, when they address the House, to inform it whether the Poor Rate has increased, and whether more persons are now receiving public relief.

In fact I trust to the Chancellor of the Exchequer, who is so able and accurate in statements on these matters, to give details from official sources in support of what I have said. My own impression from the reports on the subject is, that there is an extraordinary diminution in the number of those in receipt of public relief during the past year, as compared with that which preceded it, and a great reduction in the expense of supporting them. I believe that the number of persons now receiving relief is between 50,000 and 60,000 less.

As regards the amount of bullion in the country I do not know the exact quantity, but I am informed that there never was a time in the history of the Bank of England when the amount was greater than it is at present.

And with regard to the Revenue, there is actually a surplus of 2,000,000*l.* of income over expenditure. Of a two million surplus, or indeed of any kind of surplus, we certainly have not heard much before this year.

I have here a comparison of the commitments in the years 1848 and 1849. This kind of thing is generally admitted as good evidence of the condition of the people at different periods. In 1848, I find that the number of persons committed to prison in England and Wales was 10,352, while in 1849 the number was 9,512. In Ireland the number of offences reported by the constabulary for the same respective periods was 3,615 in 1848, and 2,501 in 1849. And as poverty and crime, which ever go together, have always been justly reckoned as two of the consequences of a want of a sufficient supply of food, these results tend to confirm still further the view of the increased prosperity of the country which I have been taking.

I am prepared for the argument which I know will be urged against me by Hon. Gentlemen opposite: namely, that though they admit (for it cannot be disputed) that trade is flourishing, and the employment of the people general, still all this results from other causes than those to which I have attributed it; that there are other ways by which the prevalent prosperity may be accounted for. I have by me a calculation which I have made of what the country now saves in the articles of food—a calculation of the difference to the country in paying for the necessary supply of food when food is cheap and when it is dear.

The people have to be fed, whatever the price of food in this country may be; and there is necessarily a certain expenditure required in order to obtain food which varies according as food may be cheap or dear at different periods. Now what I want to show the House is the enormous difference in the cost of supplying food to the country when food is cheap and when it is dear; and that when you hear of wages going further and the trade being better at the time that food is cheap, there is no difficulty in concluding that cheapness of food is the cause. I will give the House the average prices for the years 1847 and 1849:—

	Average price, 1847		Average price, 1849		Difference	
	s.	d.	s.	d.	s.	d.
Wheat . .	69	5	39	4	30	1
Barley . .	43	11	25	9	18	2
Oats . .	28	7	15	6	13	1
Beans . .	50	1	26	11	23	2
Peas . .	39	1	29	0	10	1

The following is the estimated consumption of all kinds of grain in this country:—

			£
20,000,000	quarters	wheat at 30s. . .	30,000,000
20,000,000	,,	oats ,, 13s. . .	13,000,000
20,000,000	,,	barley, beans, and peas at 18s. . .	18,000,000
60,000,000	,,		£61,000,000

Estimating the consumption of meat, butter, cheese, potatoes and other vegetables, to be equal in value to the total consumption of grain, say 60,000,000*l.*, and estimating the reduction in price to be equal to 10*s.* per quarter, the reduction will amount to 30,000,000*l.* So that there remains on the expenditure of the people for food a difference of no less than 91,000,000*l.* sterling between the years 1847 and 1849; which, as everybody must see, necessarily leaves to the community means available for other objects; and which, from whatever cause it may arise, will always be felt immediately in trade and shown in the condition of the people.

If the Protective Duty on food had the effect of keeping up the price of food, the people will know how to judge of what they have gained by its abolition, and they can calculate how much they have lost by Protection having been continued so long.

I do not want to make them more dissatisfied than necessary with the manner in which they have been treated for the benefit of a particular interest. On the contrary, I should be glad if Hon. Gentlemen opposite could show me that I am wrong. I should be glad to find that they can show the people that there has not been the injustice done to them in past years that my calculation tends to show; and that they have not derived so much benefit from Free Trade as I believe they now enjoy, seeing that in the first year of Free Trade, which is said to have caused reduction of price, such great saving has been made. If 91,000,000*l.* had been rendered available to the people by any other means than Free Trade would anybody be astonished to hear that a state of universal prosperity followed? And I say that this economy in the article of food between such years as 1847 and 1849 has been available to the people for the comforts of life; and that the prevailing state of prosperity proves that the people have availed themselves of these increased means for procuring comforts of which they would otherwise have been deprived.

Any one who entertains any doubt on this subject has only to look to such evidence as I have read in order to see that such is the case. But I must say that when Free Trade is called an experiment in this country (for I understand that Hon. Gentlemen call the liberty to buy food freely an experiment), it seems to me an experiment of justice and advantage not likely to be soon changed or departed from; or, at least, not until people prefer a limited to an abundant supply of what they require, and wish to pay an excessive instead of an adequate price for what they want to buy.

Seeing that there are many others to follow me, likely to be full of information of the kind that I have already adduced, I shall not detain the House longer on this point. To sum up what I have said on it, my case briefly is this:—That the great change in the price of food is sufficient to account for the improvement that has taken place in the condition of the people.

I would now advert to another topic in Her Majesty's Speech: namely, that contained in the following passage:—

> It is with regret that Her Majesty has observed the complaints which in many parts of the kingdom have proceeded from the owners and occupiers of land. Her Majesty greatly laments that any portion of her subjects should be suffering distress.

I think that any expression of sympathy on the part of Her Majesty with the sufferings of owners and occupiers of land will be readily responded to in this House, and indeed out of the House. I share largely in that feeling myself. I never wished ill, God knows, to the landed interest. When I advocated the repeal of the Corn Laws, I always thought that the advantage of the landed interest was involved in the removal of what was falsely termed Protection, as much as that of any other class. What enhances my regret for it now is that I cannot hold out the smallest prospect of relief that, with a view to its benefit, the Legislature can, with justice to other classes, extend to it. And this for more than one reason.

The landed interest has had great power in the Legislature; and owing to the frequent recurrence of agricultural distress, notwithstanding Protection, there have been many opportunities for trying whether it could be relieved by special legislation ; and these opportunities have not, I think, been thrown away. Indeed it would be difficult to find an experiment of this kind that has not been made. And after considering this subject attentively myself, I am obliged to conclude that there are no peculiar liabilities attached to land from which it could be relieved. There are none in fact that attach to an agriculturist in his capacity of agriculturist. The assessments for rates are upon the local and visible property in any district ; nevertheless, I have found that there have been constant exemptions made with regard to them in favour of the agriculturist: for certainly, when it was enacted that the farmer should pay no duty for his horses, none for his dogs, none for his tolls, none for his windows, none for insurance, the enactment amounted to so many favours. But what makes me despair more than anything else of proceeding further in this direction is the fact that whenever any charge of this sort was removed it gave value to the land ; that in consequence of any such reduction land would always let for a higher rent to the occupier. And yet it was said that the thing chiefly desired was to relieve the occupier!—that the owner cared little for himself! But if the kind of legislation referred to does not relieve the occupier it is of no use.

I do not state this solely on my own conviction

and authority: I am fortified by an authority in the other House, the late Lord Eldon, who said in a Corn Law Debate, that it would be needless to reduce the local charges on land, because every sixpence that was taken from them went to swell the rent of the owner. I think indeed that this is delicate ground for the landed interest to touch upon; for it will disclose more class favour in the matter of taxation than Hon. Members are perhaps now conscious of.

But I have still less hope of the possibility of relief when I observe the special claim put forward for the occupiers of land themselves; for judging by the oratory that has lately resounded throughout the country, it would seem that the farmer still calls for that of which it is impossible to assure him, and which if promised would only prove, as it did before, seductive and ruinous to himself: it is still demanded for the farmer that Parliament shall promise him a price for his wheat, according to which he could bargain for his land. In fact it is the old claim for Protection that has again been urged at the many meetings lately held on the landed interest. I am astonished at the infatuation that can make such a claim after what has passed. It shows a persistence of fallacy unequalled; and is worthy of nothing less than a place in the work entitled 'The History of Human Delusions,' where it would, unquestionably, hold supreme rank; for if anything is logically deducible from what has gone before, it is that the farmer's heaviest losses, and sometimes ruin, have been occasioned by this very promise of Parliament.

The evidence taken before the Agricultural Committees of the House is really nothing else than the details of his disappointment given by the farmer himself, which disappointment is the direct consequence of his having bargained for his land at the Act-of-Parliament price, and, not having afterwards obtained that price, being obliged to fulfil his contract by paying his rent out of his capital; ending only too often in the 'Gazette.' And yet he again urges upon Parliament to guarantee him a price for his produce!

It is just ten years ago that when making my annual Address in this House on this subject, the greater part of my speech consisted of the evidence of farmers that I had taken from those Committees, describing the manner in which Protection had deceived them; and alleging that both in the year 1822 and in 1836 they were unable to meet their liabilities from having contracted to pay for land that which the prices of produce rendered impossible. In 1822 the story was: 'We were told that wheat would sell for 80*s.* a quarter, and we are here as ruined men, having been able to get only 49*s.*' In 1836 the story was: 'Here we are deceived again; we have been promised 64*s.* a quarter, and we are actually feeding our pigs and horses with the wheat, and malting it instead of barley, having no better use for it.'

One fact particularly worthy of notice is that in 1822 the Protection amounted to 50*s.* a quarter, and in 1836 to nearly 100 per cent. And let no man imagine that then there was hope among the farmers; there was only unqualified despair: numbers were really swept away, and others deemed themselves ruined beyond recovery because they did not expect to see a higher price again. If Hon. Gentlemen opposite will turn to the Report they will see that the language was more desponding then than it is now; and that the same question that now seems specially to engross agricultural thought, then also absorbed it: namely, whether wheat could be grown at 40*s*. a quarter. The question was deliberately put in that Committee. An intelligent land-agent and farmer was asked what he believed, and what farmers generally believed, would be the price of wheat in future; and the answer deliberately given was that the farmers did not expect to see it again higher than 5*s*. or 6*s*. a bushel. He was next asked whether he thought that the farmer could do upon that. 'Well,' he replied, 'I think they will, for other things will fall in proportion.' And lucky would it have been for the farmers if they had seized that moment to abolish Protection, and to rely upon the price that they must submit to now. They would now, probably, have been a prospering and contented class instead of a disappointed and needy body of men.

But further, I cannot lead the landed interest to expect that the House will take this matter into consideration, for I do not think it is a matter that Parliament has anything to do with; for even supposing it were to consider the question and come to a conclusion that wheat cannot be produced at 40*s*. a quarter, still I do not see that it could act upon that conclusion; the time is past when the price of the people's food can be raised for the mere benefit of the producer. And if the other conclusion were come to—namely, that wheat could be grown at 40*s*. a quarter—still it does not follow that it would be grown at that price, and that the farmer would in consequence be insured against loss. For if it requires great capital, economy, intelligence and security on the part of the farmer to produce wheat at that price, it does not follow, looking to the mode in which owners of land deal with their properties, that farmers would always be placed under circumstances that would enable them to accomplish it; and if any reverse came they would be as little able to meet it as they are now. Land is not by any means regarded by many of its owners as a mode of securing the largest amount of produce at the least possible cost. Land has a value to many people quite independent of that consideration. Accordingly we find that it depends much upon the taste and objects of the proprietor what will generally be the tenure or circumstances of the farmer as cultivator of the soil. One man is a sportsman, and preserves game on his land which destroys much of the produce. Another man is a politician, and cares more for the vote than for the skill of his farmer. Another charges his estate with debt and has nothing left after paying the interest for improvements. Another looks to influence from the possession of territory; while many like to tie up the land or limit the interest of the owner for the sake of perpetuating the same property in one line of descent; and only a very few are genuine agriculturists.

All this shows how difficult it is to calculate upon the result of what could or would be done in farming in this country, and how impossible it is for Parliament to fix a price for produce. The tenant of an improving landlord may be the next neighbour of another whose landlord is of a different character; and the one would be ruined in a year like the present, while the other might be doing well. Such things prove clearly that the House cannot relieve any man in this or any other business from the conditions of success, which are found in reliance upon his own forethought, capital, skill and industry, and without which he will inevitably fail.

The farmer, then, should be told that with the best disposition in the world to serve him, this House is unable to; for Parliament cannot undertake to manage the landed property of the country or to put a limit to the amount of its produce, without which certainty with respect to price is impossible.

In the midst of the present distress of the agriculturists it will be opportune to read to this House a case that has recently occurred, showing how little able the House is to come to any practical conclusion on the business of agriculture from the statements of distress made by individuals :—

A farm in Gloucestershire of 400 acres, the land of medium quality, and distant from a market, which was formerly let at 20*s.* per acre, which has been drained and on which money has otherwise been laid out in permanent improvements, has quite recently been taken on a lease for eighteen years, by an experienced farmer, with adequate capital, at a rent of 40*s.* per acre. The tenant to be at liberty to destroy game, remove hedges, cut down trees, and, in short, to deal with the land as though it were his own; and if the landlord sees reason to fear that he is not fairly dealt by, the matter is to be settled between him and the tenant by arbitration. No other conditions in the lease. The tenant says he shall be satisfied with 40*s.* per quarter for his wheat, and prices for other produce in proportion.

[Cries of 'Name, name!']

Hon. Gentlemen seem to doubt the correctness of the case. It was given to me by persons who assured me of its being a faithful statement of what has occurred, and I have read it believing it to be true; if it is otherwise, I shall on proof be the first to admit that I have been deceived.

I do not deny that many farmers are distressed: I believe that they are. I should be astonished if they were not; for tenants-at-will, depending entirely on the price of wheat for the year, must suffer severely when the price falls. But notwithstanding the reduction of price, I do not think that at present the case of the owners and occupiers is hopeless; because there is this consolation still remaining: land has not fallen in value, but is as high now as it has been for the last twenty years, and much higher than it was previously. No farm becomes vacant without the appearance of as many or more candidates for its occupation as ever, if not more than there used to be. While, in some cases farms have lately let at an advanced rent. And the agricultural labourers are as well off as they have been, if their means have not actually increased.

And this is the condition of the landed interest after the first year of Free Trade: one not calculated,

I think, to produce despondency; nor one that precludes agriculturists from retiring from their business should they despair of it. And there is this further consolation, which will I am sure occur to the landed interest, that supposing the worst comes to the worst, and the owner is obliged cordially to co-operate with the occupier with a view to improvement, and to conduct the business of farming in the same spirit and with the same economy and energy with which other businesses are conducted, the land-owner of this country really and truly labours under no disadvantage whatever compared with any foreigner. And if his tenant is less fortunate in one respect, he is more so in many others, and there is no reason whatever why he should not compete successfully with any country in the world. In most respects indeed his advantages are superior to those of the foreigner. He has better climate, better government, better labour, better implements, more manure, superior communication, and the best market in the world at his door. But one thing is against him: land is dearer here than elsewhere. But the remedy for this is always in the hands of the landed interest, in fact of the owner himself; and I am certain that if he looked his position fairly in the face, and considered the future requirements of the community, he would come to the conclusion that it is only a reproach to him, and to the land-owners of Ireland, that we should import so much food from abroad as we do. It is my deliberate opinion that these two islands could with ease furnish us with a very much larger supply of food than they do at present; and the reproach of not doing so applies peculiarly to Ireland.

If any man were calmly to survey the circumstances of these two countries, he would say that Ireland had been laid beside England for the purpose of feeding her: the finest agricultural country in Europe, united to the largest manufacturing and the wealthiest commercial community in the world. And yet what is the spectacle presented to the world at this moment? The owners of land in Ireland more distressed than those of England, though this very agricultural interest has been what is called protected, and the people of this country better off, simply because there has been a large and free importation of foreign food. What is it owing to? Is there a man who says that Ireland could not produce more? Or that the state of things has resulted from anything but the mismanagement of landed property, protected highly for forty years? A purely agricultural country, and yet within three years one of the most awful famines that ever visited a country has befallen it; and the landed proprietors at this moment are in a state of ruin! Was there ever such an anomaly? I do not wish to reflect severely on the present proprietors, but an awful retribution has fallen upon the ownership of land, and the owners have been quite unprepared for the visitation: their lands have been neglected, the people neglected; too much of the agriculture is in a barbarous state, and the estates are encumbered with debt; while the only hope for the country now is that its recent misery having revealed to us the real cause of its past poverty, and the responsibilities that would be incurred by the landed proprietary in case of its neglect in the future being no longer open to dispute, it is unlikely that the same evils will be again suffered to recur.

Yes, regretting deeply the sufferings and the sad reverses of fortune to which the people of property in Ireland have lately been exposed, I expect that the regeneration of that country will date from the time at which we have had fully discovered and disclosed to us the past neglect and sad waste of its resources.

I have no hesitation in defending the legislation for that country in the particular that is most complained of by the Irish proprietors : I mean the Poor Law. I believe that the Poor Law was a measure of policy as well as of humanity. I believe that it has already removed from the people one great pretext for crime; that it has diminished an evil only next to crime —the frightful extent of mendicity in that country; that it has secured comparative safety to life and property; and that therefore the people have ceased to feel desperate from being destitute. And all this, taken together with the facilities that have been given to the transfer and sale of property, will, it is to be hoped, soon tempt men of capital to invest their fortunes in land in Ireland, and agriculture there will become a profitable enterprise engaged in by persons from all parts of the United Kingdom.

But above all other things, I should reckon upon the continued prosperity of the manufacturing interest of this country as the most important adjunct to the prosperity of Ireland, in affording a constantly improving market for their produce, and a great and ready vent for their surplus people; and the policy that has been adopted here with respect to trade is, I am sure, the best means for insuring their prosperity.

Attributing many of our past convulsions in commerce to erroneous policy with respect to the trade in food, I expect—and am not afraid to say it—that the prosperity of this country will endure and will increase under our present system.

I may be wrong, but I regard the affairs of this country at present with more confidence and with more hope than I ever did before. I believe that they rest upon a more solid foundation than they have hitherto done. And I ascribe this condition to the increased intelligence of the people, their constant vigilance in public affairs, the higher moral feeling that pervades all classes, together with the great and useful reforms that have taken place of late years, from all of which has resulted a greater amount of political, religious, and commercial freedom than was ever previously enjoyed by any people on the earth.

Political and religious freedom we have had for some time past, and nothing but better order and increased contentment have proceeded from it. And I can never think that anything but good can follow from that other great measure of freedom which has given us the strongest interest that there should be peace on earth and good will among men, and that our neighbour should prosper equally with ourselves.

And now I trust that I do not place a wrong

construction upon the concluding passage of Her Majesty's Speech, when I infer from it that those who are at present entrusted with the Administration of the country are duly impressed with the truth that the surest mode of maintaining the institutions of the country in the affections of the people, is to continue in the progressive course of later years, by reforming what is bad, supplying what is deficient, and showing confidence in the people, which every extension of their liberties has hitherto justified.

XXIX.

HOUSE OF COMMONS, March 15, 1852.

Lord Derby when, as Lord Stanley, he failed to form an Administration in 1851 proclaimed that had he been successful he should have had recourse to a fixed duty on corn for purposes both of revenue and protection to the agricultural interest; when he assumed office in 1852 he emphatically declared in favour of a duty on corn, and more than hinted disapproval of the Free Trade measure of 1846; and many of his supporters showed themselves of like mind. Grave apprehensions were entertained of the reimposition of a tax on food, and a reversal of the entire policy that, according to Sir J. Graham, far exceeded the most sanguine expectations of its authors and supporters. Mr. Villiers lost no time in the matter: on the Motion for Supply, March 15, he immediately demanded a distinct statement from the Government as to the policy they meant to pursue with regard to foreign commerce, especially that branch of it engaged in the supply of food for the people. The Chancellor of the Exchequer, Mr. Disraeli, who was charged by Lord J. Russell with having in his speech in Buckinghamshire promised the agricultural party a fixed duty on corn, with much circumlocution evaded the question, and said that they were not pledged to any specific measure, though they should consider it their duty to propose plans to redress the grievances of the agricultural interest.

In accordance with an intimation that I have given to the Right Hon. Gentleman the Chancellor of the Exchequer, and for reasons that I will shortly state, I wish to make some inquiry with the view of obtaining information from Her Majesty's Ministers upon a subject on which I am sure I do not exaggerate when I say that it is of vital concern to every subject of Her Majesty. I refer to the principle or the policy on which the Government propose to regulate the Foreign Commerce of this country, and more especially that branch of it which is engaged in the supply of food for the people.

This is no abstract question or matter of mere idle speculation: it is a subject so intimately connected with all the realities of English life that it affects the whole social and domestic policy of this country. It affects the finance, the trade, the labour, the capital, and the general condition of the people. I hope, therefore, that it will be treated by the Right Hon. Chancellor of the Exchequer with all the earnestness that it deserves.

The public want information on this subject. It would be incorrect to say that they have not heard anything about it; but it would be quite true to say that they would have been less perplexed if they had not. What has been said by the Government themselves, or by friends on their behalf, has created doubts where none would otherwise have existed.

For some years past there has been a Free Trade policy in force; and during the past few weeks a Protectionist party has been in possession of the Government; but what this Protectionist party is going to do for the cause of Protection is one of those mysteries that may possibly be solved to-night, but that hitherto has not been disclosed.

Now if I seem to be forward in this matter, and if I should appear to be urgent on the Government to make some distinct and candid avowal on the subject, I hope my motives will not be mistaken. I assure the present Government that I am animated by no factious motives, by no party object. And I think I have reason to expect that my motives will not be misinterpreted.

I have been for eighteen years in this House, and during that time I have uniformly manifested great solicitude on this subject: as some of my friends well know, I never in former times lost an opportunity of promoting inquiry and discussion on this matter; and, as the House remembers well, I used annually to submit a Motion to it on the Laws restricting the importation of foreign grain. I have with singleness of purpose done everything in my power to aid in promoting the success of the cause of Free Trade, having always believed that it is more closely connected with the well-being of the people than with any, if not every, other matter besides.

It would surely, then, be remarkable if those who displayed their zeal in that cause before any experience of its advantages had been acquired should now remain inactive—now, when its blessings are appreciated, but when danger and difficulty again hang round it. I was silent only when I believed the question to be safe, when I hoped that it was settled. But no man can doubt that this question is again raised in the country, and that considerable apprehensions and anxiety exist as to the intentions of the Government with respect to it.

I assure the House that I have no object to gain by embarrassing Her Majesty's Government; I have no purpose whatever to serve in placing them in any difficult situation with respect to this subject. I do not regret to see them personally in office. I believe they have as much right as any other Members of this House to their present position if they can hold it with honour to themselves and with advantage to the country. Indeed, I would much rather see them there, than engaged in the agitation that has been going on during the last four or five years; an agitation that I must describe as one of the most reckless and inconsiderate that has ever occurred in this country.

I am, moreover, quite alive to the claims that every new Ministry has to the forbearance of this House with regard to questions that they have not had time to consider, or upon which they are not in a condition to decide. But this is not the relation in which Hon. Gentlemen opposite stand with regard to this particular question. They will not be offended if I say that they are not known in this House or in the country except in connection with it; and they have been distinguished as a party by the course they have taken on the subject. They have steadily maintained the policy of protecting particular interests by law against competition; and they have as firmly asserted the failure of Free Trade. While the characteristics, as far as I have observed, by which they have been and are mainly distinguished, are the union, perseverance, and determination that they have manifested in endeavouring to possess themselves of the government of this country for the purpose of reversing the Free Trade policy. This is not stated for the first time by me: it has been stated by some distinguished Members of the party themselves, and it has been constantly repeated by those who have resisted their movements in this House.

When the late Sir Robert Peel used to oppose the Motions of the present Chancellor of the Exchequer (which as an independent Member he was not bound to do), he did so, he asserted, because the object of the Hon. Gentleman was to carry his Motions in order that he might displace the Government and occupy their place, and so be in a position to reverse the commercial legislation of the country. The Right Hon. Gentleman the Chancellor of the Exchequer himself said in one of his addresses that he might not be successful on that occasion, but that the time would not be far distant when the then Government would be displaced, and when the principles he advocated would be triumphant.

I do not intend to impute any unworthy motive to the Protectionists in what they did: I merely mention their conduct to show their zeal in seeking to reverse the policy of Free Trade. They have not sought office for the sake of distinction or position, but simply and solely with a view of re-establishing the policy of Protection. They have sought every opportunity to further their cause; they have been vigilant throughout every Session; they have combined with persons the most opposed to them; they have supported Motions the least connected with their principles; in short, they have exhibited an earnestness in their cause that I have not observed in any other political party in this House.

And now that he is in power the Right Hon.

Gentleman the Chancellor of the Exchequer cannot, I think, object to tell us how soon and in what way he proposes to fulfil his promise, made two days ago on the hustings, to establish that policy with which he was identified when in Opposition. I think, too, I may also ask the Right Hon. Gentleman the Chancellor of the Duchy of Lancaster in what way he proposes to forward the desire that he says exists in the breast of the chief of the Government to reverse a policy he describes as prejudicial to the capital of the country, and ruinous to native industry.

The Right Hon. Gentleman the Member for Stamford,[1] likewise, should not object to state, if I ask him, what course he intends to pursue with a view to reverse the objectionable change in the maritime code of the country that, according to his opinion, has been attended with results for evil far greater than he had anticipated.

Most certainly the Noble Earl at the head of the Government ought not to shrink from making a bold avowal of his intentions. If any one man in this country is responsible for the position of public affairs at the present moment it is the Noble Earl at the head of the Government. The Noble Earl seems to me to be the man who has formed the party now in power, guided their movements, instructed them in their course, and led them at last to the victory that he has always promised. He is, indeed, particularly responsible, because he is one of those men sometimes observed in this country who are so circumstanced,

[1] Mr. Herries.

and in the enjoyment of such advantages and qualifications, that many persons think themselves justified in following them blindly in the course they prescribe.

In starting the agitation that has led to the present result, the Noble Earl was peculiarly situated. He had been a Member of the late Sir Robert Peel's Government, and had enjoyed the advantage of communicating with men of the greatest experience as Ministers and statesmen. He was fully acquainted with all the circumstances that caused the great change in our commercial policy, and familiar with the special events that ultimately convinced Sir Robert Peel that, for the good as well as for the safety of the country, he was bound to renounce the Monopoly in corn that the land-owners had, with his assistance, maintained. But the Earl of Derby, as I understand, was the only Cabinet Minister who left Sir Robert Peel on that occasion; and, by leaving him, and afterwards associating with all the persons who opposed him, the Earl of Derby did practically announce to the public that, in his opinion, there was no occasion for the change of policy then made; that it was a concession to cowardice; that there was no reason why the Corn Laws should not continue; and that if they would only faithfully follow him, he would lead his party to a position in which they might re-establish those Laws.

A man in the situation of the Noble Earl cannot act but with great responsibility. He is endowed with intellect of a high order; he possesses rank, fortune, and experience, which give him exceptional weight and influence; and many who are his followers justify themselves, as I said, in following him blindly.

I state this for the purpose of showing that the Earl of Derby, above all men, should be ready to tell us the course that he intends to take. In so far as we are allowed to know or to understand from the public journals the relations existing between him and his party, the Noble Earl has been constantly guiding their movements, stimulating their hopes, and encouraging them to believe that the moment would arrive when he would be able to lead them to victory. He seems to have likened himself to a captain of a band, to an officer addressing his soldiers and telling them to be patient and to persevere: that the day was coming when he should be able to give them the signal to make their onslaught on their enemy.

But, not to misrepresent him, I will read an extract from a speech made by the Noble Earl last year, which shows that he was bent on inciting his followers to persevere, with the assurance that the day of triumph would come for them. In May 1850, the Noble Earl (then Lord Stanley) stated, at a public meeting—I do not know for what reason, but if I were to speculate I might suppose that it arose from some suspicion then current of his own fidelity—but whatever the reason, he stated that:—

If in any part of the country, if there be but one district in which a suspicion is entertained that I am flinching from or hesitating in my advocacy of those principles on which I stood, in conjunction with my lamented friend Lord George Bentinck, I authorize you, one and all, to assure those whom you represent, that in me they will find no hesitation, no flinching, no change of opinion. I only look for the moment when it may be possible for us to use the memorable words of the Duke of Wellington, on the field of Waterloo, and to say, 'Up, Guards, and at them!'

And he concluded with the promise that if they would keep up the pressure without, he would do it from within.

This took place a year ago; and looking to the disposition of parties in this House and in the country generally, it must be considered that those whom the present Prime Minister encouraged his followers to treat as the Duke of Wellington treated the foes of our country, were the manufacturing, commercial, and industrial interests of the nation.

It is therefore, I think, not unreasonable in persons who represent those interests to ask the Noble Earl to have the kindness to tell them when he is going to direct his soldiers to be 'up and at them,' and when we are to expect this onslaught upon great national interests which we cherish as of the highest importance. The Noble Earl and the Government ought to be in a position to give a reply to the question I put to them, in which the entire nation is concerned. And considering the professions they have formerly made, they are fully bound to relieve us from the suspense in which we have been ever since they attained power.

And now, I beg for a moment to call the attention of the House to the present condition of the country which, in my opinion, makes it imperatively necessary that such a reply should be given.

Looking at the state of the country as it was at

the beginning of the present year, and during the chief portion of the last, no person living could point to a period when greater peace, contentment, and confidence prevailed. There was remarkable activity in trade, industry was employed, old causes of strife had ceased, of angry politics there were none. The official returns of our navigation and trade disclosed an amount of business during the preceding year wholly unprecedented in the annals of our commerce. There was an expansion in our Foreign Trade, and an increase in our Home Trade of enormous amount: the exports of British manufacture, and the imports of articles of general consumption, were larger than the history of this country offers any previous instance of. The Revenue of the country presented a surplus of nearly 3,000,000*l.*, notwithstanding that we had had to contend with a reduction of taxation approaching to 5,000,000*l.*, to which extent the public have been relieved.

In spite of the assertions made by the Right Hon. Chancellor of the Duchy of Lancaster that the capital of the country has diminished, and native industry been injured, no fact is more notorious than that the capital of this country was never more abundant than now; and that the population of this island, though never so great before, was never better paid, better fed, or more employed.

There is also, as is usual in such cases, what is incident to an improved physical condition: less of misery, of disorder, of vice, and of all the other evils that spring from poverty. This is proved by the evidence of persons whose duty brings them in contact with persons of the poorer class. And surgeons and others state that patients in hospitals are now, from having had better nourishment, more easily cured, and are better able to sustain the operations to which they may be submitted. And not only is this general melioration manifested in towns, but likewise in villages ; for at no period during the existence of the Protective system was the agricultural labourer better off than he is now. I go further, I say that if any candid man competent to survey the agricultural districts and to institute a comparison with former periods were to inquire into the matter he would come to the conclusion that there has been no moment when agricultural advancement was proceeding with so much energy and spirit as at present, or when more skill and economy were apparent in the husbandry of the country.

It is really a relief to turn from speeches out of doors on the distress of the agriculturists, to the writings of one who understands what he writes about, and never speaks on subjects of which he is wholly ignorant. I was astonished to read a speech the other day from so able a man as the present Chancellor of the Exchequer, wherein he told his audience of the local burdens that press on them, the injustice inflicted on them, and the unparalleled distress of agriculturists in general. But now, let me refer to the able Report that the Hon. Member for Berkshire [1] presented to the Royal Commissioners of the Great

[1] Mr. Pusey.

Exhibition in which he describes the immense improvements made of late years in agriculture, and let me read one extract from it:—

The main difficulty of farming has always been in its uncertainty; but it may now be said that machinery has given to farming what is most wanted, not absolute, but comparative certainty. It seems proved, that within ten years old improvements have been improved, and new ones devised, the performances of which stand the necessary inquiry as to the amount of saving the produce, seeing that the owner of a stock farm is enabled in the preparation of his land, by using lighter ploughs to cast off one horse in three, and, by adopting other simple tools, to dispense altogether with a great part of his ploughing; that in the culture of crops by the various drills horse-labour can be partly reduced, the seed otherwise wanted partly saved, or the use of manures greatly economised; while the horse now replaces the hoe at half the expense. The American reaper effects thirty men's work, while the Scotch cart replaces the old English waggon with exactly half the number of horses; that in preparing corn for man's food the steam thrashing-machine saves two-thirds of our former expense, and in preparing food for stock the turnip-cutter, at an outlay of 1*s.* a head, adds 8*s.* a head in one winter to the value of sheep; lastly, that in the indispensable but costly operation of drains, the materials have been reduced from 80*s.* to 15*s.* —to one-fifth nearly of their former cost. It seems to be proved that the efforts of agricultural mechanics have been so far successful as in all these main branches of farming labour, taken altogether, to effect a saving on outgoing of little less than one-half. It is evident that a farmer, setting up a business, who instead of the old waggons with three horses each, should bring one-horse carts, and the smaller number of horses required by such carts, and other improved machinery, would find that, without any increase of outlay whatever, beyond the old scale, he would require all requisite modern machinery, with the exception of the steam-engine. There has been more done in agricultural mechanics during the last few years than had been attempted anywhere in all former times.

It is important to refer to this document, which should be read entire, in order to show that the agricultural interest presents no exception to the general improvement of every other interest of the country; and, notwithstanding all that is alleged with respect to the agricultural interest having undergone sacrifices for the sake of the advantages that it is now hardly denied are enjoyed by other classes, one fact is undeniable: there never was a time when people were more ready to invest their savings and their fortunes in land, or to take farms whenever any occupation became vacant.

I am glad to see that in his speech the Right Hon. the Chancellor of the Exchequer gave up altogether some of those phantom evils that many years ago were predicted as the consequences likely to ensue from the adoption of the policy of 1846. It was an old argument that our merchants and manufacturers would never find a vent for our goods in the markets of the world if we allowed the free importation of corn, and that our bullion must be exported to pay for it. The Right Hon. Gentleman gave up that altogether, and for a very curious reason. He said that the prophecy was quite just, but that it failed through an accident: a pure accident—the discovery of Californian gold. The Right Hon. Gentleman, however, forgot that one of the arguments of his friends is that everything has now become too cheap; for if there were anything like an excess of gold the result would have been that prices generally would have risen. I am sure, therefore, that the Right Hon. Gentleman felt that his argument was suited for Aylesbury, and not for the House of Commons.

Again; I think that when we refer to Official Returns, as at present one may venture to do, because Hon. Gentlemen opposite have now the opportunity of ascertaining whether they have been—as they constantly asserted they were—falsified and doctored at the Board of Trade, it will be seen that none of the serious evils anticipated by Hon. Gentlemen opposite have befallen the country through the change of the Maritime Code. The Official Returns are in our hands, and from perusing them I come to a different conclusion from that arrived at by the Right Hon. Member for Stamford.[1] The conclusion I arrive at is, that a greater amount of tonnage has entered into and cleared out of our ports than at any former period, and that a greater number of British ships were registered in 1851 than in any previous year.

Connected with this we have the cost of what we desire to consume in this country reduced by lower freights. We find, moreover, that, notwithstanding the prediction that we should be unable to compete with other countries, British shipping employed in the trade carried on between neutral countries has increased.

We have had some communication to-night with respect to the colonial policy intended to be pursued by this country. It seems that the Secretary of State for the Colonies[2] is still of opinion that the cause of suffering in some of our colonial islands is the reduction of the Protective Duty: he adheres to his opinion, but he gives up his Measure for continuing the Duty. The Right Hon. Baronet was

[1] Mr. Herries. [2] Sir J. Pakington.

on the Coffee and Sugar Plantation Committee in 1848; and I am convinced that the evidence there produced must have led him to the same conclusion that the Noble Lord, who was Chairman of that Committee [1] and whose loss I deplore, came to: the Noble Lord told me that all the evidence went to show that it was not so much Protection, but the restoration of slavery, or more power over the free labourers, that would, according to the view of the witnesses, benefit the parties complaining. I think, however, that the Right Hon. Baronet will admit, that notwithstanding the Free Trade policy, there has been less complaint heard during the last twelve or eighteen months than at any time since the abolition of slavery. I do not say that the West Indies are prosperous, or that they have yet recovered from the consequences of the great change to which they were submitted; but that during the last year we have heard fewer complaints in the matter of labour, and proprietors have received remittances, though before they were obliged to send out money. In many respects the general aspect of our West Indian colonies has improved; while our dependencies, whether in America or Australia, commercially speaking, never promised better.

Looking, then, both at home and abroad, the empire, under the Free Trade policy, is not declining, but prospering. I do not know that I may not say that this policy has produced a better feeling towards us in foreign countries; where, whatever may be the

[1] Lord George Bentinck.

political feeling towards us on the part of Governments, the people who used to think us selfish in all we did, are now satisfied that our commercial policy towards them is a generous one; and the prospects of more amicable relations between us are thereby improved.

And this being a fair picture of the condition of our country in its various aspects and relations both at home and abroad, and whereas but a few weeks since we were thoroughly appreciating our advantages and progress, what, I ask, is the state of feeling prevalent now? Is there not from one end of the kingdom to the other a feeling of distrust, anxiety, apprehension, and uncertainty? And why is this, but because people anticipate an attempt to reverse that commercial policy, with which they connect so much of their present peacefulness and prosperity? No change is demanded by the people; but they apprehend that some will be attempted. They believe that the men now in power are all pledged to reverse the policy of Free Trade, and they anticipate with considerable anxiety the struggle about to be made at the General Election, when all the influence of the Government at present in power will be used to accomplish their object.

There are, indeed, men connected with the landed interest itself, who now view with alarm the possibility of such a change of policy. The tenant-farmer, I venture to say, will not now ask the Government to reverse the Free Trade policy. He would rather be let alone than have this 5*s.* fixed duty that has been promised at the hustings. He may well think it a scheme devised by the landlords for the purpose of raising the rent of land again. The tenant-farmers generally agree with an intelligent proprietor, a Member of this House, who stated last year that they would get only 2*s.* on a quarter of wheat by a duty of 5*s.*, while it would enable the landlord to come down upon him and say: 'I have got you back Protection, you must now return me the 10 per cent. I abated of your rent.'

This feeling is very general in the agricultural districts. If any are conscientiously opposed to a Free Trade policy they are, of course, justified in endeavouring to procure its reversal; but the attempt will disturb the business of the country and unsettle men's minds. Where peace and confidence existed before, apprehension and uncertainty now prevail. No one knows on what principle to proceed. Contracts are not completed, orders are not sent home; agents abroad and at home are in doubt how to act for their principals. Foreign merchants, I see from this morning's newspapers, are accepting the change of Ministry as a change of policy. During the last three weeks the country seems to have been labouring under a sort of paralysis. Is this state of things to continue? The return to Protection is looked upon by many as the coming of some pestilence that is to blight or to blast all that has been blessed by the bounty of Heaven. Men are startled by doctrines propounded by Members of the present Government, and especially by the Noble Earl at its head, who declared that he could not, for the life of him, see the difference between a tax upon food and a tax on any other article.

If the Noble Earl cannot perceive the difference, it must be because his position in the world is so immeasurably distant from any apprehension of want, that he cannot appreciate the anxieties of poorer men on this account; and he fails, therefore, to see a difference only too obvious and too notorious to his humbler fellow-creatures. I should have thought, indeed, that wisdom no less than humanity might have suggested the distinction to the Noble Lord. I should have thought that a First Lord of the Treasury would have known that unless food in abundance is provided the Revenue must diminish, because our taxation falls chiefly on expenditure; and that on the price of food must depend the sum left to expend in other ways. If he cared for the comforts of his fellow-men, he ought to know that bread is the first necessary of life, and that the more that is spent on this, the less would be spent on all that conduces to the comfort and elevation of man. Men who have only wherewithal to satisfy their bare wants are little better than mere animals; but whether they are better citizens when reduced to such a condition, the Noble Lord perhaps can judge.

The Noble Lord at the head of the Government once publicly gave a definition of the effects of a tax on foreign corn. In answer to a question addressed to him, the Earl of Derby said that a corn-tax raised the price of land, raised the cost of living, but did not increase the remuneration of the labourer. If the Noble Earl would now consider that statement, it might assist him to understand the difference between taxes on food and other taxes.

The Right Hon. Gentleman the Chancellor of the Exchequer, also, was not happy in an illustration bearing on this point that he made out of the House. He talked of a poor man going into a coffee-house and having a chop and some bread for which he might be charged half-a-crown, and observed that it was of little importance to him whether meat were a little cheaper, or bread a little dearer. The Right Hon. Gentleman is not familiar with the habits of the poor when he talks of their going into chop-houses and spending half-a-crown on their dinner. It depends very much on the price of bread whether they can have any meat at all. It is only lately that any one heard of the labouring classes consuming meat. If they consume it now, it is because the cheapness of bread gives them an opportunity of buying it.

But we are told that all these matters are to be decided in a constitutional manner. The people are not to be taken by surprise ; the opinion of the country will be consulted, and the most intelligent portion of the community must decide the question at issue.

In the same speech, however, in which he referred the question to the decision of the country, the Noble Earl at the head of the Government stated a fact that is in no way consoling to the poor man : namely, that bribery and corruption have increased enormously during the last twenty years. He might have said with a nearer approach to the truth that influence and intimidation were never more unscrupulously used, and that therefore it will afford but little consolation to the poor man who wishes to have his bread cheap, to know that the rich, some of whom are interested in its being dear, are going to call a new Parliament to settle the question.

The Right Hon. Chancellor of the Exchequer told us on a former occasion that the history of this country is the story of reaction; that no sooner do the people obtain some great right or liberty than they become indifferent to it and are ready to surrender it. I differ from the Right Hon. Gentleman on this point; but I believe that the people are often too confiding, and take it for granted too readily that when a great question is once settled it will not be disturbed. The people are often imposed upon; and those who have yielded them a right that they never ought to have withheld, are ever on the alert watching for a moment to recover what they have lost.

The Right Hon. Gentleman will probably refer to the present state of Europe in support of his theory of reaction. The people of the Continent made a gallant effort, but a short time since, to obtain their political rights; but now they are again trampled under foot, and are in a more prostrate condition, comparatively, than they have ever been known to be in the history of the Continent. But they have not been so reduced by fair means: what they had gained they have lost by treachery and false pretences. The state of Europe should be a warning to the people of England. The people of the Continent are now watching to see whether the people of this country—the last asylum of freedom—will allow their liberties, in like manner, to be filched from them.

From what I know of the spirit of the English people, they will not submit to be deprived of the boon conceded to them at last by a statesman whose loss the nation now deplores; claimed for them long before by their friends; and sustained and extended by the Government that has recently left office. If the people should prove to be so little alive to the advantages conferred on them, if they should prize so lightly the policy that has rendered them prosperous and happy, we cannot help it; but at least we can give them warning of what they have to expect; we can make them aware of the danger that is approaching them in the most insidious way; we can tell them that the precious gift that they have enjoyed for the last few years is about to be taken from them; and that it becomes them to be at this moment most strictly on their guard against those whom they have so much reason to suspect.

On these grounds, then, I now distinctly ask the Right Hon. Gentleman to come forward in the face of this House—of the country, and make a candid, manly, and open avowal of the intentions of the Government on the subject of their policy with respect to our Foreign Commerce. I ask the Right Hon. Gentleman to tell us whether he intends, under any pretence whatever or for any reason whatever, to re-impose a duty on foreign corn; and whether, in case of a dissolution of Parliament, he intends to propose any scheme of legislation that will raise the question of commercial policy generally and as affecting the food of the people particularly, so that the judgment of the electors may be taken on the subject? And so little am I actuated by party motives in making this appeal to him, that I declare solemnly that the answer most satisfactory to me, as I believe it would be the most gratifying to the country, would be an avowal from the Right Hon. Gentleman that the Government have not the least desire to disturb the existing arrangements under which the country is prospering. The country wants no change of policy, it wants no Dissolution, no disturbance or struggle of any kind. People desire only to be allowed to remain in their present peaceful, prosperous condition; and for this nothing is necessary but a declaration on the part of the Government that they have not any intention of disturbing the policy of Free Trade.

XXX.

HOUSE OF COMMONS, November 23, 1852.

The ambiguity regarding Protection of the Queen's Speech when the new Parliament met on November 11, 1852, coupled with the equivocal proceedings of Lord Derby previous to the dissolution of July, caused Mr. Villiers, immediately after the Address was moved, to give notice of Resolutions [1] that should not only pledge the Legislature for the future to a Free Trade policy but also bar the Government from any further efforts for 'compensation to the agricultural interest,' by an explicit approval of the Act of 1846 establishing the free admission of corn, as a wise, just, and beneficial measure. The Resolutions were brought forward on Nov. 23. The Chancellor of the Exchequer (Mr. Disraeli) scouted the idea of returning to any thing so out of date as a Protection policy; but nevertheless moved an Amendment to completely supplant Mr. Villiers's Motion, and omit the 'three odious epithets,' as he termed them, 'wise, just, and beneficial.' Lord Palmerston, anxious at that moment to avoid a defeat of the Ministry, to the surprise and regret of the Whigs and Liberals stepped in with the suggestion of an Amendment conditional on the withdrawal of the original Resolutions and the Government Amendment: a *via media*, so he would have it, also free from the three odious epithets, thereby giving a loophole to the principle of compensation, and cutting off the retrospective force of Mr. Villiers's Resolutions. Men like Mr. Milner Gibson and Mr.

---

[1] The Resolution moved by Mr. Villiers on this occasion was as follows:—

That it is the opinion of this House that the improved condition of the country, and particularly of the industrial classes, is mainly the result of recent Commercial Legislation, and especially of the Act of 1846, which established the free admission of Foreign Corn, and that that Act was a wise, just, and beneficial measure.

That it is the opinion of this House that the maintenance and further extension of the policy of Free Trade, as opposed to that of Protection, will best enable the property and industry of the nation to bear the burdens to which they are exposed, and will most contribute to the general prosperity, welfare, and contentment of the people.

That this House is ready to take into its consideration any measures consistent with the principles of these resolutions which may be laid before it by Her Majesty's Ministers.

Bright strongly protested against the attempt to wrest the final decision of the great question from the hands of the one man in the House entitled above all others to settle it. The Chancellor of the Exchequer withdrew his Amendment in favour of Lord Palmerston's; but Mr. Villiers consistently adhered to his maturely considered and carefully worded Resolutions, and went to a division on his Motion. It was rejected by a majority of 80, and then Lord Palmerston's Amendment was carried by a majority of 415. The Ministers were pinned to a Free Trade policy; but they were still at liberty to indulge in the vagaries of 'compensation to the agricultural interest,' to which the dwindling body of Protectionists tenaciously clung.

In rising to submit to the House the Resolutions of which I have given notice, I think it right to state why I have deemed it my duty to persevere in my Motion in face of the request made to me by the Right Hon. Gentleman the Chancellor of the Exchequer to postpone it until a time subsequent to his proposal of some measure which he said he wished to lay before the House. For this purpose I beg first to remind the House of its own position with respect to the great matter that we are specially summoned at this unusual and, perhaps, inconvenient season to settle.

It will be remembered that on the first night of the Session there was a sort of general concurrence in the propriety of not moving an Amendment to the Address; occasioned chiefly, I think, by a feeling that, as the Session was a special one, a more deliberate consideration might be given to the subject on some future or distinct occasion. It was under these circumstances that, on the first evening, I gave notice that I should bring the matter distinctly under the notice of the House on a future occasion.

But one of the consequences of the unanimity that prevailed on the first night of the Session was, that the House became bound by the contents of the Address; and with respect to that particular matter on which we were supposed to have been summoned, the House was specially bound by the paragraph or passage in the Speech that had reference to it, which at the time was the subject of observation; which, indeed, I may say was justly and generally objected to by the House on that night, and which I may add without exaggeration has since been universally condemned. Something like an official intimation of the opinion of the Government upon the great matter on which the last Parliament had been dissolved and the new Parliament had been called together, was expected. Persons were hoping either to hear that opinion intimated through the Speech, or the view entertained by the Government of the opinion that the country had expressed on the subject; but where they expected to have this information nothing was found but what I think has been properly designated, an unworthy evasion of the whole matter. Whereas a distinct statement was looked for, only something of a very questionable nature was implied in a paragraph couched in terms that I venture to say not a man present considered were used otherwise than with a deliberate purpose of showing disrespect to the House. I say this advisedly. I do not believe that in the modern days of Parliament, at least, there has ever been another such a paragraph penned or addressed by any Ministry to this House.

We all know what is meant by a reference to 'the wisdom of Parliament.' Why, it is the cant sarcasm or cynical reflection commonly made upon the character of this House! Whenever anybody wants to satirize this House he refers in a sneering tone to its wisdom. That may or may not be just; but I say it is the custom, and I say also that there was not a man in the House, and I believe there was not a man out of it, who did not recognize this object in the terms used on the occasion. And this is the paragraph in the Speech that was intended to satisfy the country on a question distinctly put in issue when Parliament was dissolved, to which an answer is said to have been given, and on which Parliament has been summoned expressly to pronounce.

I am at a loss to understand how Hon. Gentlemen opposite can honestly say that they supposed for a moment that such a passage in such a Speech would be in any way satisfactory to what they themselves have described as 'the great majority of this House.' And still more am I surprised to learn from what has recently passed in another place, that it was not only expected to be satisfactory, but that anybody who contests the point, anybody who is not satisfied with such an allusion to the great matter in dispute, is factious, and raises a discussion upon it for the purpose of opposing the Government, or resisting the measures that are in contemplation for the benefit of the country.

It is on this account that I consider it most important that the House should come to some positive declaration on the momentous question at issue. The House has been placed in a position anything but satisfactory by the decision of the other night. I said before, and I repeat now, that no Amendment having been moved to the Address, the House has become bound by its contents ; and, with reference to the condition of the country, it is bound by the passage in the Speech to which I have referred. Is that a decent or satisfactory way for this House to represent the opinion so strongly expressed by the country upon a great question submitted to it ? But the Right Hon. Gentleman the Chancellor of the Exchequer suggested to me to waive the Motion of which I gave notice, for the purpose of first hearing the measures that he had to propose. I really do not understand the logic of such a proposition.

The House is met at the present time, as I have said before, for the purpose of receiving the answer of the country upon a matter distinctly referred to it : the policy that is to regulate the commercial interests of the country. I am only insisting upon that which was stated by the Prime Minister at the beginning of the last Session and repeated by him last night, when I assert that this is the purpose for which we are assembled at this unusual time of the year. The Right Hon. Gentleman, without anything having been conveyed in the Speech as to the opinion of the Government upon the subject, or with regard to the elections that have taken place, proposes or at least suggests to me that I should waive the proposition I now make for a distinct decision of the House until he brings in certain measures. I do not know what those certain measures have to do with the principal purpose for which we have now been summoned. I do not remember that the last Parliament was dissolved with the view of appealing to the country on any particular question beyond the great measure to which I have adverted.

I do not deny that certain intimations were made in another place of measures that were to please everybody if only a reasonable time were given for their introduction. All that may make a very good story for Gentlemen to tell their constituents, or for Cabinet Ministers to announce to their party; but it will not do for a House of Commons assembled to ascertain whether the recent great change effected in our commercial policy is to be maintained or repudiated by the present Government. The object for which Parliament was dissolved is fresh in our recollection; it was, as we heard the other night, because the First Minister of the Crown could not make up his mind to change his own opinion on this important subject, and thought proper to assume that there was a doubt on the matter in the country, and he desired to learn whether he had been right or wrong in the course he had adopted. As far as I could understand him last year, he consented to an appeal to the nation; he submitted himself (I will not repeat the irreverent addition he made) to that ordeal; he said that he would be tried by his country. And this is sufficient to justify my Motion. He has been so tried and, as it appears to me, has been found wrong, though now he seems to start afresh, and say: 'Well, if that won't do, I must attempt something else.' 'Certainly,' he begins, 'you differ from me in this matter; but,' he goes on to promise, 'if only you give me a little time, I have got a colleague so fertile in his resources and of such transcendent abilities, that he will soon prepare a new scheme for you, one that you will be delighted with, one that, if only he is permitted to produce it, is sure to be satisfactory to all parties.' I do not deny that this is possible. There are geniuses, particularly in connection with medicine, who discover remedies for every evil that flesh is heir to; and I have no doubt but that this colleague is preparing measures that will be universally palatable if only he has plenty of time to produce them. But in the meantime we must think of the business for which we are assembled, and come to the decision for which we have met.

I am perfectly astonished to hear that a Motion so obvious, so reasonable as that which I am about to submit to the House, that one so strictly consistent with the purpose for which we are assembled, and the object with which we were dissolved and dispersed through the country—I am perfectly astonished to hear that the very mention of such a fair, common-sense proposition is considered by Her Majesty's Government and their supporters to be factious. Framed for the purpose of overthrowing the Government! Framed for the purpose of thwarting Ministers! Really, I do not know why I am implicitly to trust this Government, or to rest satisfied with their reputation for consistency! I do not see why such faith in them should be expected from any man. I dare say that before this debate terminates we shall have plenty of reasons given why we should all agree; but nevertheless I cannot think that my offence deserves the name of factiousness, or, seeing that the Government has not yet intimated its opinion, why I should not submit a Motion in order that the House of Commons may have an opportunity of expressing its collective opinion in obedience to the directions its Members have received from their constituents.

Moreover, I have no idea what the measures are that the Right Hon. Gentleman is to propose with a view of silencing a factious opposition. I certainly have read the public papers and have endeavoured to collect the information that is open to everybody, but I have found the same difficulty that I believe has been experienced generally to trace out the real character of these measures. I have read carefully the speeches of persons supposed to be in the confidence of Her Majesty's Government. One of them, a Noble Marquis, when addressing an agricultural audience said that he had received no distinct intimation of what the Cabinet contemplated, but that he felt perfectly convinced that they in some way or other intended to advance the agricultural interest; whether by a tax on spring corn or by meddling with the Currency he could not say; but relief in some way or other was to be afforded.

Turning our gaze to Essex, we see a gentleman there who has given his attention particularly to the Currency, and he intimates that there can be no justice for the farmers until 'that most unwise measure,' the law of 1819, is repealed.

Again; a gentleman high in the confidence of Government, one in fact holding a most important position in the Government, goes down to Lincolnshire and enlightens the farmers there: I do not allude to his original speech in which he stated, as the grounds of his confidence in Lord Derby, that he knew his Lordship to be a thorough Protectionist, who had nothing at heart but the re-enactment of a Protectionist Policy—I do not allude to that speech, it is too old, it was made some months ago; but I allude to the speech of a week ago, which I consider to be important. In this speech he says that there are only two courses open to the Government: either to return to Protection or to give the agriculturists in its place something as good, which, as I venture to read it, would be something quite as bad.

These are the only sorts of measures shadowed forth by Members in the confidence of the Government, and yet the Right Hon. Gentleman expects to be allowed to bring forward his measures before my Resolutions; and begs to have precedence of me. Of me, when my special object is to obtain the explicit adhesion of the Legislature to the principles upon which the country ought to regulate its commerce, or, according to an expression used in the House of Lords, its interests! Before you do that, says the Right Hon. Gentleman, let me introduce my measures. And he asks me to assume that some mischief has been done and that some reparation is required, which, he must be aware, I deny *in toto*: I declare the direct opposite to be the case.

Then I am told of recent converts. I hear of Members who are honestly desirous of supporting our policy, Members, too, who on both sides of the House are tender on the subject; and I am told that we have framed our Resolutions purposely to offend these converts. Let it be shown first that they are honest converts and that they adopt our views of commercial policy, and certainly they shall receive all forbearance from this side of the House. But, as far as I can understand, these converts to Free Trade, if converts at all, are so from necessity. They dissolved the last Parliament and got a verdict against themselves; and now—to use their own phrase—they bow to the verdict of the country. Certainly I must say that I never heard of a more convenient course for a party than, after having dissolved Parliament for the purpose of obtaining a verdict from public opinion as to whether they were right or wrong, to adopt such a plan as that now proposed. One cannot but be amused at it. It is simply, 'Heads I win, tails you lose.' If Protection succeeds, so much the better; we are all right. If Free Trade is successful, we 'bow' to the verdict of the country, but in any case we remain in.

I never should have made these observations, or have taken this line of argument, had not my Motion been stigmatized as factious. I want to justify my course, and to show the country that I am reasonable in calling for a distinct declaration of the principles that are to guide the Government. I believe that the country has declared itself to be perfectly content with its experience of the recent commercial policy, and does not want to have it changed. On the contrary, they want to have it declared settled, and even extended. And I cannot understand why the Government should hesitate to declare itself satisfied also, and ready to carry the policy out to its fullest extent.

If I am to understand the arguments or speeches of the Right Hon. Gentleman, or at least of the First Minister of the Crown, they mean that the latter has not abandoned his opinions; but holds them unchanged. This being the case, I cannot see that there is anything unreasonable in the people's declaring likewise that they still adhere to their opinions, and that they expect them to be faithfully represented in this House.

I do not believe that a public meeting could be called in any part of the kingdom at which the persons assembled would not, if they were independent, affirm that they had derived the greatest advantage from the changes the Legislature has made in our commercial policy; that they had confidence in them; and that they did not wish to return to the old system. And why, I want to know, is the House of Commons the last place in which such opinions are to be declared? Why are we to come here with 'bended knee and bated breath' to whisper something conditional and equivocal like this paragraph in the Queen's Speech, which seems to intimate that evil has resulted from our commercial legislation, and that the first business of Parliament should be to remedy that evil ? This paragraph is vague and mysterious : we do not understand it. We, the majority of this House, think and have declared elsewhere that the recent changes are wise, just, and beneficial ; and such we are assembled here to declare them.

There is one thing, moreover, that encourages me and that convinces me of the propriety of my Motion : it has already done some good—it has produced the Amendment of the Right Hon. Gentleman. I can assure the Right Hon. Gentleman that I have derived the utmost satisfaction from seeing his Amendment ; which, certainly, is a great amendment of his own politics and that of his party, particularly as they are propounded in the Queen's Speech and in a speech recently made by the First Minister of the Crown. But I cannot withdraw my Resolutions for the sake of it, because great though the improvement it marks in the Right Hon. Gentleman's course is, nevertheless, any man of common sense seeing the two propositions would, at once, I think, say that mine is the Amendment, and the Right Hon. Gentleman's the original Motion. The good that my Resolutions have already done amply justifies them. Indeed I do not despair that before the close of the evening, or of the week, the Right Hon. Gentleman himself will adopt them—nay ! perhaps vote for them.

There is one point in the ministerial Amendment that brings us so near to an agreement that I am in hopes that we shall have but one Division—perhaps none. It is a most valuable admission : namely, that one of the Acts of our recent legislation has cheapened provisions, and thereby greatly improved the condition of the working classes. I so entirely agree with the Right Hon. Gentleman on this point that I have expressly named the Act he referred to, and characterized it as a wise and just measure. If the Right Hon. Gentleman still requires me to withdraw my Resolutions, he will be obliged to tell me why an Act that, according to his own Amendment, has conferred such an inestimable blessing on the people, should not receive the character which I have given it. I should be surprised if there were any hesitation on the part of his friends to admit that character to be correct; for, having long considered the subject, having many times assisted in its discussion in this House, I have a distinct recollection that the recent legislation alluded to, which used to be called the total repeal of the Corn Laws, was opposed solely on account of the advantages of those Laws to the poor. It was always a labourers' question. 'Prove to me,' the Members for counties whose seats depended on upholding them were wont to say, 'that they are not for the good of the poor, that the labourers won't suffer from their repeal, and I am in the lobby with you directly; for it is on their account I uphold them; it is because it is a labourers' question that I vote for the Corn Laws.'

It was a poor man's question essentially; and used to be discussed by Gentlemen opposite from that point of view. I am sure that if any foreigner had been present when our discussions were going on he would have thought that all the benevolence was on that side of the House and all the heartlessness on this. He would have thought that those charitable men cared nothing for their own kindred or their own property, but were all ready to be sacrificed for the benefit of the humbler classes ; whereas their opponents were hard and flinty-hearted men, ever grinding the faces of the poor and seeking profit by their misery. If such an observer were to appear to-night, and to learn that we have not only changed the Corn Laws, but have admitted that the change has greatly benefited the working classes and greatly improved their condition, yet nevertheless that a great party—the majority that used to be, the disinterested and humane that seemed to be—now object to designate the Act that has abolished those Laws as wise and just, I believe that he would be led into some doubt as to the sincerity of their sympathy with the poor. And if I must offer a word of advice to the Right Hon. Gentleman the proposer of the Amendment, and his party, it would be to accede at once to my Resolutions. It is not much to ask of them ; I hardly see how they can do less ; for if ever there existed Laws that had the effect of raising the price of provisions and, consequently, of impairing the condition of the people, they must have been the most odious and execrable Laws that were ever passed ; and no one will understand why an Act that has repealed such Laws and produced such consequences as the Right Hon. Gentleman asserts it has, can be other than I have described it in my Resolutions.

I cannot conceive a more guilty exercise of authority than that of tampering with the subsistence of the people; and if a law having that effect existed for the benefit of a few members of the community I cannot conceive anything more vile than such an enactment would be. What is it that you mean by an Act that has raised the price of bread and provisions, and limits the amount to the poor? Such an Act involves everything that regulates and gives character to the whole condition of the people. The amount, more or less, of food that the people enjoy, determines the condition of those millions who earn their daily bread by their daily toil. Whether a man shall lead the life of an animal or of a civilized social being depends entirely on the means he has of obtaining not only sufficient food to meet the bare requirements of existence, but that also which enables him to provide for his moral and social wants. The condition of the bulk of mankind is literally civilized or the contrary, just in proportion as food is easily accessible to them or the reverse; and in the present state of the world the most important circumstance connected with the moral nature of man is that which affects the plenty or scarcity of his food.

What is the first business of life? Look round at the millions upon millions that cover the surface of this earth, and consider if it is not to exchange labour for food? The terms on which that exchange is made, decides whether a man shall be debased or raised; and, here amongst ourselves, whether he shall uprightly and freely pursue his calling in life, or become the occupant of the workhouse, the gaol, or a premature grave. It is a clear apprehension of this that has produced the universal conviction now prevailing as regards the importance of an abundant, I had almost said of a superabundant, supply of food in this country.

If, therefore, any Minister or man in authority should again try to persuade any portion of his fellow-countrymen that an Act having for its purpose to increase the abundance of food has had the effect of increasing crime and pauperism—if any man, I say, announces such an opinion, he excites the wonder if not the indignation of the people throughout the land.

There are men in every parish of this country whose experience satisfies them that the extent of crime and destitution among the people depends greatly upon the amount of food available for their support; and in making the reference I do now, I am perfectly satisfied that the Right Hon. Gentleman the Home Secretary will feel that it is necessary for him to make some explanation to this House of the statement he is represented as having made when he recently addressed his constituents. I myself am sure that the Right Hon. Gentleman has been misrepresented or misreported, for I believe him to be the last man in this country who would misstate a fact, or mislead his countrymen. But with his high authority he is supposed to have suggested to the people whom he addressed, that in consequence of recent legislation, crime and destitution had increased. [Mr. Walpole: 'No!'] I readily believe that denial of the Right

Hon. Gentleman; and I am glad at the prompt manner in which he expresses it, for it shows his conviction of the opposite opinion.

It is the knowledge of the great importance of this matter—the greater or less amount of food in this country, that now makes the power or control of it a circumstance so terrible, so momentous in the hands of any authority ; and I think there can be no greater manifestation of heartlessness, I had almost said of barbarity, on the part of any body of men, than to attempt to limit the amount of the subsistence of the people for the purpose of benefiting themselves.

Nevertheless, I am obliged to ask what it is that we are here assembled for upon this occasion ? I am obliged to ask whether such Laws have not existed, or did not exist, in this country for upwards of thirty years ; and whether we are not now about to recognize the enormous advantage to the community of having repealed those Laws ? Laws for which there is nothing in the vaunted institutions of this country or in the wealth that it may have conferred upon individuals, or in any other circumstance connected with this country, that could compensate to the working classes for the enormous injury they inflicted on them. And yet, if I understand the difference between this and the other side of the House to-night, it is that I propose to designate the repeal of such Laws as wise and just whilst you consider such a designation as 'factious,' and that it is utterly incompatible with the honour and credit of some Hon. Gentlemen to acknowledge the policy and advantage of such a change.

Indeed, I received information within a few moments of entering the House, that if it should be declared by a majority of this House that the repeal of the Corn Laws, which has had the effect the Right Hon. Gentleman the Chancellor of the Exchequer has stated, and which I have so often stated in this House, was wise and just, that then we shall have a prospect of the resignation of this Government.

I can assure the Right Hon. Gentleman and his colleagues that, whatever they may think of the motives of the person who proposes this Motion, and though Lord Derby may think it factious, I have not the smallest desire to see them dismissed. I do not deny that the Noble Earl at the head of the Government is a great authority as to what is factious. He has been, as he stated last night, thirty years before the public ; the public have had the opportunity of witnessing his conduct for the last thirty years ; and I, as one of the public, do not dispute his authority in such matters ; but I can assure the Noble Earl that it is still possible for a man to be single-minded on a matter of this sort—to have but one purpose before him ; still possible for a man not to be ready to adopt every principle and abandon every party for the sake of power.

I care, however, very little whether credit is given or not by Hon. Gentlemen opposite to the statement I have made ; for most surely I believe that this great country would survive the calamity with which it is said to be thus contingently menaced by Right Hon. and Hon. Gentlemen opposite resigning their places. I should be very sorry to see it happen; but even if it did I should not be without hopes for the country. I have heard of such things happening before, and I have seen them happen, without any evil ensuing in consequence. In fact, I myself am not disposed to attach so much importance to the existence of any particular Ministry as some people are. I have seen four or five Ministries in office since I have been in Parliament, and, so far as I have been able to judge, there has been a strong family likeness between them all. The country never suffers much from any of them; those who accede to power generally do that which they resisted in opposition, which is pretty much what their predecessors did before them. My own impression is, that no great genius is required to administer a Government. I believe that all the real business in the public offices is done by a certain number of public servants—able and valuable men—of whom we hear very little; and that it must be owing to some lack of judgment or some want of capacity, whenever a Government becomes sufficiently unpopular to be displaced.

That I may not be misunderstood, however, I beg to state again, that in making this Motion I have no intention of displacing the Ministry. I do not act as a partisan on the occasion. ['Oh, oh!'] Well, then, as Gentlemen opposite do not seem satisfied with what I say, I will add that, were that displacement to occur, I should be quite reconciled to the event.

If, however, I might offer a word of advice to the Right Hon. Gentleman the Chancellor of the Exchequer, it would be that he do no such thing as resign, but rather, if this Motion be carried against him, that he accept it with thankfulness and make use of it in adopting the course that he apparently wishes to pursue. He seems to be about to enter upon a career of usefulness, and I would advise him not to be deterred by the novelty of that course from doing so.

He takes very much the same views with regard to the financial policy of the country that those whom he used to assail took before him ; and with his talents, which seem to be available for the purpose, I should be really sorry to see him removed from office by my Motion. I am still more hopeful of the course he is likely to pursue from what I see shadowed out in his Amendment. There was reason to expect good from his statements when he produced the Budget last year. He stated facts very candidly ; and, though his friends were then extremely anxious to relieve him from the imputation of deducing any conclusions from those facts, it seems that he concluded something from them, and formed opinions from them that he really means to maintain.

The Right Hon. Gentleman declared that the commercial policy that had been followed in this country for the previous ten years had had the effect of greatly relieving the community, without injuring the Revenue. He admitted that these were facts that it was his duty as a Minister to declare ; that duties had been repealed or reduced to a very large amount; that the Revenue had not suffered much; and that the community had benefited a great deal. Facts such as these were obviously distasteful to his supporters; but still the Right Hon. Gentleman, with the responsibilities of office upon him, felt bound in candour to state them. I must say, that in his present Amendment he seems to have laid the ground for advancing the policy to which he then did homage: a policy that consists in reducing, or altogether removing first of all duties on articles of necessary consumption and then on articles of general consumption; so that the people might, in easily satisfying the wants of first necessity, have the means of also obtaining articles of secondary importance.

This was a policy distasteful to Hon. Gentlemen opposite to accept; but nine months' gestation has done a great deal, and, among other results, has given birth to the Amendment that admits the case of this side of the House: that when you reduce the tax on food and do nothing to raise its price you may venture to reduce other duties; because then the people will be able to consume the commodities on which they are laid, and the Revenue will recover itself. This is an intelligible principle, and we want the principle acknowledged by this House. We want the Chancellor of the Exchequer to recognize it, and fully to carry it out.

I justify the Resolutions that I am going to propose, on the ground that at present the Chancellor of the Exchequer's intentions on this main subject are not known ; that we cannot understand from anything that has taken place officially, whether he is going backwards or forwards, or what course he is going to take ; whereas if he adopts the Resolutions that I shall move to-night, there can in future be no doubt on the matter : they are a full and clear recognition by the House of the advantages that we have already experienced from the new policy.

Some time ago I startled Hon. Gentlemen opposite when I attempted to show how available the means of the community would be for further consumption if duties on necessary articles were reduced ; but lately some of those Gentlemen when occupied in agitating the counties and remote districts on the subject of Protection made great use of the statements I put forward, and applied them in support of the proposition that 91,000,000*l*. had been abstracted by recent legislation from the pockets of the farmers, and that consequently the farmers were entitled to indemnity. Now, what I spoke of was the vast difference between the means of the community available for general expenditure in a year of great scarcity and a year of great plenty ; between their means in such years as 1847 and 1849—years in which people paid respectively a great deal for little food and paid little for a great deal of food : a difference of means quite sufficient to account for great differences in the demand for articles taxed for Revenue, and the condition of the people generally.

I did not stoop to contradict Gentlemen who made this use of my statement, for they exposed themselves to this question: If 91,000,000*l.* have been taken from the farmers, who gave the farmers the 91,000,000*l.* in the first place? I have here in my hand a calculation (smaller in amount and one therefore I trust that will startle Gentlemen rather less) that exactly illustrates the advantage of the policy that I hope the Chancellor of the Exchequer intends still further to carry out.

This metropolis alone affords a most conclusive illustration of the enormous effects that are produced by a reduction in the price of articles of food upon the availability of the people's means for purchasing other articles. The population of London, according to a moderate calculation, is 2,300,000. From July 1828, when the Sliding Scale was enacted, up to the end of 1841, when it was abolished, 14,787,990 quarters of wheat were admitted; of which 12,452,562, or 84 per cent., were not admitted until the price exceeded 70*s.* per quarter. 70*s.* per quarter for wheat gives 60*s.* per sack for flour. The quartern loaf would then be 11*d.*, it is now 7*d.* The consumption of the population of London is not less than two quartern loaves per head per week, so that the saving is 8*d.* per head per week, or 1*l.* 14*s.* 8*d.* per annum, being, in round numbers, for the whole population, 4,000,000*l.*

Again, as to articles that come next to those of necessity—sugar, for instance: in London, where the consumption is greater than in the country, the allowance to servants is half-a-pound each per week for breakfast and tea alone; the middle and upper classes consume not less than 50 lbs. a head per annum; so that the average may fairly be taken at about 30 lbs. The soft sugar, that, up to 1845, was 7*d.*, is now 4*d.* to 5*d.*; the loaf sugar, that was 10*d.* and 11*d.*, is now 5*d.* to 6*d.*; and probably half the consumption of London is loaf sugar. Take the reduction, as a low average, at 3½*d.*, the saving is 8*s.* 9*d.* a head per year; or, for the whole population, 1,093,750*l.*, the entire amount consumed giving above 26½ lbs. per head. In coffee, on a similar calculation, the gain to London is 166,666*l.*; and in tea, 125,000*l.* Both these gains are due to the recent reduction in the price of coffee and tea, and represent a total of 5,739,583*l.* in London alone—there being also, of course, a corresponding gain throughout the country, and in every town, from the same cause.

The reason why I wish to impress these facts on the Government is, that the First Minister of the Crown does not appear to be informed on the matter. If anything were needed to justify my present Motion, his speech on the first night of the Session would suffice.

The Noble Earl cannot understand, it seems, what difference there is between taxing food and any other article (he said so last year), and his notion is, that if the amount of food increases, the condition of the labouring classes is deteriorated; or, as he pleases to express it more shortly, if the price of food falls, wages will fall: he stated this only the other night. Now I want to impress upon him that the difference between food and any other article is, that food is a thing of first, of necessary consumption; and that it depends entirely on the price, or rather on the abundance of that article, what there is left for further consumption.

But perhaps the Noble Earl will say that he is occupied with the Revenue ; that he is not talking about humanity or about the condition of the people ; and that he does not see why food is not as good an article to tax as any other. But, taking merely the financial and economical view of the subject, it is, as I have shown, of the greatest possible importance that, while you tax expenditure generally in order to collect a vast revenue, food should be cheap and abundant in order to facilitate all other consumption. The Noble Earl keeps to the point that if the price of food falls, wages also must generally fall ; but I cannot offer so great an insult to the intellect of an able man like the Noble Earl, as for a moment to suppose him to be in earnest, in uttering a fallacy that could only be entertained by the most ignorant person : no amount of sympathy with the labouring classes could lead an intelligent being to suppose that they would be injured by an easy access to the first necessary of life, or that a fall in the price of provisions must impair their condition. Against such statements and such views, if honestly held, it would be necessary to show what the general condition of the country is under a fall in the price of provisions. But not knowing exactly what view the Government will take on this occasion, I do not like entering very much into details ; I still hope that on both sides of the House we are agreed as to the general fact that with food cheaper, and with various duties on articles of consumption reduced, the country is in a prosperous state.

I have, indeed, since I gave notice of this Motion, had more information on the matter sent to me from all parts of the country than I could well carry—papers and documents, containing facts of every kind, proving the great prosperity that in all directions now prevails. If I thought there would be the least dispute on the point, the smallest difference of opinion expressed as to the fact, I should feel myself bound to read to the House more or less of this information, because it certifies from literally every part of the kingdom, the wonderful prosperity of every interest measured by every recognized test—by full employment, by diminished pauperism, by decrease of crime, by loyalty, by contentment; and it is confidently given by competent judges who have witnessed and watched the course of the change from its commencement. Formerly, I should have felt it necessary to lay all such information before the House; but I shall, for the present, abstain from doing so, because I will yet venture to hope that we are in effect, and substantially, agreed upon the main point of the Chancellor of the Exchequer's Amendment: namely, that by the recent legislation abolishing Protection on food the people are well off.

I want the Chancellor of the Exchequer to go further; for he seems to have confined his proposition to the working classes. I do not know why he does so; but I suppose he will explain his reason. I myself do not confine it to the working classes, because there is no possibility of really benefiting the working classes by legislation that does not also beneficially affect the whole community; and on the same principle the Corn Laws could not formerly injure the working classes without every other class being injuriously affected. The same legislation that facilitates and extends to the merchant the market at home for foreign commodities, increases for the manufacturer the demand in exchange for his manufactures, for the agricultural producer it increases the demands for his produce by means of greater consumption, for the labourer the demand for his labour; and thus all classes are in fact mutually benefited.

It is for this reason that in my Resolution I propose to the Right Hon. Gentleman as Chancellor of the Exchequer to accept the principle that the property and industry of the country are better able to bear their burdens under a policy of Free Trade, than they are under that of Protection. And it is on this point that I am anxious to get a declaration of his opinions; for as yet, I repeat, we have not got his real views on the respective benefits or evils of the two policies. This is one of the chief purposes for which I propose my Resolutions. I want to know whether he thinks Protection the best means of enabling those who are protected to support their burdens; and whether he thinks Free Trade a mischievous system, which, if it must be endured, it will be his duty, if possible, to mitigate. These are points which I desire to have definitively settled in this House, but which, as far as the Government is concerned, are still left uncertain by the Amendment.

My opinion is, as I have often stated it before in this House, that Protection is an unqualified mischief, unjustifiable in principle, vicious in practice, and peculiarly injurious to the interest it purports to benefit. If the Right Hon. Gentleman, in the course of the changes that he is undergoing, has come to the same conclusion, it is highly important that we should know the fact without loss of time, since the character of future legislation will probably turn upon this point.

Further, it is my distinct impression that no compensation whatever is due to any interest that was protected, because, as regards every such interest (I speak of the interest, and not of individuals in particular cases connected with it), my conviction is that it has only been served by the change of policy.

My belief is that previously every protected interest had been withering under Protection. The experience of the last few years has proved to us the vast advantage of setting all interests free ; and if we want one illustration of this fact more convincing than another, more completely demonstrating how injurious Protection was, and how beneficial the relief from Protection is, we have it peculiarly and most conclusively in the case of the agricultural interest. I do not speak rashly or without book ; it has ever been my strict habit, throughout the long discussion of this question, to take the utmost possible pains to assure myself that I was right in the data upon which I based my views and my statements; and in preparing for this debate I have not departed from that rule.

Throughout the struggle for the total repeal of the Corn Laws, in seeking to ascertain whether the change could be effected with safety to the country and without injury to the particular interest in question (and if any one doubts the truth of what I say, I would refer to the evidence I adduced before this House in 1844), I made it my business conscientiously to procure information from every one who was competent to give an opinion, and I have done so since. I have questioned persons intimately acquainted with the present state of agriculture in this country, and I have sought their views of that condition, and have received their solemn and conscientious opinion that the agricultural interest was never in a more healthy condition than at this moment. [Cries of 'Oh! oh!'] If Hon. Gentlemen doubt me, I shall be obliged to produce my authorities. I can adduce one of them now whose credit, were I to name him, the Government could not dispute, and whose competence others would admit to be unquestionable; for he is a man who besides being a large occupier and farmer of land himself, is employed by many noblemen and gentlemen as their land-agent, and is generally intrusted with the purchase and sale of land. I asked this gentleman what he thought of the condition of the landed interest: he told me that he had not known it for years in so good a condition as it is now. His expression was: 'I never knew it in a sounder state.' I asked him whether land now sold for more than it used to fetch ; and he replied : 'Most undoubtedly ;' and that, speaking from twenty-five years' experience, he had never known land sell so well as it sells now ; that he himself had sold within the last few months a great deal of land ; that it is rising in value ; that he should say that it is selling now at thirty-seven years' purchase ; and that some pasture land which a few years ago sold for twenty-eight years' purchase, had recently fetched, under his hand, thirty-three years' purchase.

As to the farmers ; where they are distressed it is because the landlords have not done for them that which they properly require ; nothing that the Legislature can do for them will remedy such evils ; and this they now understand. They do not expect a restoration of Protection ; they no longer have any faith in Protection ; they all refer their difficulties to causes of a more domestic kind : to matters that must be settled between them and their landlords, but of which we hear little in this House.

I have said that I will not weary the House with details, and I shall keep my word ; but there is one statement which I have verified that does so immediately bear upon the question closely concerning so many in this House—the effect of the recent legislation on the landed interest—that I cannot forbear reading it to the House. I happened to see it in a public journal, and I took the trouble to test it so that I might not mislead Hon. Members. It is a very remarkable case. It seems to me to be precisely in point : it is the case of a land-owner who was supposed to have been ruined in 1846, and who, from having been an old supporter of Sir Robert Peel, supposing that his rent and the value of his property entirely depended upon the Corn Laws, was extremely indignant at his Protection being taken from him. He charged the Ministry of the day with all the losses that he should have to incur, and in his distress sent for an agent to consult with him in what way to dispose of his property. The statement is as follows :—

At the time the Government made known the intention to repeal the Corn Laws, which is now nearly five years since, the owner of an estate of about 4,000 acres, situate in the centre of England, alarmed at the prospect which Free Trade presented of reduced rent and diminished income, had his attention drawn to the necessity of preparing his tenants for the lower prices they would have to take for the produce of their farms, and sought, in the improvement of his estate, for means to enable them to continue its successful cultivation. The success which has attended his proceedings offers so valuable an example to others, that I trust I shall be excused for giving some account of it. At the period mentioned the estate was divided into farms of 180 to 300 acres, which, tithe-free and arable, with valuable pasture, were let at rents of from 15*s*. to 30*s*. an acre. The tenantry, although ancient, had held only by the year; the land, which is naturally fertile, had had scarcely anything done to improve it, and the farmers had little idea of any capability in the soil beyond what their inferior practice had developed. The quantity of pasture upon each farm allowed of a considerable quantity of stock being kept, but as the cattle were grazing all the winter in the meadows, and no provision of winter food, except hay, was given them, the arable land had no benefit from the stock; and its cultivation being upon a course without root crops, and but little assisted by manure, gave only very moderate returns. To tenants so farming, Sir Robert Peel's announcement of Free Trade created considerable alarm, for they, as well as their landlord, saw little chance of their continuing to do as they had done; but in the improvement of their inferior practice, and in the amendment of the general state and ill-condition of their farms, the proprietor was told there would be found ample scope to cover their reductions from Free Trade, and on this he was told to rely. The assistance of a new land-agent, and from a distant district, was obtained, and he at once saw how much of the imperfect success of the tenants was owing to the ill-condition of their farms, and their ignorance of the improved practices which the cultivation of inferior soils had elsewhere called forth; he knew the difficulty there would be in introducing the different practices which he considered essential to the future successful cultivation of their farms, and he could only hope to effect this by at once destroying their confidence in their past practice, and making them place a higher appreciation on the capability of their soil. He determined on a course which should at once drive them to adopt a different system, and at the same time should encourage them to enter into improvements of their farms. It was with these views that at the first audit the tenants were informed that they would each receive notice to quit, but that leases for twenty-one years would, at the same time be offered them, at an advance of rent of 20 per cent.; that permission would be given them to break up certain portions of the pasture of their farms, after they had been drained, upon plans that would be given them; that draining tiles would be allowed them to drain all their land, but that the draining was to be done at depths and upon the plans to be laid down; that their homesteads would be improved, and sheds built to give them accommodation for wintering their stock in yards, and fattening cattle in stalls; and they would be allowed to remove all unnecessary hedges and trees injurious to the corn; but at the same time their leases would forbid their existing practice of taking two white corn crops in succession; and they would be obliged to dress a fourth of their arable land every year, and other restrictions would be introduced on what they had been in the habit of doing. It was expected in this way they might be made to adopt a more advantageous course of husbandry, and that their farms might be put into better condition, and made more productive, so as to become cheaper to them at the increased rents than they had been under the old. I must pass over the difficulties of the next three years, the stand made against these measures, the obstacles thrown in the way, the withdrawal of some of the tenants, the objections raised to the deep draining, and the attempting the cultivation of roots where roots had never grown, &c. Fortunately, some of the tenants left, and the readiness with which the vacated farms were reoccupied, and at still higher rents, and the example which the new tenants afforded, who, directed by their leases, at once proceeded to grub hedgerows, to deep-drain, and raise turnips and green crops, and better clean the land, were answers to many of their objections. And now it is to the result I would call attention, which is as follows:—this estate now affords a clear rental of 23 per cent. advance on the rental of 1845. The rents are now better paid than they ever have been; the last two audits were held quicker than ever after the quarter-days, and at each the whole of the rents were collected without an arrear; and the tenants, with scarcely an exception, admit they are doing well, and their farms are cheaper than they were to them at the old rents: and well they may say so, for such crops as they have had the last two years were never before seen in their parishes. I am aware that such an instance of meeting the requirements of Free Trade is little likely to have the approval of tenant-farmers, and yet how far more truly beneficial has been the course here adopted than would have been that of the proprietor seeking to afford relief by reducing his rents! No reduction could have given the same relief, but would have been mischievous.

This is a case that cannot be singular, because I find it constantly stated by agriculturists who are properly so called and referred to in their own periodical journals, that, notwithstanding the long duration of Protection, the land is still in most places in a terrible state; that the buildings are dilapidated and wholly unsuited to the occupations; and that if the outlay and improvements actually required were only made, the occupiers of the land might be now in as good a position as ever they have been.

I need only allude to the journal of the Royal Agricultural Society, with which every gentleman opposite must be familiar, and to the prize essays that are written every year upon the husbandry of every county, to confirm my statements. I have seen those essays. There is not one within these two years that either refers to Protection or to legislative relief; but they speak of that relief which a landlord is able to bestow upon his tenants by improving his own estate, and which he has not yet afforded.

My object is to establish that Protection has been an evil to agriculture, and has not promoted improvement, and for this purpose I will just read a few extracts from these essays. ['No, no!'] Hon. Gentlemen may be disinclined to have such facts published; but I wish to show that no relief can be given by reverting to Protection which has done unqualified mischief, and that if agriculture is to be improved, it must be by the owners and occupiers of land themselves.

In the prize essay of the Royal Agricultural Society on the farming of Kent, after stating 'that the further advancement of agriculture in the cold clay districts of Britain essentially depends on draining,' the writer says:—

Before draining can be successfully carried out on the Weald and other enclosed portions of the county, the small fields must be enlarged by grubbing hedges and felling trees. Not less, perhaps, than an *eighth* of the entire area of the entire arable land of this extensive district is occupied by hedges and trees, taking into calculation the ground that is injured by their roots and shade. Many of the fields consist of only three or four acres; the mere mechanical disadvantages, therefore, of cultivation are obvious, especially when it is considered that upon this heavy soil four horses are usually worked at length in ploughing. . . . .

Lost fallows, as they are aptly termed, not unfrequently occur in wet autumns in small enclosed fields, where light and air are in a measure shut out. Thus nearly a whole year's expenses, and perhaps a dressing of manure, are almost lost. There are many thousand acres in the Weald of Kent which cannot, under existing circumstances, be cultivated without a positive loss, that might be made to yield of most kinds of corn a full average of the kingdom. . . . .

The fatal mistake characteristic of this district is to allow high wood and trees to grow in the hedges of arable land in small inclosures. . . . . It is common to see very inferior trees do more injury in three or four years to the crops than the whole value of the trees will amount to after continuing the mischief for half a century.

The district possesses within itself the means of its own amelioration. All that is required is to go about the business in a judicious manner. . . . . The cheapest and most effective way of carrying out the great object (the improvement of the district) would be for owners of land to commence their operations systematically, and do nothing by piecemeal. . . . . The best way would be for the landlord to pay the whole expense of the draining, conducting it under his own superintendence, and to charge a fair percentage on the rental. A judicious outlay might be made to yield in many parts of this country five or six per cent., with a great advantage to the occupying tenant.

Now these observations are in a great measure applicable to all our heavy land districts.

I will not read the essays from other districts; but I have them here from the different counties—from Norfolk, Northamptonshire, the West Riding of Yorkshire, and Cumberland. Their contents have the authority of a journal that I am sure Hon. Gentlemen opposite must read, and they all acquiesce in the opinion that the only thing necessary to make the agricultural interest prosperous is, that the owner and occupier should agree on those obvious improvements that in many instances have already been employed with the greatest success. And, I repeat, if ever we see reported what the farmers say or require, it is almost invariably something else than a return to Protection.

I do not say that they would not like high prices

if they could have them without a rise in rent. But looking at the published reports of their meetings, you will see that the farmers complain, but that their grievances are not such as the Legislature can remedy. They have very distinct grievances ; and I feel the same sympathy for the farmers that one has for any other class of one's fellow-subjects that is aggrieved. I say that they are a most valuable, not the most, but a most valuable portion of our community ; a portion of the great middle class, the productive class who invest their capital in the cultivation of the soil. Who can be, or who ought to be, more respected for their usefulness ? Can any man, indeed, who pretends to dilate on the rights of the community at large exclude those of the farmer's and treat their interests with less regard than those of any other class ? My judgment at least does not lead me to do so. I think that they are a most deserving class. And, in my judgment, the time has come when their real interests must be more considered in this House than they have been.

I cannot help thinking that the farmers have not been fairly dealt with. In my opinion their distress has too often been made capital of by certain Gentlemen for political purposes. I do not know any class of people who have been so deluded. It is not their fault if they are not so quick as other people. Circumstances determine men's intelligence and characters ; and the circumstances of the farmers have not been likely to make them more intelligent than other classes of the community. But that does not justify their being imposed upon. I say that the farmers have too often been misled to believe that they had friends in Parliament, friends who would secure to them some advantages, though at the expense of the community, by which they would be able to live, succeed, and prosper. Those promises have been held out to them for thirty years and upwards by persons in this country who have lost nothing by making such promises. They held out to the farmers, that if they returned them for the counties and gave them political support, they would either pass Acts of Parliament or maintain Acts of Parliament by which they, the farmers, would be enabled to get high prices and to live comfortably. The farmers in this respect have been grossly deceived. They had promises made to them in the name of Parliament, which have not been fulfilled. They have been promised first one thing then another; now this price now that; but they have invariably been deceived. And never more deceived than of late years; because they have been encouraged to think that under the altered circumstances of the country they need not help themselves; that they had only to rely on their friends; that they must go to Parliament again; and that what had been taken from them ought to be restored to them. I say that when people have been so grossly deluded, any independent man may well feel sympathy for them.

But when I listen to their own story, I find that it is not Protection, or Acts of Parliament, or want of political friends, that they principally dwell upon. There are certain things always specified at farmers' meetings, but if any one mentions them here he is either told that he knows nothing of the Agricultural Interest, or that he is intruding matter irrelevant to the subject.

There are a few things, I say, invariably mentioned. One is the Law of Distress. Another is the Law of Settlement. Another is, that the Law should be better defined that awards compensation to outgoing tenants for crops or unexhausted improvements. And again, another is the privilege that is given or maintained for keeping up or increasing that which destroys the tenant's produce: namely, game. If you refer to any farmers' journal, you will find that these are their grievances; and yet they are never discussed in this House.

The Law of Distress operates injuriously to the farmer. His credit is seriously impaired by it. The landlord always comes in before any other creditor. And who, under such circumstances, likes to advance him money on the security of his stock—money that he needs to make improvements? Another evil of this Law is, that it causes the landlord to be much more careless whom he selects for his tenant; and this produces a very mischievous kind of competition: all sorts of people come into the market for the land; and the landlord is generally safe, for there is always enough on the farm for six months' rent.

Then again, I really thought, judging from some of the opinions expressed by certain Members of the Government, that the Law of Settlement, the law that affects the farmer most materially and is a positive evil in this country, would have been one of the measures dealt with by the Government. There is nothing that the farmers complain of more than this, on account of its mischievous effect on the character of their labourers.

Then, with respect to game, and what they term 'Tenant Right,' but which may be interpreted by having the law better defined than it now is with reference to compensation to outgoing tenants; these are real mischiefs that the farmer complains of, and real relief cannot be given to him, whether by the Legislature or otherwise, except by remedying them.

And next to turn to the owners of land; for I allude to all the different branches of the landed interest to show not only that Protection cannot be restored with any advantage, but that it has not been removed with any ill effects; and that if you want to benefit the agricultural interest it cannot be by the agricultural relief which we hear of in this House. Well, as to the landowners. Generally they are well off in this country at present. The Noble Marquis the Member for Leicestershire,[1] who knows a great deal about the agricultural interest, admits that the landowners are very well off, and that they have nothing to complain of; otherwise he thinks they would take care to remedy the evil for themselves. They are, in fact, very far from having anything to complain of. They have great advantages. Everything tells in their favour. At no time was there such a desire to purchase or to occupy their land as at

[1] The Marquis of Granby.

present. There never was a time when they obtained money so easily, whilst everything has been made cheaper to them than it was before.

And the labourers, by the admission of every person, are better off now than they used to be, and have been so ever since the price of provisions fell. I have here a proof of it in a letter from Wiltshire, written by one in a position to know the views of all classes. He says :—'There is nothing that many of the labourers have more at heart now than getting a picture of Sir Robert Peel to hang over their fire-places—they are so well off.' For two years past Hon. Members have been told of this improvement in the condition of the labourers, and now they say : 'It is owing to emigration.' Doubtless, in certain places, the emigration of some of the labourers has ameliorated the lot of those remaining at home ; but the generally improved state of the whole class is chiefly due to the great improvements in agriculture which create a demand for labour ; and to the fact that with food and wages at their present prices the labourer has a greater command over the necessaries of life.

Before I proceed to make any further statements as to the immense advantage of removing Protection from every interest, I challenge the Right Hon. Gentleman the Chancellor of the Exchequer to prove that any injury to any important interest has resulted from its removal. I do not deny that there are individuals who may under the peculiar circumstances of their case have been unable to endure the transition ; but that is a very different thing from the way in which the interest generally has been affected. I do not deny that there are things affecting important interests in this country, and thereby the country at large, that ought to have been done long since and should no longer be delayed. These things may severally affect the shipping interest, the agricultural interest, or the colonial interest. But such things are entirely independent of the removal of Protection, and ought not to have been allowed even while that system prevailed. What I contend for is, that Protection is a positive evil in itself to the nation and to the interest protected, and that, as six years' experience has now established, nothing but advantage has attended its removal.

I challenge the Right Hon. Gentleman to disprove what I have said ; and until I understand that he does so, until I hear any statement from the opposite side of the House controverting my position on this subject, I shall not weary Hon. Members with any illustrations of fact. I am—as I have already stated, and cannot too often repeat—in possession of the most extraordinary details of the well-being of the country. And the House cannot be too strongly impressed with our state of unexampled prosperity : the manufacturers and producers in every part of the country are unable to execute their orders ; the people never were so well off before, owing to the wages they receive and the control those wages give them over the comforts and necessaries of life ; and all this is owing to the emancipation of Trade and Manufactures from restriction in most important particulars, and the stimulus thereby given to production and employment, and in no way due to those other causes to which the Earl of Derby and his colleagues are pleased to ascribe the present condition of the country.

I think that it is unworthy and ungrateful when we see this great prosperity, and when we see that it is so obviously connected with the changes in the commercial policy of the country to which I refer, that there should be a poor attempt by vague and indefinite expression either to underrate it or to ascribe it to any other cause. And I call on the Right Hon. Gentleman to explain distinctly to us what it is the Earl of Derby means by the influence that the discoveries of gold in Australia and emigration have had in producing the national prosperity of the last two years. Let us have it clearly defined, and not left a mere vague assertion. I beg the Right Hon. Gentleman to state to us explicitly the influence that the influx of gold into Europe or into England has had on the present condition of this kingdom. I am perfectly willing to admit that the recent discoveries of gold, like the production of any other article, has given activity to trade between England and the countries where it was produced which, as concerns that article, did not previously exist; but such activity only as would have resulted from the increased production of any other article in general demand—nothing more. The new gold has been useful for commerce, available for immediate exchange with every part of the world, and, therefore, a most valuable product to the countries where it is found, giving them a means of receiving in exchange the products of other countries, but of no more special value to us than any other article of exchange in general demand.

The Noble Lord at the head of the Government, however, seems to ascribe the present position of the labouring class chiefly to the recent discoveries of gold in Australia and other parts of the world. I want to have this explained; because, if I read the statement of the Noble Earl aright, it was that inasmuch as the influx of gold into this country has raised the value of every article in the country, it has therefore raised wages and improved the condition of the people.

But the opinion of the Right Hon. Gentleman opposite and of the Government generally—as I understand it, and according to the Amendment they propose—is that the improved condition of the people is owing to the cheapness of provisions. Now, which is really the case: Is it the Australian diggings that have raised the price of wages and every other article, or is it the cheapness of provisions? The Right Hon. Gentleman will, I am sure, make all this clear.

Then with reference to emigration: that statement of the Noble Earl's is not very distinct; there is a sort of ingenuity in confounding Irish emigration with English emigration. I want to know what effect emigration has had upon the condition of the people of this country. As far as I understand it the great amount of emigration that has taken place from this country has been within the last six months.

Emigration, therefore, will not account for the improved condition of the working classes for the last two years. Besides, if any man examines the returns of the countries from which the people emigrate, they will find that whereas England and Scotland supply something like 100,000, all the rest consist of the Irish who have gone to America—not to Australia. How does that account for the improved condition of the country by the efflux of the people? Then he has not told us what class of our countrymen it is that has gone to Australia. It happens to have been a class distinct from that to which he refers: persons above the labouring population—men who have taken capital with them, and who belong to the middle rather than to the ordinary labouring class.

To underrate but to admit the prosperity and ascribe it to other causes than the adoption of Free Trade, is consistent with adherence to the principles of Protection; and this may be the purpose of the language employed by Hon. Gentlemen opposite. I hope the Right Hon. Gentleman will not overlook the point in his speech, for it is part of our business this evening to solve the question whether the abolition of Protection has been attended with any evils, or whether it alone has not produced the good fortune of the country that we all observe. We must have an opinion expressed to-night on this point, and learn from the Government, composed of men formerly Protectionists, whether our prosperity is not fairly to be traced, directly and indirectly, and beyond all fair dispute, to the operation of the commercial policy that was adopted by the late Sir Robert Peel, and continued by the Noble Lord the Member for the City of London.

And now I will bring my remarks to a close. In doing so I again beg to say that I have no other object in view than that which since I have been in this House has ever guided my course on this question, and which has reference to the great matter in dispute, and to that alone: it is not to serve a party, it is not factious, it is not personal. I say once for all, in language that shall not be misunderstood by anyone, that my object is not to displace Right Hon. Gentlemen opposite. I do not want any of their places myself, and I do not want the House to take this Motion as necessarily a Motion of want of confidence in Her Majesty's present Ministers. [Cries of 'No, no.'] They have themselves said, they have themselves volunteered the declaration, that they do not possess the confidence of this House upon the great questions on which the last Parliament was dissolved. They said at the opening of the Session, and they have repeated it since, that they have not changed their own opinions, and that the opinion of the country remains against them, which I say is tantamount to an admission that they have not the confidence of the House as at present constituted. This being a Free Trade House of Commons they might, if they had changed their opinions, be said, as Ministers of the Crown, to have the confidence of the House; but if Lord Derby does truly represent the rest of them, then, inasmuch as he adheres to his former views, they are in an undoubted minority in the present Parliament.

For what I believe to be great national reasons I want to have these Resolutions carried, and to have the views of the House of Commons on this question most distinctly, and most explicitly, expressed; and most especially do I want these Resolutions to be placed on record, in order that we may at least during the existing Parliament have a settlement of a matter that, while unsettled, leaves men of business in the country uneasy, and the rest of the world in doubt as to what the permanent commercial policy of England is to be.

I hope, therefore, that the Right Hon. Gentleman the Chancellor of the Exchequer will not attempt to evade the real question by talking of factiousness or by impugning my personal motives; but that he will address himself in a straightforward way to the question before the House, and will not sit down without letting us at last know what he really means.

Enormous mischief has already been done by the course taken by Hon. Gentlemen opposite ever since 1846. I know from what I have heard and from what I have seen on the Continent that there people exaggerate the importance of the party to which the Hon. Gentlemen belong; they imagine that Lord Derby represents a strong section of the English political community, and that he has acquired or will acquire power to reverse eventually the policy of Sir Robert Peel. Indeed, it is notorious that in those instances where foreign nations are disposed to change their own commercial policy, the movement is retarded because their Governments are compelled to notice the continued existence of the so-called Protectionist party in this country.

There are people both here and abroad who will never adapt themselves to the altered circumstances of our commerce while doubt is allowed to exist as to our retention of a Free Trade policy ; and constant mischief is still being done by the agitation and assertion of Protectionist and Anti-Free-Trade views. And therefore I contend with the Right Hon. Gentlemen at present in power, that the importance of some distinctly-worded Resolutions such as those I propose, to be taken as a final decision of Parliament and of the country, cannot be over-rated. I now conclude by moving my Resolutions, and once more emphatically state that I have no other object in urging them upon the House than that which has influenced me during the last fifteen years, in my constant efforts to establish the commercial policy of 1846.

INDEX.

THE END.

www.ingramcontent.com/pod-product-compliance
Lightning Source LLC
Chambersburg PA
CBHW031810270326
41932CB00008B/368
* 9 7 8 3 7 4 4 7 2 4 0 6 7 *